For more information, email stillstanding385@gmail.com
ISBN: 978-1-7752396-7-3

rmkipublishing.com

Finding Hope

Finding Hope

For Those Without A Voice

Finding Hope is a true story. Names have been changed to protect the identity of those depicted in this book.

Dedication

I dedicate this book to the victims abused by someone they love and trust. I am so excited to share this book to empower abused victims who are afraid to speak out.

I hope this book will bring awareness to every victim and let you know that you are not alone.

Everyone has a story to tell. What's yours?

Contents

I.

Chapter One

Hope is the eldest of three children. She grew up with her mother, Grace, father Princeton, and brothers Ricardo and Austin. She was a shy girl with bold black eyes and long curly black hair that she loved when her mom put it in a braid. Hope had a slim build, and people in the village called her 'thinning' because of her skinny shape. They all lived in the small farming community of Vermont on the beautiful Island of Saint Vincent and the Grenadines. It was a place where the villagers were friendly and caring for each other. Most people in the village were also related to each other. The children loved going to the rivers to bathe. They found joy at night when the moon was high in the sky, and they played ring games such as "A-Brown-Girl-In-The-Ring," and "Hide-And-Seek."

Saint Vincent is a small island located in the Caribbean, and it is known for its national dishes of Breadfruit and Jackfish. It is very mountainous and has many beautiful beaches. It was settled first by Amerindian adventurers, travelling northwards along the lesser Antillean chain from South America. They named the island Hairoun, meaning "the land of the blessed." Saint Vincent and the Grenadines are friendly and always welcome others not from the island. The children in the community were always taught to be respectful of elders and were forbidden to get involved in an adult conflict.

Hope travelled to the mountains with her parents to help on their farm when she wasn't at school. She never liked it but had no other choice. Her classmates started fights with her because her family was poor. Hope always protected her brother Ricardo at school from bullies. Her mother taught them to never get in trouble with anyone but fight back if they must. So, Grace would punish both Hope and her brother if they came home defeated.

Hope and Ricardo had to walk many kilometres to get to school. On their way, they met with their friends. There was a river path to get to the other side, and their friends would tell them, "Let's take the river path to get to school faster." One such day, the river current was very heavy from the storm the night before, and Hope and Ricardo decided to listen to their friends and cross the river. When they arrived, construction was going on as a crew built a bridge to get to the other side. While Hope tried to get across the temporary bridge, a boy pushed her, falling into the water. Ricardo, who was in front of Hope, reached the other side safely. But Hope was in the water, screaming "Help," but no one could hear but Ricardo, and he ran to get help.

There was a machine cutting the stone and pumping out the water for the construction workers to build the bridge in the water. Hope was in the water, and she didn't know what to do. She prayed that someone would hear her or that her brother would find someone to rescue her. She could hear the machine getting closer and closer. She gave up Hope that anyone was going to save her, but suddenly a man came pulled her out of the water in the nick of time. Hope hugged the man and thanked him for saving her life. She held her brother and cried; Hope and Ricardo couldn't go to school that day because their uniforms were wet. Ricardo wasn't going to school without Hope, so they went home. Hope knew that she was supposed to take the long way to school, but she didn't, and now her parents were going to be mad at her. They told their mother what happened when they got back home, and Grace was angry but happy that Hope and Ricardo were both alive.

When Princeton came home, he was also mad when Grace told him what had happened. He took out his leather belt, and Hope knew she would not get out of this one. Even though she had almost lost her life, Princeton punished Hope. He beat her so hard that her skin bled. When Princeton was finished beating Hope, she looked at her mother and cried, "look what dad has done to me!" Hope could see that her mother wanted to cry. Grace threw a bucket of water on Hope to revive her. Hope fell to the ground with the many cuts from the belt.

It was stormy that night, and there was rain, lightning, and thunder. Hope could hear her parents fighting, and she wished the noise of the thunder would drown out the sounds so that she wouldn't be able to hear her parents' fighting. But the sound of their arguments wouldn't stop. So she held Ricardo close to her until the fighting stopped.

The following day, Hope didn't want to go to school. She had been awake all night replaying the fight between her parents in her head. She wished it would rain all day so that she and her brother wouldn't have to go to school because she was afraid for her mother. The school was essential to Hope, but Mrs. Pear's teacher didn't like her. She tried to be a good student, but Mrs. Pear didn't care whether she was trying or not. Hope knew that she would never be a teacher's pet. The only thing she could do was work hard to be a good student. Whether Mrs. Pear would eventually like her, Hope would never know.

To escape from all the chaos in her home and school, Hope turned to music. She loved to sing and write music, and she dreamt of one day becoming a singer. Hope wanted her music to touch people's lives, but she was just an ordinary girl, scared of the dark and always getting into fights with her brother Ricardo. Even though Hope feared her father, she was still a happy girl. Her brothers and her mother were everything to her. She thought that everything in her life was perfect. Although much of her family is poor, there was always food on the table and clothes on their backs. Besides farming in the mountains, her parents owned the corner shop in the village. Hope's mother was the most caring person she knew. She was a giver, and everyone loved her. Hope's father was an upstanding family man in the villagers' eyes. She wanted to believe he was a good man even though he frequently punished her and her brother Ricardo. They could never bring home a failed report card from school. Princeton never liked repeating himself more than once while talking, and he would punish them for it.

Hope's parents always seemed happy. Grace was a good mother and partner to Princeton. They were together for 14 years but never married. She made sure that Hope and her brother Ricardo got ready for school and had breakfast in the morning. Brother Austin was the baby in the family. Princeton would leave early for work, and then Grace would go to the farm to join him. They raised animals like goats and sheep planted produce on the farm. They also had a chicken farm at home for income to support their family, and they worked the chicken farm as well. Working on the farm was hard work, but Grace never complained. She knew that it was their only source of income outside of the income from the corner shop, and if there were no income from farming, the shop would have to be closed. But still, Princeton never married Grace.

As Hope got older, she started seeing things go wrong. While her mother seemed happy on the outside, she was hurt by her father on the inside. Princeton abused her mother behind closed doors, but Grace never said anything. Hope would hear her parents fight more and more at night, and things started getting worse. Her mother did everything to please Princeton, but it was never enough. He always wanted more.

At Christmastime, when Hope was just ten years old, a lady came to their house with a child stating that it was Princeton's. The child was the same age as her youngest brother Austin. The child's name was Rebecca. She was the most beautiful baby; her dark skin was smooth to the touch. Hope was happy that she was a big sister and had a little sister to call her "big sister." Hope's mother welcomed Rebecca with open arms. Not every woman would do what Grace did. Hope's new sister spent Christmas and New Year's with them. "That was the best Christmas ever," Hope said. Things were going well until New Year's Day when a man came to Hope's house, claiming that Rebecca was his daughter, and he took her away. He knew that her sister was Princeton, her father's child, but he didn't care. The man knew that he loved Rebecca as much as Hope's father did, and that was the last time Hope saw her sister.

Hope always wondered if Rebecca was happy, and she hoped that no one was abusing her. The last thing they heard about Rebecca was living in England. Hope made up songs about her sister Rebecca. She wrote in her diary, "I wish that I could go back to when we first met. I'm sorry I never got to tell you that I loved you. We are sisters forever, no matter how far away you are. You're always close to my heart."

Things didn't go well with Hope's mother and father. Even though he brought another child into the family that wasn't hers, Grace still loved him. When her mother thought things were improving with Princeton, he started seeing Suzette from the village. Anytime Princeton was at the shop, Suzette would visit him at night. They would go to the river for moonlight swims. Grace knew about it but still stayed by her father's side.

One night, Hope's mother and father started fighting. Hope and her brothers got scared, so they hid under the bed and cried for their mom. Everything eventually calmed down. Hope saw her mother, but Hope didn't recognize her. She looked as though a demon had possessed her body. Her eyes were coming out of their sockets. Princeton didn't know what to do. Hope and her brothers started crying. No one knew what was going on that night. Hope was angry, and she blamed Suzette for what her mother and father were going through. Finally, her mother couldn't take it anymore, and her parents' relationship ended.

Things were never the same after they broke up. Hope's father and mother closed the corner shop, and Princeton turned it into a house for her, her mother, and her brothers to live in. They moved into their new home, but Grace was cooking and cleaning for Princeton like they were still together. Many nights, Princeton would come around for sex from Grace. Sometimes, she would say yes; other times, she would say no. People might ask, "how does a child know these things?" Hope was a child who feared the dark, and at night she would be scared to sleep. She would hear her mother opening the door for her father. When Hope's father didn't get sex from Grace, he wouldn't take care of her and her brothers.

Hope was angry when her parents broke up. She would write her feelings in her diary. There was a children's song that she wrote to her dad that went like this; "Bring back, bring back, bring back my daddy to me, my daddy went over the ocean my daddy went over the sea, my daddy went over the ocean so bring back my daddy to me."

Princeton moved on with his life and married a woman named Liz. Unfortunately, he didn't invite Hope and her brothers to his wedding. She never understood why her father didn't marry her mother but married Liz.

Liz was a selfish woman. She wanted everything for herself and Hope's stepsister Kizzy, who wasn't Princeton's child. Even though Grace wasn't working, Princeton wouldn't give her any money to help take care of Hope and her brothers. Hope and her brothers didn't have anything to eat. Grace told her to go over to her father's house and ask for money. He gave Hope ten dollars. Grace got mad and went over to Princeton's and got into an argument.

In their community, ten dollars wouldn't take care of three kids. But Liz didn't care if Princeton gave them anything. Instead, she told Grace, "Whatever I give Princeton to give to his children, that's what he'll give."

Hope would see her mother and father arguing from a distance. She knew it wouldn't end well, as she had seen from her past, growing up as a child. Her mother once came back home with a severe cut to her hand. Her mother said Princeton had pushed her, and her hand got cut from his gate when she tried to stop herself from falling. Hope asked herself, "why doesn't my father love us anymore?" She picked up her diary and started to write, with tears in her eyes. She always listened to a song on the radio called "Mind You Pickney" by the group called "Touch." The song's meaning was that men need to take care of their children. Hope loved the song and knew what it meant. In her diary, she wrote the lyrics to the song, "A man stands up to his responsibility and mind your pickney (kids), children need their daddy, later you'll be sorry." She also wrote, "It's crazy how a man can have kids and say he loves them, but when he finds another woman, he forgets all about his children."

While the tears were falling from Grace's face, she said, "I rise, I fall, and I learned. That was part of your game. The anguish that I felt made my heart bleed. I get down on my knees, asking God to heal my troubled soul. I'll say I don't mind the pain because I had a lot to gain. Remember, my tears were not in vain."

Liz gave birth to Elizabeth, and Hope got jealous. Princeton gave all his love and attention to his new family, forgetting he had three other children. So Hope and her brothers were left in the cold.

Hope's mother couldn't afford new clothes. For school, Hope and her brothers only had three uniforms each. Sometimes Ricardo would wear Hope's shirt, leaving her with two shirts for the week. Hope felt different from the other kids. She hated being poor, and the school kids treated her differently. Hope was tired of pretending to have the best lunch in school like the cool kids when all her mother could give her was buttered bread.

At home, Hope tried to be a good daughter. She cleaned the house, cooked, and helped care for her brothers. Everyone in the community admired how she cared for the home and her brothers. In addition, her friends in the village would come over to her house, cooking food for them. Hope may have been less fortunate, but she never said no to anyone. Her mother also did whatever she could to support Hope and her brothers.

Eventually, Liz went to America, leaving her father all alone. Princeton asked Grace to let Hope come to clean his house. She cleaned the house's yard, washed his clothes and cooked for him. Hope was angry with her mother for letting her clean for him after he didn't want to be a father to her and her brothers.

One day Princeton saw her on the steps of her stepfather's house, and he asked Hope why she was sitting on the steps in the hot sun? Hope replied, "there isn't anything to do." He said, "walk with me to my house." He wanted to give her five dollars. Hope went into the house, and Princeton sat her down and talked to her. "Do you have a boyfriend," he asked. Hope said, "no, dad, I don't have a boyfriend." Princeton said, "very good." He then asked her, "are you a virgin?" Hope answered nervously and said, "yes, dad, I'm a virgin."

Princeton then told Hope how much he loved her and her brothers. He hugged her so close, and she felt uncomfortable. Princeton said to Hope, "Go into the bedroom, and I wanted to check to see if you are a virgin like you said." With fear on her face, she went to the room. Her father pulled her pants down then he began to search. When he was finished, he said, "you're a virgin like you said." Hope thought he was finished, then he took his pants off and said to her, "you're a young lady now and do you know if you have sex with a boy, you could get pregnant?" Hope said yes with confusion in her voice. Princeton pulled his pants down and began to have sex with Hope. While she lay on her back feeling hopeless, with tears running down her face, she wondered why her father was doing this to her, his firstborn child. He saw Hope's tears flowing but didn't stop. He wiped the tears on her face, then he discharged her tummy, saying to her, "this is what gets you pregnant."

Hope looked at her father with sadness on her face. She pulled her pants up. Princeton gave her five dollars and sent her home. Her mother wasn't there when she got home, but her brothers played outside. While she was in her room crying, everything was replaying in her head. What her father had done to her came as a shock. First, she said to herself, "my father will pay for what he did to me." Then, as she picked up her diary, she wrote, "You will reap what you sow."

2.

Chapter Two

Grace kept sending Hope over to her father's house to clean and cook for him. She would cry so she wouldn't have to go, but Grace would get angry. Hope thought, "what if I told my mother what my father had done? Would she believe me?" But she was too scared to find out. Hope felt alone in this crazy world. Finally, she looked up to the sky and said, "Lord, give me the strength to carry on."

Hope started to act out at home and school. She blamed her mother for what Princeton had done without Grace knowing what had happened. Hope had no control. She said, "if my mother were spending more time with me, my father wouldn't hurt me." When Hope talked to her mother, she would give her attitude. Hope didn't care if they punished her for it. Inside, Hope was crying out for help, but Grace didn't understand the pain behind her daughter's change of attitude.

Grace worked in the mountains with farmers in the community to support Hope and her brothers. She also worked with the government to clean the roadside in the city and other villagers to put food on the table. She made little money, and there were times when they didn't have much to eat, and Grace went hungry just so that Hope and her brothers could eat. She hid her pain to prevent Hope and her brothers from seeing the tears that she was holding back. Grace knew they would be hungry, but she didn't know what to do.

Hope washed clothes every Saturday morning at the river as the sun rose. It was the least she could do to help her mother around the house, so she skipped breakfast to start her morning early. Hope came back from the river with a smile on her face, happy that she had finished one of her chores for the day. After she hung the clothes on the line in the yard, she made her way to the kitchen, only to discover that her brothers had eaten everything. Ricardo and Austin ate everything they could find. It was hard on Grace, not having a steady income with three children to feed.

Even though Grace put more responsibility on Hope, Hope still tried to play with her friends. She would invite them over to her house and cook and share. She never refused anyone even though her family didn't have much.

After being heartbroken by Princeton, Grace fell in love with a farmer in the community. His name was David. She would leave Hope and her brothers at home to visit David. Hope was happy her mother had found love again but wished she would spend more time with them.

Hope and her brothers visited Grace at David's home, but it wasn't the same as having her home. Every morning David drank water from the river. So, at the crack of dawn, Hope and her brothers fetched water at the river close to David's house. Then, they went to the farm to help David. Hope washed his clothes but was angry she had to do so much for him. Of course, she couldn't show it, or her mother and David would get upset, so she hid her feelings with a smile. Hope was tired that her mother wouldn't take the time to see how much she was hurting. Her hate towards her mother began to grow. She took care of her brothers while her mother was away. They slept at home alone. She still wanted to tell her mother what Princeton had done, but Grace was too busy with David and her friends.

One day Princeton came over to Grace's house and asked, "Can Hope come by and clean for me?" Hope said under her breath, "I thought he wouldn't show his face again after what he had done to me." Grace said, "go and help your father." Hope was angry. She didn't want to go, but what could she do? She was just a child who had to listen to her parents. So she went with her father. On the way, Princeton told her, "Go to the shop and buy me a cigarette."

On her way to the store, Hope worried about what to expect from her father. Her mind wandered, "does my father just want me to clean for him?" But she didn't know. Hope returned from the store, and her father was sitting, waiting for her. She gave him the cigarette. Princeton told Hope, "Go into the bedroom when she arrived at his house." Hope was scared but said, "ok, dad." He went into the room, laid her down and did it again. While Princeton was on top of her, tears ran down her face. He wiped them away and continued. She cried even more while he looked at her with shame. Finally, he shook his head and got off Hope with sadness on his face. Princeton knew what he did to his daughter, and he knew that it was wrong. As he lay there, he lit the cigarette, and he began to smoke. Hope looked at her father while pulling her pants up. He told her, "You can go home now." Hope tried to hold back her tears while walking home. Her friends saw her and asked, "can you come and play with us?" Hope said to them, "I'm not feeling well, maybe next time."

Hope just wanted to be alone. She picked up her diary and wrote, "I hate you," as the tears ran down her face. In her room and talking to herself, Hope said, "because of my father, I'll know what it's like to be with a man that I love, for the first time." Her hate for her father grew. She said to herself, "I hate you; you took my innocence." Only Hope and her bedroom walls saw her tears.

Hope wanted Princeton to feel her pain, to feel how much he had hurt her. She asked herself, "how can I make him pay for what he had done?" She questioned herself, "should I call the police on him?" She thought to herself, "that won't work because he's friends with the police." She continued to ponder, "should I let my mother and everyone know? Will that ease my pain?" The fear of her father took her over, and she said, "I can't; my father will be angry at me and deny it."

Hope blamed herself for what Princeton had done. She never knew how to protect herself from him. But, she wrote in her diary, "my father was supposed to love me, not hurt me. Now I must live with the scar that my father raped me for the rest of my life."

Grace was a god-fearing woman and went to church every Sunday. There were times she would take Hope and her brothers to church. When Grace went to church at night, Hope and her brothers were left at home, ensuring they were ok before she left. When Grace left for church, she discovered that the VCR was broken one Sunday. She knew it was the only thing that kept Hope and her brothers home while at church. Grace told Hope to go to Fred's house and ask him to come over and fix the VCR. Fred was Hope's cousin who lived on the other side of the community, and he knew how to fix electronics. Hope gave the message to Fred. He told her it would take a few hours before fixing it. Hope returned home while Grace was at church that evening, thinking to herself, "the children wouldn't be leaving the house because Fred would finish the VCR for them."

Hope had a cousin named Meesha. They were close friends and cousins, and they did everything together. For example, they would go around in the community to see what they could find to sell at the market. Meesha came from a low-income family, too, both understanding how it was to have very little. Yet, nothing could break the bond they shared. They knew each other's secrets. But there was the one secret that Hope didn't know how to share with

Meesha. She was afraid that Meesha would treat her differently, so she didn't tell her what her father had done. She was ashamed, and she feared him.

Meesha came to Hope's house to keep her company while Grace was at church. Her brothers were in their room while Hope and Meesha were in the living room. There was a knock on the door. Hope opened it, and it was Fred. He said, "I came to fix the VCR." Hope said, "come in, Fred." While he fixes the VCR, Hope and Meesha begin to play around with Fred just for fun. He said, "the VCR is fixed. I'll be on my way." Hope and Meesha weren't ready for Fred to leave. Hope wanted Meesha and Fred to stay till her mother came home. She knew that her mother would be home late from church, and she wanted company.

Hope and Meesha had fun with Fred. They hid his shoes so that he wouldn't leave. He pleaded, "Come on guys, I have to go home." Hope knew that Fred didn't want to play, so she gave him his shoes. When he was getting ready to leave, there was a knock on the door. Hope said, "who is it?" but there was no answer. Then, there was another knock, but Hope wasn't scared because Meesha and Fred were there. She opened the door and was slapped across her face, and she fell on the couch. When she caught herself, she looked up, and it was Princeton. He held her shirt and asked with anger in his voice, "what is going on here?" Hope answered and said with fear in her voice, "nothing, dad." Her father replied, "what I saw didn't look like anything." Hope was confused. She didn't know what he was talking about. He then let go of Hope and grabbed Fred by his collar. Fred was also confused about what was going on. Princeton pulled him outside, and they began to argue. Finally, Fred said, "I did not do anything wrong.

I came to fix the VCR because Grace asked me to." Princeton said, "I saw you from the hole in the house touching Hope and her cousin." Hope's house was partly made of wood, and she knew there was a tiny hole at the back of the house. But Hope didn't know anyone could see into the house. The neighbours heard the commotion and came out to see what the noise was all about. Princeton told the neighbours that Fred was touching Hope and her cousin. Meesha got scared, and she ran home, leaving Hope to defend them against Princeton. Princeton didn't want to hear what Hope had to say.

The following day, the news of what happened spread throughout the community like wildfire. When Grace returned from church later that night, Hope was already asleep. She told her what had happened the next day. Grace wanted to hear from her father and took her to Princeton's house. Princeton told Grace what he believed to be accurate, but Hope denied it. Princeton was not pleased.

Eventually, Grace and Princeton went to family court to address what happened that night. Princeton told the court what had happened with Hope, Meesha and Fred and that he believed Fred molested Hope and Meesha. Hope denied it and, to get to the bottom of it, the social worker at the family court told Grace to take Hope to a doctor to determine if she was still a virgin. The social worker asked, "will that be ok with you, Princeton?" Princeton said, "yes, it's ok with me." Hope looked at her father with anger. She mumbled under her breath, "how could my father be such a wicked man?" Everyone looked at Hope, and the social worker asked her, "did you say something?" Hope said, "No."

It was Friday, so Grace had to wait until Monday to take Hope to the doctor. The social worker made an appointment to see Grace, Princeton and Hope the following Wednesday to give Hope time to see the doctor.

When Grace took Hope to see the doctor Hope was scared because she knew she was not a virgin. Her mind wandered, and she said to herself, "the truth is going to come out; how am I going to tell my mother it was my father who took my virginity?" The nurse called Hope, and Hope's heart began to beat fast. She could feel her heart beating faster and faster. The doctor asked Grace, "what are you here for today?" Grace said, "I came to see if my daughter is a virgin." The doctor said, "I don't do those things. You'll have to see another doctor who does." The look on Hope's face showed a sigh of relief. She knew if the truth came out, it would break her mother's heart, knowing that the man that she once loved raped her daughter. Grace didn't get another doctor to check Hope to see if she was still a virgin.

On Wednesday, in the meeting with the social worker, she asked, "what was the result of the doctor visit?" Grace lied and said, "the doctor said Hope was a virgin." Hope looked at her mother with shock and surprise. Princeton looked at Grace, then at Hope. He knew it couldn't be true. He wanted to give the blame to someone else for what he had done. Something inside of Hope was telling her to tell the truth about her father, but she was a scared little girl.

Grace said it was a surprise because Hope knew she didn't see a doctor. The social worker asked Princeton, "are you pleased with what the doctor said?" With a surprised look on his face, he said, "yes, I am."

Hope was angry that she couldn't tell her mother what her father did when she had the chance. But, the fear of her father was overwhelming, so Hope picked up her diary and wrote her feelings down.

"I am searching and looking to find a way out. I can't look at myself in the mirror because all I can see is what he has done to me, and the shame I'm feeling is too much for me. So now I'm asking myself, did I deserve what he did to me? Did I make him so mad that he took my innocence from me?"

Hope continued:

"Tell me why? Tell me why you hurt me like that? Tell me why? Tell me why? I tried so hard to protect myself from those guys out there. I never knew I was supposed to protect myself from you. Tell me why?" Hope was crying out for help. She wanted the pain to stop, but no one could hear her. She prayed to God, asking him to take her out of this world. She didn't want to live anymore. Hope knew she survived the river for a reason, and one day God would show her why she should live.

When Grace found out she was pregnant, she kept it a secret from Hope and her brothers. Hope could see that her mother wasn't feeling well. They didn't know what was going on. She thought her mother wasn't feeling well, and it was just a bug. But as the days went by, Grace's belly started to grow more and more. Grace finally told Hope, Ricardo, and Austin that she was pregnant, and Hope wasn't happy. She knew she would have to take care of that baby. She was angry that her mother was having a baby because things were already hard for her. She barely had enough money to send Hope to school. Hope was in high school, and Grace tried hard to pay her school fees. There were times Grace didn't have the money to pay her school fees. It was a blessing that Ricardo and Austin were still in public school. Grace had to ask her friends for money to send Hope to school. They also gave their kids' old school shirts to Grace so that Hope could wear them to school. Hope knew having another baby would make it even harder for Grace to take care of them.

Grace gave birth to a beautiful baby girl. Grace and David named her Leah. They brought her home from the hospital, and the anger Hope had felt, disappeared when she saw Leah. The twinkle in the baby's eyes melted her heart. Hope helped her mother with Leah. She went to the river to wash her baby sister's clothes. She would hold her and bathe her at times, for Grace. While her mother went to the farm to get in a day's work, Hope stayed home with Leah.

Eventually, Hope had to leave school because her mother couldn't afford her school fees. She was angry, but she accepted that she couldn't go to school and that her father Princeton wouldn't help. Grace took him to family court, but it wasn't of any help. While Grace worked with the farmer to help take care of Hope and her brothers, Hope made sure that Grace had dinner ready when she came home. She cared for her brothers and baby sister, and life was hard for her. Still, she couldn't do anything to change things. She prayed that God would make way for her to go back to school. But for now, all she could do was pray and hope that he would answer her prayers.

3.

Chapter Three

One day, Hope's Aunt Alexandra, her mother's sister, came for a vacation. Hope had heard many stories about her Aunt but had never met her. Alexandra came to their house and told Grace that she wanted to take Hope to Canada. She said, "I've heard many great things about Hope, and everyone admires her in the community." Grace was very pleased. She called for Hope and asked her, "would you like to go to Canada to live with your aunty?" Hope smiled and said, "yes, I would love to go." Hope said, "thank you, Lord, for answering my prayers."

Alexandra said to Grace, "I have a friend that wants someone to help her with her two girls." She also said to Grace, "Hope will get to go back to school and further her education." Hope was pleased to know that she would finally go back to school. Hope was happy to know that she was leaving this place, where there was so much heartache and pain. She was delighted and said to herself, "I'll never look back when I'm gone."

Hope had been angry with her mother for putting so many responsibilities on her shoulders. She blamed her for what her father had done to her. Hope would miss her brothers and new baby sister but was happy she was leaving. She never got to do anything fun, and she spent most of her time at home helping her mother. However, one summer night, her cousin Keith came by their house with a handsome young man. The first thing Hope saw was his smile that lit up the room. Keith introduced him to Hope. He said, "meet my friend Neal from Barbados."

Hope was a shy girl in the community. Besides her family, she didn't talk to anyone else, but that night Neal changed everything. They laughed and talked like they had known each other for a long time. The full moon was bright and lovely that night. Hope, Keith, and Neal made plans for the next day. They went to the nature trail, a beautiful place that attracted a lot of tourists. Everyone loved it there. It was a long walk to get there, but Hope didn't mind because she was with Neal.

The next day Hope, Keith, Neal, and some of her friends got ready to go to the Rainforest. Grace wanted Hope's brother to watch over her, but Hope didn't want her brother there. However, Grace insisted that if he didn't go with her, she couldn't go. On the way to the trail, Hope and Neal walked and talked, getting to know each other. While talking to Neal, Hope fell in love with his accent. It was Hope's first-time hearing from someone with a different accent.

Hope showed Neal some of the trail's most beautiful things during the walk. They sat together and laughed. Neal had become Hope's first crush. But the day had come to an end, and Neal asked Hope, "can I see you again?" Hope said, "for sure!" Hope and Neal went to the river together and had as much fun as possible the next day. They promised each other that they would keep in touch. But would they ever stay connected? Time would tell. Regardless, it was a memorable summer with Neal.

Grace and Leah's father eventually broke up. Now, Grace had four children to take care of. Grace didn't have the time to see how Hope was hurting. Now she had no money to take care of them.

At Hope's house, they didn't have a TV. So they would watch television at the neighbour's house. Princeton later financed a TV for Hope. He said to Hope, "take care of this TV; it's yours." After what Princeton did to Hope, it seems to Hope that he was trying to make up for what he had done. But a TV couldn't take away the pain Princeton placed upon Hope. She would never forgive him.

Since Princeton's wife went to New York, he tried to get with Grace again. Hope wondered why he would try to get with Grace after what he did to her. Grace didn't pay any attention to him because he was married. She wouldn't get involved with a married man. She just wanted him to take care of his children. Princeton's wife didn't take the kids with her when she went to New York. She left them with her mother. Princeton had to care for her children while they were in his mother-in-law's care. He gave her money all the time but wouldn't do the same for Hope and her brothers. Princeton gave Grace very little money and said he would make the TV payments. Grace knew Princeton could do better by taking care of the children, but he wouldn't.

As months went by, Grace started dating again. She met a man named James, but Hope didn't like him. He just wanted to control everything in the home. Grace was having a hard time finding a steady job. Hope had to cook food without meat many times because Grace could not afford meat for her family. Hope went to her father's farm to get food items to cook when there was nothing in the house. She would go to the river where there were many coconut trees, just to find a dry coconut. She came home with the coconut in the shell to remove the shell and grind the coconut to get the coconut milk. Hope will then get some flour and make porridge for her and her family to eat. When they didn't have any coconut or milk, Hope would make the porridge without it. They did whatever they could just to survive. It was hard on Hope and her family when they didn't know where their next meal was coming from, and now this man, James, comes into their lives acting like he was sent from God.

Hope's cousin Kat comes to her house every day, or Hope will go to play. When Hope was at her house, her grandmother, Hope's great Aunt, would always give her something to eat. Kat and her sister lived with her grandmother, cousins, and uncles. It was a big family. When Kat came to Hope's house to play, Hope would feed her, but James didn't like it. He never wanted anyone to come to the house. James didn't live there but acted like he was the head of the house. "James thinks sleeping at the house once in a while gives him the right to tell me what to do," said Hope to Kat one day. James was a Barber. He worked in town, and he came to the house every day drunk. Hope said to herself, "wherein the hell did my mother find this guy?" Hope only talked under her breath. If her mother heard her, she would get a whooping.

Hope never heard her mother talk about James. He just showed up out of nowhere. Hope thought her mother should have said something to her and her brothers to prepare them for James. But what did Hope know? She was just a child. One day Grace didn't have any food in the house. James told her that he would buy food for the home. She told him, "Take Hope with you." James was going to work after shopping. Hence Hope went to town with him. Hope didn't like him, so she went because her mother told her to.

James told Hope that everyone would look at them and wonder what he is doing with this little girl while walking to the store when they got to town. James smiled at Hope and said, "I know everyone might think you're my girlfriend." Hope thought, "Is he serious?"

James bought a quarter bag of rice, sugar, and flour. He decided he wouldn't work anymore, so they came home. Hope went to the kitchen to make flour porridge for everyone. Kat came by, and Hope gave some to her. After Kat left, James got angry. He said to Grace, "I don't want to give anything I bought for the house to anyone but your family." Hope was surprised when her mother started arguing with her because when they had nothing to eat, she would go to

Kat's house, and Kat would give her something to eat. Grace was just angry because James was angry. Hope started to dislike James even more. She went to Kat's house and told her what had happened after she left. Hope told Kat that James got mad because she gave her some porridge. "James acts like he's doing something," Hope said. She also told Kat that James was wrong and didn't like him. She didn't think he was suitable for her mother.

Ricardo and Austin also disliked James because Grace always took his side. She always made excuses for him, and he was never wrong in her eyes even when he came home drunk. James talked to Hope and her brothers however he liked, and Grace wouldn't say anything. In time, Hope's anger towards her mother grew. Grace was so busy looking for love that she couldn't see what was going on with her.

When Grace went to church, she left Hope to take care of her brothers and Leah. James wasn't at home; he left for work and didn't come back before Grace went to church. When James came home, Hope wished he didn't. But, Hope, her brothers and her baby sister were already in bed and sleeping. Leah was in Grace's room. Hope and her brothers were in her room. Hope never liked sleeping alone while her mother was out.

When James came home late that night, Hope heard the door open. She thought it was her mother, and she listened as the movement got closer. Hope thought it couldn't be a mom because she sang while coming through the door. Hope pretended to sleep. It was James, he came into her bedroom, and she felt him come over to her. She barely opened her eyes. She could smell the liquor on his breath. He was looking into her face while squeezing a washcloth in his hand. Hope was scared. She didn't know why he came into her room. He knew her mother wasn't at home and would not be happy with him going into her room late at night. Eventually, he went back outside and, because James was drunk, it scared Hope even more.

Hope wanted to tell her mother the following day but wasn't

sure she would believe her. Grace knew Hope didn't like James and wanted him gone. James woke up and said morning to everyone. Hope looked at him and wondered if her brothers weren't in her room, what would he have done to her as drunk as he was. She wondered, "would he have raped me?" Hope didn't want to find out, not after her father had done.

Princeton didn't like it that another man was sleeping at their house. He got jealous. Hope thought, "why should he get angry," because all he ever did was mistreat her mother, Hope and her brothers." He has a wife, but that didn't stop him from getting jealous.

Princeton couldn't get with Grace, so he stopped paying for the TV. Grace tried to keep up with the payments independently but couldn't. The store eventually took it back. It was an embarrassment for Grace in the community. Hope was sad because it was the only thing keeping her and her brothers at home. Grace went to the store to try and get the TV back, but they told her she had to come up with half the money to get it back. However, she didn't have the money and could not get the TV back.

Hope wished that James would leave. But, she felt like he brought more problems into their lives, and her mother gave all her time to him and had none for them. In time, James got "under Grace's skin," so to speak. However, even though she couldn't stand his drunkenness anymore, she stayed with him.

Hope tried to spend more time out of the house. However, she couldn't stand being around James and wasn't doing anything for herself. She spent most of her time taking care of her baby sister when Grace was not around. Hope loved Leah, but it was too much for her when she wanted to go to church and had to take her sister. Hope wanted to be a teenager with fewer responsibilities. She was happy to be leaving, no longer living with her mother and couldn't wait to be with her Aunt Alexandra in Canada.

With everything going on at home, sometimes at night, Hope would sit outside by herself and cry at her neighbour, Mrs. Lewis' house. She just wanted the burden she carried around to go away.

One day, Hope's cousin Kirk saw her sitting alone at Mrs. Lewis' house. He asked, "what are you doing here all alone crying?" Hope dried her tears and said, "I just want to be alone." Kirk was Hope's second cousin, and he lived in the countryside. He was dating the neighbour's daughter. Hope just wanted someone to talk to but didn't know if he would understand what was happening with her. Whenever he came to the community to see his girlfriend, he would check in on her from that night on.

Kirk saw that Hope was not happy. Hope wanted someone to share what was going on with her. Inside, she felt like she wanted to die. They became close as Kirk gave Hope a shoulder to cry on. She told him what her father had done to her. He was the first person she had told since it happened. Finally, Hope found a person she could trust. Kirk was angry when Hope told him what her father had done. He wanted to kill Princeton. "Are you sure your father did that to you," he asked? With tears rolling down and the shame on her face, she said, "yes, he did." Kirk told Hope, "You have to tell your mom." She replied, "I don't know how to explain it to her; she wouldn't believe me anyway."

Later, Kirk went to Hope's house with her and told Grace he wanted to talk to her. Kirk starts the conversation hoping that Hope will say something. He looked at Hope, trying to tell her mother what her father had done. But Hope couldn't say anything. She was too scared of her father and how he would react or what he would do to her. Kirk was angry, and he didn't want to be the one to tell

Grace what was going on. All Hope wanted to do was get out of that place. She couldn't wait for her Aunt Alexandra to send for her.

Hope understood that Kirk was trying to be there for her. He was like a big brother and a protector to her. Everyone thought Hope was sleeping with Kirk in the community, but Hope'sreputation was ruined in the community because of Princeton. When he lied, saying Fred molested her that night.

Hope was home with her mother, sitting on the porch one afternoon. She looked down at the neighbour's house and saw that Kirk's girlfriend, Abbey, was looking at her. She came over and said, "good afternoon, Grace." Grace answered, "good afternoon, Abbey." Then she said to Grace, "I want to bring something to your attention." Grace said, "go right ahead." Abbey continued, "Kirk has told me he is having sex with Hope." Hope looked at her like, "what the hell." Grace said, "what are you talking about?" Hope was confused, wondering if Abbey had lost her mind. Hope said, "why would you say such a thing." Hope looked at her mother, afraid of what she would say. Grace looked at Hope and said, "Hope is that true what Abbey has said?" Hope said to her mother, "no, it's a lie." Hope continued, "Kirk is my cousin. I can't have sex with my cousin." She started to cry. She knew Abbey was jealous of the bond that she and Kirk shared and that she just wanted to stir up problems. Abbey fought all the time with Kirk because of her insecurity. Hope didn't know what she was trying to accomplish, but she would not be a part of her drama.

Grace said to Abbey, "you know that Hope and Kirk are cousins. Why on earth would he say that about Hope?" She continued, "if Kirk told you that, I don't believe it. I know my daughter, and she said it's not true." Abbey then walked away. Hope was angry with Kirk. She wondered why he would say something like that. She asked herself if he did say that to Abbey to make her jealous? Why would he do that? Hope couldn't wait to ask Kirk those questions when he came down to visit her. Hope sighed while taking a deep breath.

Abbey didn't want any woman around Kirk. So, she came up with the lie just for Grace to tell Hope to stay away from Kirk. But it didn't work. Kirk was the only person in Hope's family she could talk to about anything, and she didn't want to lose his friendship. So, Hope prayed about what Abbey had said. When Kirk came by the house to check on Hope, Grace told Kirk what Abbey had said about him. Kirk said it was a lie. Hope prayed that he never said that because he was the only one she could talk to when she felt down about her father.

Hope loved to visit her Aunt Les every summer. She would spend weeks at her house. She didn't know her mother's family that well because of her dad. Princeton did not like Grace's side of the family, so he kept Hope and her brothers away from them. However, he made sure that Hope knew everything she needed to know about his family, whom she loved. Hope loved being around her Aunt. Her Aunt treated her differently. She never put a lot of responsibilities on her, letting her just be a kid.

Hope met three sisters while visiting aunt Les. Their names were Lana, Rose, and Abigail. They were also friends with Les, and they were neighbours in a small, close-knit community. They visited aunt Les every day. Hope would sit back and enjoy how friendly they were. Lana and Hope became friends first since she was the youngest of the three, and she was easier to talk to. Lana showed Hope around the community. Then, she would go to the river with Lana, her sisters and Aunt Les.

Hope was surprised that Kirk came to the river too. Kirk lived in the same community. He was now dating Rose. Then all the secrets came out about him and why he and Abbey argued so much. Abbey visited Kirk at times, and he and Rose would have it out. Abbey knew that Rose was with Kirk and Rose was happy to let her know that she was with her man, and she was not going anywhere.

Rose and her sisters came by Les' house. They were talking about Abbey and Kirk's son. Rose said he was an ugly child, but Hope didn't like what she said. "No one should attack a child when women are fighting over a man; a child should always be off-limits," said Hope.

Hope went to visit her grandaunt, who is Kirk's mother. Abbey was at home, and even though Hope didn't like that Abbey came to her house accusing her of sleeping with Kirk, Hope could not hold back when she overheard what Rose had said. Hope told Abbey what Rose said about her son. Abbey was angry. Hope didn't feel she owed Rose any loyalty, and she didn't know her that well. However, Abbey didn't confront Rose, and she had to go back home. Hope, Lana, and her sisters were getting close. Rose turned out to be a nice person. Hope didn't like that she was dating a guy who had already taken, but she was kind to her. Hope felt guilty about what she told Abbey. She hoped Abbey wouldn't bring it up to Rose, but who is she kidding. No one would keep that to themselves when they hear someone talk bad about their child.

The following weekend, Abbey came to visit Kirk. She saw Rose the next day. Rose didn't like Abbey at all, so they started arguing. Abbey said that she heard Rose was talking bad about her child. It was a big blow-up. Rose went down to see Les. She saw Hope, and she said to her, "Hope did you tell Abbey what I said?" Hope held her head down. She didn't want what she had said to come out while building a friendship with Rose and her sisters. Finally, Hope said, "yes, I did; I regret it." Hope knew Abbey told Rose what was said to her while arguing. Abbey didn't care about Hope. She still believed she was one of the girls sleeping with Kirk.

Hope wondered if Rose and her sisters would trust her again. Aunt Les said to her, "Hope if you want to keep visiting me, you have to hear things and keep your mouth shut." Hope couldn't get into an argument because she knew her Aunt was right. She messed up. She still hung around Lana, trying to figure out if Rose and Abigail were mad with her. As it turned out, Rose didn't care that much about what happened. She said to Hope, "I'm glad you told her what I had said." Hope looked at Rose and said to her, "Is that a joke?" Rose smiled. Her friendship with the sisters grew after that.

Hope spent a lot of time with Rose and her sisters. They played games on the roadside, never seeing one without the other. Always barefoot, they called themselves the 'Barefoot' Crew. Rose called the popular radio station and sent a shout-out to the Barefoot Crew. Hope heard it on the radio and was excited. She never thought she would hear her name on the radio. Sadly, it was time for Hope to go back home to see her mother. Rose and her sisters asked, "can we come with you and visit?" Hope knew her mother wouldn't mind. She said, "sure, come along, we'll have so much fun." Apart from Hope worrying about what was going to happen when Rose got to her house, where Abbey, her neighbour, is, Hope thought, "Oh boy, that's not going to end well."

Hope invited her friends Lana, Rose, and Abigail to her home and introduced them to Grace and her siblings. Grace liked them right away. Hope showed the sisters around the community, just like they did with her. Hope, Lana, and Rose all have something in common, they loved the river and went to bathe, then came back, but they ran into Abbey. She came in front of Grace's yard and started arguing with Rose. Grace wasn't expecting what she heard. Hope told her mother that Kirk was dating Rose as well. Grace said, "oh," and that was her last words.

Rose started to lose interest in Kirk. She grew tired of the back and forth with him, and she loved him, but Kirk couldn't decide between her and Abbey.

A week went by, and Lana and Abigail weren't ready to go home. Rose said that she had to go and see what her parents were doing but that she'd be back. Lana and Abigail stayed, and all the boys from the community came around Hope's house because they heard that she had new friends visiting her. Grace wasn't happy about this. She didn't want any boys around her house. However, they played with the family cards to get away with it.

When Rose came back, it was the end of the week, and Hope and the girls loved spending time together. Rose had her eyes on one guy in the community. Kirk was ancient history. The guy she liked was Hope's cousin Keith. She liked him a lot, and Keith saw her as eye candy. He couldn't get enough of Rose, and Hope couldn't get rid of him. She loved her cousin, but he was always there. Hope was happy that Rose was no longer in the love triangle with her cousin Kirk. Everything was going well with Rose and Keith, but Keith's mother didn't want the relationship to work. She didn't believe that Rose was good enough for her son. She came to Grace's house and began to cuss Rose. But Rose didn't back down. She did not care that it was Keith's Mother. All she knew was that Keith's mother was disrespecting her.

Keith's mother always wanted to control her grown kids' decisions with their lives. Keith's mother said to Rose, "I don't want any women for a daughter-in-law, who can't walk in heels." Rose and Keith never worked out. The relationship never got the chance to bloom into something extraordinary. Rose, Lana, and Abigail finally went home. They told Hope, "We'll keep in touch." Hope was sad that they were leaving, but they never came to stay; they had a home to go back to.

Weeks went by since Lana, and her sisters went home. Hope was in the house when she heard someone call her name, "Hope, Hope." She looked outside to see that it was Abigail and a guy from the other side of Hope's community. Hope was excited to see Abigail but more surprised to see her with this guy everyone knew loved the ladies. Abigail was always about having fun and about a guy who had a car. Hope pulled her aside and asked, "what are you doing with him?" She said, "That's my boyfriend, Mikey." Hope knows Mikey, and she asked, "do you know who Mikey is?" Abigail looked at Hope like she was weird.

Hope didn't tell Abigail what she heard about Mikey because he would hear about it. Abigail told Mikey she was going to spend the day with Hope so he could pick her up later in the evening. Hope was happy for the little bit of time with her to tell Abigail about Mikey before it was too late.

Hope finally told Abigail that Mikey had AIDS. Abigail looked at Hope and said, "What?" Hope said, "I'm sorry, but that is the news going around." Abigail didn't believe it. She said, "it's just a rumour." Hope looked at her and said, "all right if you say so, even if it was just a rumour, I don't want you to be close to him."

Mikey's best friend liked Abigail. He told her that the rumour was true. He didn't want to be with Abigail, and he knew that she and Hope were friends. He was Hope's cousin Fred, and he was looking out for Abigail. However, Abigail didn't want to hear anything anyone had to say. She was a girl who loved guys with cars, and Mikey had a car, and even better, he was a bus driver.

Mikey knew he had AIDS but didn't want to tell Abigail. Finally, someone gave it to him, and he shared it with anyone he came in close contact with. Anytime Abigail was in the community, she visited Hope. She came by one afternoon with Mikey, and she asked Hope if she wanted to go for a ride. Hope said yes because she didn't think it would hurt her by riding in his car.

Hope came home one day, and her mother told her that Mikey had died in an accident. Hope wondered how Abigail took the news.

Finally, Hope's cousin told Abigail to see a doctor because AIDS killed Mikey, not the accident. He went to the doctor because he didn't want her to go through it alone.

A week later, Abigail got her results. She was HIV positive and fell into the cousin's arms and cried. She didn't believe what everyone was saying, which is how it turned out.

What happened to Abigail could have been prevented. But instead, it was a lesson learned. A man with a fast car doesn't mean he's got his life together.

4.

Chapter Four

The time had finally come for Hope to move to Canada. She was so happy to leave. Alexandra said to Hope, "I will get you back into school and help you get your status in the country." Hope was so excited about it. She said her goodbyes to her family and friends. She was going on a plane for the first time, and she was terrified and happy at the same time. Even though she was angry at her mother, the tears began to flow. Hope knew she would miss her family.

Hope saw her aunt at the airport, and she was happy to see Alexandra. She was glad to get away from her father. Hope's aunt introduced her to Mrs. P, the lady with whom she would be living. She was happy that she was there. When they got to Mrs. P's house, they all sat down and had dinner. Mrs. P introduced herself and her two daughters. Their names were Fatima and Lisa. Hope didn't say much; she said hi and lowered her head. She started to miss her family, and Alexandra could see that Hope was sad. She told her, "you'll come to my house every weekend and meet your cousins."

Mrs. P showed Hope what she had to do around the house the next day before leaving for work. Hope would be working as a live-in caregiver. Mrs. P paid Hope $200 per week to take care of her two girls, clean the house and wash their clothes. On the first day of her new job, Hope made the girls breakfast before they got ready for school. The school was far from the house, so Hope walked them to school.

Hope returned before Mrs. P left the house, and Mrs. P asked her to cook some chicken. In Hope's country, when they told someone to cook chicken, it meant to cook with seasonings for flavour, and that was it. Hope cooked the chicken and looked around the house to see what else she had to do. She noticed that Mrs. P's kitchen floor had a white and black carpet with the white part being dirty. So she got a bucket with soapy water, and with a stiff brush, she got down on her knees and scrubbed the floor. After finishing, Mrs. P's sister Mary came by the house. She came in the kitchen door, looked down on the floor, and asked, "did you wash the floor?" Hope looked at her, smiled, and said, "Yes, I did." Mary looked at Hope with a smile, and Hope knew she was pleased and that Mrs. P would be pleased also.

Hope said that she would forget about her mother when she left home. However, Hope remembered what little they had to eat and how hard her mother had to work at any small job to feed her and her brothers. Hope couldn't turn her back on her mother. Every week, she sent money to her mother from the two hundred dollars she received for caregiving. It wasn't much for doing all that work, but she thought it was better than nothing at all.

Hope didn't understand the meaning of long-distance on a landline. She would call her family and friends back home to get updates on how she was doing. She would call her friends and stay on the phone for 30 minutes at the most. Hope did it for two weeks, but Mrs. P called Hope into her bedroom when the bill came. From the tone of Mrs. P's voice Hope knew she had done something wrong but didn't know what it was. With anger in her voice, Mrs. P asked, "did you make long-distance calls on the landline?" Hope didn't understand what Mrs. P was talking about. Hope said, "no, Mrs. P." She asked again, angrier this time. She said, "Did you make calls to your country on the landline?" Hope replied, "yes, I did; I called my mother and my friends at home." Mrs. P was in a rage, and she said to Hope, "you are not allowed to make long-distance calls on the phone. How are you going to pay this bill? It's $900?" Hope began to cry, she didn't understand how long-distance calling worked, and now Mrs. P was angry with her.

Hope began babysitting Mrs. P's friend's son. Hope would get the girls ready for school, and the little boy would come in the morning and wait for Hope to take him to school. Hope didn't mind because every penny counted. When it was payday Hope got excited. Finally, she would send money to her mother to buy food and help pay the bills. Mrs. P gave the money to Hope, and she went into her room to count the cash. However, Hope was displeased. Mrs. P only paid her $80 to care for the little boy. She didn't pay her for what she was doing around the house.

Hope visited her aunt on the weekend, and she loved being around her family. She and her cousins, Jessie and Lena, became close. They took her to see different places, and she wished that she could be at her family's home more than at Mrs. P's. However, Hope couldn't see her family because Mrs. P wanted to go out with a guy, and Hope had to stay at home and care for the girls. Hope felt like her job was never done. She would rather be at her aunt's house than at Mrs. P's, even though her aunt's mother, Mrs. Lewis, didn't like her coming around. Hope didn't care; she just wanted to be with her family.

Many nights Hope cried. She was just fifteen years old with a significant role to play in a home that wasn't hers. Hope wondered why she wasn't in school yet like her aunt and mother told her she would. She hated doing Mrs. P's laundry. Her underwear had poop stains, and she thought, with anger, "why would a grown woman have poop in her underwear?" Hope always ironed the girls' clothes, folded them, and put them away even though they were never remained folded. Still, Mrs. P would not pay her enough money to send her family back home.

Hope reached the breaking point and wanted to leave Mrs. P's house. All Hope was doing was working in the house. Mrs. P stopped paying Hope and only paid her to care for the little boy she was taking to school, then picking him and caring for him till his mother picked him up. Hope cried. She had her family back home depending on her, but she couldn't take care of her and her family with only $80 she was getting from Mrs. P. Hope did everything she could so that Mrs. P would send her to live with her aunt. She started to act like she no longer wanted to live with Mrs. P. Finally, Mrs. P could see that Hope no longer wanted to be there. She said to Hope, "I can see that you don't want to be here," but Hope said, "I do want to be here." Hope knew she was lying, and Mrs. P could see right through her lies. Mrs. P said, "I'll call your aunt, and you can go live with her."

Hope was happy because she was tired of the way she was living there, always caring for the home and never feeling appreciated, so Hope moved in with her aunt. Her cousin Jessie was living there as well. There was a storage room under the stairway, and Hope and Jessie would share that space. The room was as small as a tiny box, but Hope was happy with her family.

Hope's aunt had six children; two of her adult children were married and living independently. Hope's aunt's mother was living with her as well. Mrs. Lewis didn't like Hope very much, nor did she like Hope living with them. Hope didn't know what she had done for Mrs. Lewis to dislike her. Hope thought that living with her aunt was the best thing for her, but she was wrong.

Mrs. Lewis didn't want Hope to eat anything she cooked; she kept track of the meat to see if Hope ate any. Hope wondered, "how can she know who eats any? Five other people are living in the house?" Hope knew if anyone else ate the meat, she would get the blame. Hope asked herself, "why does nobody love me." She thought that leaving St. Vincent was the best thing to happen to her, but she was wrong.

In a strange country without any status, it was hard for Hope to get a job. Her aunt didn't want her or her cousin Jessie sitting around doing nothing. She said to them, "both of you need to go and get jobs." Lena was the lucky one. She didn't need to get a job because she was in high school—every day at 6 am. Hope and Jessie went to an employment agency looking for a job. Hope knew she had to get a job to support herself and her family back home.

Hope and Jessie went to the employment agency and didn't get any jobs. Sometimes Hope gets a job for one or two days. Hope and Jessie grew tired of going to the agency and not getting as much work as wanted. Jessie didn't have any status as well, so they knew they must stick together. They were both tired of waking up early to look for work and not having much luck, so they decided to stay at home. But they had to hide from Mrs. Lewis because she never missed anything for an old lady. One morning Hope and Jessie were hiding in their room when they heard Mrs. Lewis coming downstairs. So they didn't go to the agency. Hope and Jessie knew they couldn't hide in the storage, so they ran into their cousin Brian's room.

Mrs. Lewis looked around the house. She knew she heard a noise, and she tried to open her grandson's room, but Hope and Jessie had locked themselves inside. They began to laugh. The TV was on. When Mrs. Lewis walked away, Hope turned the TV down. Mrs. Lewis turned back to the door and said, "I know you guys are in there."

The evening came, and Hope and Jessie came out of the room, pretending they had just returned from the agency. But, instead, they said, "We spent the whole day at the agency and got no work." Mrs. Lewis then said, "you were not at the agency. You were in the bedroom all day." Hope and Jessie learned something that day – you can't fool an old lady with lots of knowledge.

Hope thought a lot about her family back home as time went by. With no job, she couldn't send money to them. She knew it wasn't easy for her mother, but Hope prayed that she would get a job soon to help her mother.

Hope, Jessie, and Lena would go out and meet up with other friends with nothing to do. Lena was dating a guy, and she took Hope and Jessie to her boyfriend's house. Hope saw this man looking at her from across the room at the house. Hope looked back with a shy look on her face. He said, "my name is Randy." Hope answered with her soft voice, "nice to meet you, Randy. I'm Hope." They looked at each other and exchanged numbers. Hope didn't have a phone, so she gave her cousin Lena's number. Lena knew him, so she didn't mind. Hope and Randy got close. She would go to his house, where he lived with his sister. Hope was happy that she met someone she could talk to and get out of the house since Mrs. Lewis didn't like her living there.

Hope and Randy started dating. He seemed like a genuinely nice guy. He listened to her and about all her problems at her aunt's house. He had a good relationship with his sister, with who he lived. Hope started to believe that she and Randy could be a couple since they both hit it off from the start, but Hope was wrong. One day while at home, she went outside on the balcony. She could see Randy's place where she saw a girl on his balcony. Hope thought that it was one of his sister's friends. She was curious to find out who the girl was. She kept watching Randy's balcony but was hit with a shock. Randy came onto the balcony and held the young lady very close. Hope couldn't believe her eyes. She tried to call Randy, but he wouldn't take her calls. Hope had her first heartbreak from Randy.

Hope wouldn't let what she saw on the balcony get her down. She was sad that Randy hurt her also that she didn't have a job to take care of her family back home. Her aunt came home one day and told Hope that she got a job for her. Hope was happy now that she could go back to sending money to her mother. Alexandra got a babysitting job for her at her friend Lisa's. The person was a good friend of Alexandra's, so Hope didn't mind babysitting. Hope had to work Monday to Friday, starting at 7 am before Lisa left for work, and she finished at 5 pm. She had to make sure the kids were fed then allowed them to watch tv before lunch.

There were times Hope was late for work because of the bus. Lisa didn't like it, and she gave Hope a phone so that, if she was going to be late, she could call her. Hope was happy she got a phone because she couldn't afford one herself. Lisa said to Hope, "make sure you use the phone after 6 pm; that's the time the phone will be free to use." Hope understood. Hope would turn the phone off during the day and carefully use it. She didn't have many friends besides her cousins, so not using the phone during the day wasn't a problem.

Hope tried hard to get Mrs. Lewis to like her, but still, Mrs. Lewis always found a problem with Hope. She didn't understand why this sweet old lady she knew back home before coming to Canada didn't like her that much. You see, Hope knew Mrs. Lewis when they were neighbours back in Saint. Vincent. Mrs. Lewis would come to her house asking for some sugar while bringing the nice fry cakes Hope loved. Hope was confused about what she had done wrong. Every day Hope came home from work, she would go to the pizza shop to buy herself two slices of pizza for her dinner because Mrs. Lewis wouldn't let Hope eat the food she cooked. Hope would call her mother and cry. Hope said, "I want to come home, Mother," as the tears rolled down her face. Her mother told her not to cry on the phone; she said, "my child, you have to 'suck salt' if you want to make it in life, things will get better soon." Her mother tried to encourage her as she continued, "dry your tears." She quoted a Bible scripture "weeping may endure for the night, but joy cometh in the morning."

Hope felt those words her mother spoke to her. She dried her tears and began to smile. She said, "thank you, mother."

Hope went to work the next day. Lisa was waiting for her to come through the door, and Lisa gave the phone bill to Hope. The bill was $100. Hope was shocked. She didn't understand why the bill was so high. She knew she didn't use the phone until 6 pm. She said to herself, "that's not possible." It was payday, and Lisa didn't give Hope the two hundred dollars she earned., Lisa said to Hope, "I took $50 for the phone bill, and I will take $50 off of every pay until the bill is paid ."

Hope knew that it wasn't possible what Lisa was talking about. Lisa gave her the phone bill because her name was on both. Hope cried inside. She couldn't show how angry she was. She remembered the words her mother said to her, "Weeping may endure for the night, but joy cometh in the morning."

Hope was trying to make things work in a country for which she had no status. She wondered how she would get a permanent resident card. Everything her aunt told her didn't happen as she had said. She didn't know what to do. Hope thought Randy was a nice guy but turned out to be a liar, but she still liked him. Randy called her up, and he didn't know Hope saw him with that girl because he didn't pick up the phone when she called. Hope asked him, "who was that girl on the balcony?" He answered and said with anxiousness in his voice, "it was my sister's friend." Hope then asked, "why did you hold her so close?" He replied, "I hugged her to say hello." Hope knew he was lying, but she liked him a lot, and besides her cousins, he was the only friend she had, so she let it go for now.

Hope was glad that she met Randy and his sister. After work, she would go to his house even when he wasn't at home. His sister welcomed her in. Hope just wanted to get away from everything at home. She was somewhere else. Hope would go there after work just to hang out before she went home. She eventually found out that Randy was a liar and a cheater, but what came next? She wasn't ready for it. Randy started to ask Hope for money, and she gave it to him. He started by asking for $20, and it wasn't hard to give. Then he asked Hope to pay his phone bill. Hope didn't mind because she cared for him. Randy didn't care that Hope had a family back home to care for. Hope forgot for a second that she had a family that depended on her, all because she liked Randy.

Any time Hope came from work and saw Randy, he had different girls around, and he would look at Hope as if to say they were just friends. Randy was the first guy Hope liked, and he played her for a fool. Still, it didn't stop Hope from caring for him. When he called her, she ran to his side. Hope was a weak girl looking for love in the wrong places. She wasn't getting the love she wanted from home, so she sought it elsewhere.

One evening Hope was at home in her room, hiding from Mrs. Lewis, when Randy called her over to his house, so she went. Randy wanted to have sex with her. He said to Hope, "I want you to suck my pee-pee." Hope looked at him and said, "are you mad?" Randy started pushing Hope's head down so she would do it. Randy kept pushing, and she did it because she liked him so much.

One night, Randy was with his friends and Hope, and he started arguing, and he said to Hope, "I don't want a girl that will suck my dick." Hope felt hurt and betrayed. She did not know that it was his plan all along. Hope cried. After what he did, she knew that he was not the guy for her. She had too much going on at home to let Randy be another problem in her life, and she no longer wanted to see him anymore.

Hope began to go out with her cousins, Jessie and Lena, spending less time at Randy's house. Jessie was dating a guy, so she invited Lena and Hope to her boyfriend Mac's house. Mac's brother, Omer, was at his house. Looking at Hope, their eyes met. Hope then looked away with a smile on her face. They were all at the table laughing and talking. It was a fun night; it helped Hope forget about Randy, even if just for the night. Before the evening was over, Omer gave Hope his number. They spoke on the phone for a while, but Hope didn't feel any connection with him. Then he asked Mac for her cousin Lena's phone number. Mac told Jessie to give him Lena's number. Hope didn't care but wished she would have known that Lena had liked him. Hope didn't know that Mac's friend at his house was looking at her that night. Jessie told Hope about Alex and how much he liked her. Jessie said to Alex, "my cousin won't date you cause you're white." Hope laughed when Jessie told her what she had said.

Alex was black, but he was mixed with white and had a Jamaican background; tall and handsome. Hope began to pay attention to Alex, now that she knew he liked her when she and her cousins went over to Mac's house. Alex invited her to his house. Hope went. Alex just lived in the building next to Mac's house. Hope started to go to his house, but Hope didn't find him funny when he tried to crack jokes, and there wasn't much to talk about. At times, while Hope was at his house, she asked herself why she was there. He wanted more than a friendship with Hope, but Hope decided they should just be friends.

Hope still cared for Randy even though he had hurt her. She just didn't know why. Hope started going back to Randy's house. Randy said that he wanted things to work between them. Hope fell for it; she thought Randy was for real. She found out that Randy still saw the girl from the balcony and had his baby. Hope felt like a fool to believe his lies once more, but she was still going to his house. While there, she met Bryan, a family friend to both Randy and his sister Susan. Hope wanted Randy to get jealous, so she talked to Bryan the whole time. Bryan and Hope exchanged numbers but knew things were not going anywhere but a friendship. Hope just wanted to make her soon-to-be-ex jealous. That night Bryan asked Hope, "can I make sure you get home safe?" Hope said, "yes, you can," and she looked over to Randy and saw he was unhappy about it. Hope said her "good nights," and they both went on their way. While talking on the phone, she found Bryan a sweet guy. He worked nights and would call Hope while on his lunch break. In the morning, before Bryan went home, he went to Hope's house to walk her to the bus stop while working. If Hope didn't have enough money to buy a bus pass after sending money home to her mother, Bryan made sure Hope got her bus pass for work. Hope knew he would make a great boyfriend, but Randy was not. Nevertheless, Hope was still into Randy.

Bryan thought that Hope was his girlfriend. He told Randy and Susan that Hope was his girlfriend, but to Hope, he wasn't. She said, "how can I be his girlfriend when we never have sex or kiss?"

5.

Chapter Five

Hope was home one night, just spending time with her family, even though Mrs. Lewis didn't like her. They were the only family she had in Canada. Bryan was at Randy's house. Hope didn't know that he was there. Randy called her over to his house. Hope didn't know he was getting jealous of her friendship with Bryan. Hope went over and knocked on his door. Randy opened it, and she heard Bryan's voice. She went into Randy's room, but Bryan didn't know she was there. Hope and Randy enjoyed each other's company when Randy's brother came into the room. "It's my turn now," he said. He came onto the bed and started touching her. "Stop it," Hope said, but he wouldn't stop. Finally, Hope yelled at Randy, "make him stop!"

Randy's brother pulled his pants down, and Hope cried out, "make him stop, Randy!" Randy said to Hope. "Give it to him just once." Hope shouted at Randy's brother, "if you have sex with me, it's rape!" Randy finally told his brother to stop. He pulled his pants up and left the room with an angry look on his face. He took Hope's underwear and told her, "I'm going to tell Bryan you were here." Randy's brother brought Bryan into the room. He took Hope's underwear and put it on Bryan's head. Hope was so embarrassed. She didn't know Randy's brother was going to do it.

Bryan stood at the door watching while Hope was under the sheets with Randy. She couldn't get from under the sheets because Randy's brother had taken her underwear. Hope saw that Bryan was hurt. He looked at Randy and Hope, but she didn't know what to say.

Bryan walked away. Hope felt terrible for what happened. She knew how he felt about her, but she never told him they could only be friends. It was the last time she ever saw him.

Hope was angry with Randy and his brother. She couldn't understand why he let his brother do that to her. It was like he wanted her to have sex with him. Hope stayed away from Randy's house after that time. She spent more time with her cousins again, going out every weekend. They found it odd that she was spending so much time with them and asked, "why aren't you going to Randy's house anymore?" Hope replied, "no reason." Hope was embarrassed by what Randy and his brother did to her. She didn't know how to tell them what happened without being judged.

Hope's aunt got angry that Jessie, Lena, and Hope were going out so often. They would go to parties with Lena's brother, a DJ, who worked most weekends. When Hope and her cousins weren't at a party, they would go to Jessie's boyfriend's house. Aunt Alexandra said, one Saturday morning before she went to work, "if any of you girls leave this house today, I'm going to kick you all out." Hope was so afraid. She told her cousins, "Maybe we shouldn't leave the house." But her cousins didn't care. They didn't believe that she would kick them out. Jessie said they would meet up with her boyfriend and brother to play pool. "Are you coming?" said Jessie and Lena. "I'm staying," said Hope.

Hope left the house because she wasn't feeling wanted at home. Mrs. Lewis did everything to make Hope want to leave. She just wanted to go somewhere where she felt happy, even for just a moment. But when her aunt warned them not to leave the house, Hope listened. She didn't want to end up on the street with no papers and nowhere to go. So when Alexandra came home from work, she asked, "where are Jessie and Lena?" Mrs. Lewis said, "They went out in the afternoon." So Alexandra went back outside and came back with a new lock for the house door and changed it. "No one is to let them in," she announced.

When night fell, Jessie and Lena weren't home yet. Hope was upstairs in the living room but couldn't sleep. "Where could they be at this time of the night," she wondered. Jessie and Lena didn't get home until midnight. They tried to open the door, but with no luck. Finally, they threw a rock at the window, and Hope heard the sound. She looked out the window and saw them. Hope opened the door to the balcony and talked with them. "Aunty changed the lock and said not to let you in." Lena and Jessie told Hope to open the door. Hope knew she was not to disobey her aunt, but she couldn't leave her cousins outside. She opened the door, and they came upstairs quietly so they wouldn't wake up Alexandra.

Hope and her cousins were in the living room whispering. They told Hope how their day went and how much fun they had. "We wish you did come with us," said Lena. While talking, Hope, Jessie and Lena heard someone coming up the stairs, so they hid. It was Alexandra looking for them. She checked their room, and they weren't there. Hope hid because she didn't want her aunt to know that she had disobeyed her. Alexandra went back to bed, not having any luck finding the girls. The following day Alexandra investigates Hope and Jessie's room, where she finds them sharing one small bed as they always did. Their aunt left for work and didn't say anything to Hope and her cousin. So, they got up and went on with their day making their breakfast and cleaning the house.

They thought they were clear, but she was angry when Alexandra came home from work. She went into Lena's room and started packing her clothes into garbage bags. "You are all leaving my house today," she demanded. Jessie packed her clothes while Hope watched her aunt pack Lena's clothes. Hope knew she didn't do anything, so she stayed home as her aunt wanted. Alexandra said, "All you girls want to do is go here, there and everywhere." Hope asked if she had to leave too. Alexandra said, "yes, you too." Hope got very scared. She worried about where she was going to live. She cried, "where am I going to live? I have nowhere to go!" Hope thought to herself as she cried, "is this the reason she took me from my mother, to treat me this way?"

Alexandra threw Lena's clothes outside. Hope and Jessie took their belongings outside, and a lady next door heard the noise and came out to see what was going on. She asked, "what's going on?" Hope and her cousin said, "We got kicked out of the house."

The lady's name was Judith. She said, "my kids are on vacation; they will be home next week. I will take you all in until they come back. We are family." Hope and her cousin didn't know they had other family members in the same building. But God sent Judith to save them from being on the streets, even if it was just for the week. Hope and her cousin took their clothes to her place. It was just the lady and her husband at home since their kids were on vacation. Judith took them to her kids' room and said, "you girls can stay in this room for the week." They thanked her.

The following day, Judith and her husband went to work. They couldn't stay in the house while they were gone, so they had to find somewhere to go until they returned. Judith was kind enough to let them stay there for the week, but she wouldn't let them stay alone. Hope and her cousin would go to Alexandra's house while at work, but Mrs. Lewis wouldn't let them in. So, they went to the Community Center, where they met with a social worker named Susan. She was a lovely lady, and she gave them each a ten-dollar gift card. Then, they went to 'No Frills' to see what they could buy to eat. Ten dollars wasn't enough money to buy food, so they used both cards and bought some food so that the three girls could share.

Lena met her father while going to the Community Center. He asked, "where are you going?" Lena told him, "Mom kicked us out of the house." He replied, "I'm sorry to hear that, but I can't help you girls; I'm looking for somewhere to live myself." Lena's father, Hammer, was Hope's uncle. Their family history was a little complicated, and that's a story for another time. Her father's name was. He couldn't help Lena, Hope, or Jessie because he lived with his son. Lena's brother and her father were not happy where they were living. Lena could see that her father wished he could help them. "Something will work out," said Hammer, and he went on his way.

Hope and her cousins did the same thing every morning that week. They went to the Community Centre, put their gift cards together and bought food. They would find something to do until Judith came home, and they went back into Judith's home. With the week almost over, Judith told them, "Remember, the kids are coming home on Friday." Hope and her cousins said to one another, "we have nowhere to go." They worried about whether they would be living on the streets. Hope and her cousins went to the Community Centre the next day as they always did. Susan was always friendly to them every time they went there. Susan could see that they were not happy. "What's going on with you girls," she asked. They told her that they were not to leave their house, and they stayed with a family member while their kids were on vacation, but now that the kids are back, they have nowhere to go. Susan said, "come and see me tomorrow. I'm going to see how I can help."

The next day they went to see Susan. She said, "sit down; I've got good news and bad news." Hope and her cousins had worried looks on their faces. Even though Susan said it was good news and bad news, they were worried about the bad news. Susan said to Hope, Jessie and Lena, "I have found a shelter, but only Lena can go there." Hope and Jessie couldn't go because they didn't have any status in the country. But Jessie and Hope didn't want to go to the shelter because of the bad things they heard about it.

Susan asked Lena if she wanted to go, and she said, "yes, I'll go," with a sad look on her face. Lena worried that Jessie and Hope couldn't go with her, and she wondered where they would go. Susan told Hope that she could live with her but had rules. "In my house, you're not allowed to talk to any boys on the phone, and you're not allowed to go anywhere you want, but I'll try and help you get your life together." Hope didn't feel that living with Susan was right for her. She wants her freedom because she is still young. Would she live to regret it? Time would tell.

Lena went to the shelter. The cousins said their goodbyes and promised to keep in touch. But now Jessie and Hope had nowhere to go. Hope said, "what are we going to do?" They only had one more day at the house before the children came home from vacation. So Jessie started making calls to see who could help her. She called her boyfriend, who lived alone, but he couldn't help. Jessie was disappointed. They were both afraid that they were going to be homeless. They cried because they didn't know what to do. The only family Hope had was her aunt, and her aunt didn't want her. The lady who took her in for the week talked to her aunt, but Aunt Alexandra said no.

The day Hope and Jessie had to leave the house, the lady said to them, "I spoke with a friend of mine, and I told her of your situation. She wants both of you to go and see her." Hope didn't know the lady but was happy someone was considering taking them in. Her name was Carmen. Hope, Jessie, and the lady went to see Carmen. She sat and talked with them to get to know them. Finally, Carmen said to Hope, "I'll take you in; all you have to do is help me with my boys." Carmen turned to Jessie and said, "I spoke with one of my friends, and they're willing to take you in." Hope and Jessie were both happy that they had somewhere to stay. They returned to the lady's house and collected their belongings.

Living with Carmen was God-sent. She was a genuinely lovely lady who took in a stranger when she didn't have to. She treated Hope like she was part of her family. She helped her around the house and helped her take care of her two boys. Things were going well, living with Carmen. Hope could be an actual teenager now, but she wanted more than just living in the house and caring for the home, the kids and going to church.

Since her cousin lived just ten minutes away, Hope wanted her to come over and visit. But Carmen didn't allow anyone to come to the house. Jessie was going through the same thing where she was living, but it was worse than Hope's situation. She wasn't allowed to have friends over or use the phone. Jessie did use the phone when the lady left for work. She would call Hope and cry because she didn't want to stay there anymore. She said, "I can't even call to see how you're doing. She won't allow it." The lady checked the phone when she came home from work to make sure Jessie didn't use the phone. Jessie made sure she finished everything around the house before the lady returned home and told her when she could eat.

Hope listened to Jessie and felt sorry for her. She realized that her situation was not that bad, at least at times. Hope felt like she was losing her mind living with Carmen. She had to go to church every Tuesday and Friday night, Sunday morning and Sunday night. She was still friends with Alex. He asked Hope if she could braid his hair. Hope asked Carmen, and she said yes. When Alex arrived, he called on the phone and told Hope that he was downstairs. Carmen said, "I want to meet this young man." Hope wondered why she would want to meet him. Hope didn't have any status in the country, and Carmen said she would help her. She didn't get too excited because her aunt made that same promise, and it never happened. Hope called Alex and told him that Carmen wanted to meet him. He said, "why does she want to meet me?" Hope replied, "I'm not sure."

Alex went upstairs and sat down. Carmen introduced herself and asked, "what are your intentions towards Hope?" Hope looked at Carmen with a shocked look on her face when she said to Alex, "could you marry Hope and help her get her papers in this country?" Alex said, "I'm not ready for marriage; I'm still in University working on my career." Hope was thinking to herself, "is she crazy?" She knew Carmen wanted what was best for her, but she believed that getting married was a bit too much. Hope didn't want to get married at such a young age and for the wrong reason. Alex was her friend, and she wanted to keep it that way, he wasn't ready for marriage, and neither was Hope. Eventually, they left, and Alex took Hope back to his house.

Meanwhile, Jessie couldn't take it anymore, living with the lady, so she decided to leave. Lena's brother Brian was leaving for Montreal, and he was going to give up his apartment where he was living with his girlfriend. Jessie decided to take over the place to leave the lady's house. Brian gave her the apartment. Jessie was happy to go, but the lady was angry. She didn't get to mistreat Jessie anymore. But Hope was still living with Carmen, helping her with her kids. Carmen said to Hope, "you have to look for a job." Hope said, "ok." Hope went to the agency to get a job, but she had no luck. She hadn't sent any money to her mother for a while, but she needed to take care of herself first. Hope started to lose faith. She didn't know what else to do. Her life wasn't going anywhere.

Carmen was mad that Hope wasn't working and acted like she no longer wanted her there. Her children were getting rude and disrespectful, and Hope couldn't take it anymore. "Can I visit my cousin Jessie for the weekend," she asked. "Yes, you can," said Carmen.

Hope visited Jessie for the weekend. She was living by herself and by her own rules, and Hope wanted that as well. She didn't want to go back to Carmen's house, and she stayed at Jessie's for the week. Even though she had to go back to the shelter before nightfall, Lena visited. She had fun spending time with Hope and Jessie. Hope didn't tell Carmen she was staying there for a week.

Carmen wasn't pleased and told Hope to go and live with her cousin. Hope was happy. She wanted to leave but didn't know how to make Carmen understand how she felt. Carmen was kind to her, but Hope didn't like the rules of her house. Thus, Hope moved in with Jessie. The apartment was small. It was just a bachelor's apartment. The storage room was the bedroom, and it had no windows. Lena visited Hope and Jessie every day. She missed spending time with them. She talked about the experience she was facing at the shelter. She didn't like it there but had no other choice. Lena decided to leave the shelter and live with Jessie and Hope. Now they were all together again.

Hope and Lena were not working. Jessie had to find a job to keep the apartment after Brian left because he was about to be evicted. Jessie worked as a masseuse at a small plaza at night. Hope and Lena didn't have jobs to help with the bills or food. Fortunately, Jessie had a Social Insurance Number but worked under the table. She found it hard to support Hope and Lena. But Jessie was the eldest of the three and felt it was her responsibility to take care of them. The three girls were living a life of not having to listen to anyone but themselves. They weren't always behaving like family because there were times when they wouldn't speak to each other, but that's what families do.

They didn't have many friends in the building. But one day, there was a knock at the door. Hope opened it, and it was a guy who asked, "is Brian home?" Hope said, "No, he doesn't live here anymore." Jessie came to the door and told him, "Brian moved to Montreal." The guy asked, "Who are you, girls?" Jessie replied, "we are his cousins." He replied, "I'm Brian's friend; we go way back." He said bye, and Jessie closed the door.

Hope and Jessie thought it was the last they would see of Brian's friend, but he came to the apartment one day and asked if he could hang out with them. Since he was one of their cousin's friends, he seemed friendly, so Jessie let him in. They all sat and talked. He told them how he and Brian met during their school days. The girls thought it was good having someone else around to talk to. After that, every day, he went over to visit with them. Jessie worked at night, and Hope and Lena still didn't have jobs, so they didn't mind him being around.

One day while Brian's friend was at their apartment, someone knocked on the door. Jessie opened it, and Hope heard a lady's voice ask, "is my boyfriend up here?" Jessie replied, "Who is your boyfriend?" The guy listened to her voice and knew it was his girlfriend. She told Jessie who her boyfriend was, and Hope let her into the house. While the guy went towards the door, the lady came in. In her Jamaican accent, the lady said, "way yo ah do up ya," in her Jamaican accent. The guy left, and she turned to Jessie and started arguing with her. She said, "ah, so your ah makes 'people man' come to your house?" The lady grabbed Jessie and started a fight in the living room.

The kitchen was close to the living room, so Hope came out and asked the lady, "why are you fighting my cousin? Nobody wants your man!" The lady grabbed Hope while she was holding Jessie. She held Hope by her neck and started squeezing it. Hope screamed, "let me go!!" but she wouldn't. Hope didn't know where she found the strength, but she pushed the lady into the kitchen corner, trying to release her and Jessie. The lady was a big girl, but Hope didn't care that she was twice her size. Hope weighed just a hundred pounds. The lady finally let go of Jessie and left.

That same day when Jessie went to work, she saw the lady, and the lady told Jessie, "I'm sorry for earlier on; my boyfriend explained everything when I got home." Jessie told her, "Your boyfriend and we are just friends." She told Jessie, "Tell your cousin I'm sorry too." The lady laughed and said to Jessie, "your cousin is small, but she's strong. She moved me across the room; I hope we all can be friends." Jessie smiled and said, "yes, for sure."

Lena started dating a guy, so she wasn't home when Brian's friend returned. Jessie and Hope told her what had happened. They all laughed because it was funny. Jessie and the lady went from enemies to friends all in the same day.

Jessie got a new job at a restaurant as a dishwasher. She was just trying to get by. Hope and Lena were still not working. Jessie met a Spanish guy while working there and an old lady there. The old lady was very friendly to her. She showed Jessie how to do different things in the restaurant, other than using the dishwasher. When Jessie came home from work, she told Hope and Lena about her new job and the guy she had met. Hope and Lena could have seen that she was very into him. Would they get together? Time would tell.

6.

Chapter Six

As time went by, things finally started looking good for the girls. Hope got a job, Jessie met a new guy, and she got a new job. And Lena, while she was in the shelter, she applied for housing through the government program, which helps young adults find a home. Lena moved into her new one-bedroom apartment, but she often visited Hope and Jessie. One night they were having fun. Jessie went to bed while Hope and Lena were outside talking. Suddenly Jessie came out of her room with a terrified look on her face, saying, "something was choking me!" Tears were streaming down her face. Hope and Lena were scared. The three of them held each other close. They were afraid to go to the kitchen or the bedroom. They decided to do an old tradition they had seen done by their mothers and grandparents. Hope, Jessie, and Lena took the broom and put it upside down at the door. They knew that back in the old days, and it's what their ancestors did to keep evil spirits away. Hope and her cousins ran to the bedroom, and Jessie said, "let's say a prayer." Jessie said a prayer, then Hope, but when it was time for Lena to say a prayer, she said, "I don't know what to say."

Growing up, their mothers and grandmothers taught them how to pray, but Lena didn't know-how. Hope and Jessie laughed out loud and said, "what do you mean you don't know what to say?" Lena repeated, "I don't know how to pray." They all took a scary night and turned it into a joyful one that Hope and her cousins would never forget.

After almost a year, Jessie and Hope lived at the apartment Brian left them with because he no longer wanted to live there. The apartment had been $3,000 in arrears, and Jessie worked hard to clear $2,000 of the debt to continue living there. But one evening, when Hope and Jessie were at home, there was a knock on the door. Hope opened the door. It was Brian, his girlfriend, one of Hope's grand-aunt's husbands and Brian's friend. Hope said hello, and they came inside. Jessie asked Brian what he was doing there. "I thought you were in Montreal," she said. He replied, "I've returned." Then, Jessie asked, "did you come back to stay?" Brian said, "yes, I'm here to stay."

Brian said to everyone, "welcome to my home." He didn't care how Jessie felt about him moving back without giving her a heads-up. Then, Brian and his girlfriend took to the bedroom. Hope's aunt's husband took the couch-bed, and his friend took the other couch. Hope and Jessie had to sleep between the walkway from the bedroom to the bathroom. The walkway was narrow, but Hope and Jessie had to make it work.

The next day Brian said to Jessie, "can I get the keys?" He didn't thank Jessie for almost clearing the arrears on the apartment. Jessie had less than a thousand left to pay off before Brian returned for his place. Jessie was furious with Brian. She said to Hope, "how could he just come in and take over after all that I have done?" Hope could see that Jessie was furious, but she could do nothing. She was in the same situation as Jessie.

Once again, Hope and Jessie didn't have anywhere to go. They had to sleep on the floor where everyone had to step over them to use the bedroom or wake them up from their sleep to get to the kitchen. They weren't happy. Hope and Jessie went out every day to see if they could find somewhere to live. Lena's home wasn't big enough for Hope and Jessie to live in, as well they didn't want to live with her because she could be bossy. When Hope and Jessie returned to the apartment, they didn't have a key for the door, so they knocked, but there was no answer. It seemed like no one was at home. They went into the staircase closest to the apartment door, so they could see when someone came home. Every time Hope and Jessie heard a door open, they would look to see who it was.

While waiting, Hope and Jessie heard a door open and close. They looked and saw Brian's friend come out, and he went to the elevator. They knocked on the door again. Hope said, "maybe someone's home by now." They knocked on the door again, and Brian's girlfriend opened it. Jessie and Hope told her they had knocked earlier, but there was no answer. She told them that she didn't hear the door because she was sleeping. Hope and Jessie found it strange because they saw Brian's friend come out of the house. They were in the apartment all along but never answered the door. Hope and Jessie looked at each other and said, "hmmm, something's up."

Jessie grew tired of sleeping on the floor after working hard to pay the rent arrears. Jessie and Hope had a cousin living in the building beside where they were staying. Jessie went to her cousin's house to hang out. Sometimes she would sleep there, leaving Hope to stay at the apartment by herself.

One day Jessie came over from her cousin's house and told Hope, "I'm moving in with my cousin Lovely." Hope now thought, "where can I go?" Hope and her aunt started talking again. She didn't want to call her, but she had no choice. Jessie moved in with Lovely and her other cousin Lin. Hope wasn't close to them like Jessie was. Hope talked to her aunt to see if she would take her in once more. Her aunt said, "I'll talk to Lena so you can stay with her," Hope didn't want to live with her, but she had no other option.

Hope moved in with Lena. It was bittersweet because she knew Lena was kind enough to stay with her, but she didn't really like Lena. So when Hope moved in, she asked Lena, "what would you like me to do around the house?" Lena told Hope, "clean up after yourself!" "I could do that; it wouldn't be too hard," Hope pondered to herself. Hope then asked, "where do I sleep?" "You can share the bed with me," said Lena.

At night Lena's boyfriend would come around when Hope was sleeping in the bedroom. Lena would go into the bedroom and wake Hope up to ask her to get up to get one of the mattresses from the bed. Lena took the mattress to the living room for her boyfriend to sleep. When he came around, she would sleep on the bed with Hope. Sometimes Hope went to her aunt's house to spend the day, even though Mrs. Lewis still didn't like her. Hope got used to knowing that Mrs. Lewis would never love her. Hope didn't know that Lena was having a problem with her. She thought everything was going great between them. They laughed and talked, remembering the days' things were bad between them.

One day, when Hope visited her aunt, her aunt asked her, "what's going on between you and Lena?" Hope was confused by the question. She thought things were going great. Hope said, "nothing's going on; everything is ok there." Her aunt replied, "Lena says they had to sleep on the floor every time her boyfriend comes over." Hope paused for a minute and said, "Lena never told me anything about that; if Lena wanted the bed, she could have said something, but when I'm sleeping, she just takes the mattress."

Lena would not say anything to Hope, and It was always the elephant in the room when at her place. Lena complained to her mother about Hope all the time. Then, when Lena's boyfriend didn't come by to sleep, Hope and Lean shared the bed, and when he was around, Lena took one of the mattresses off the bed and took it to the living room for her and her boyfriend to sleep. So Hope didn't understand what was going on.

One day when Hope visited her aunt, her aunt told her, "I want you to move back in with me." Hope didn't hesitate; she moved right back in. Hope's aunt helped her get her job back with her friend. She didn't mind going back to work for Lisa even though she was unfair about the phone bill. Hope went back to work Monday morning, but nothing changed. She had to do the same old things she had to do previously. When Hope got there, Lisa's older daughter would be at home for a bit before she went to work. Hope was only allowed into the kid's room to get their clothes after their bath, the bathroom, and the kitchen to fix their lunch. It was complicated.

Hope and Lena stopped speaking after Hope moved out. However, Hope would hear from Jessie occasionally and visit her when she could. Jessie didn't like that Hope and Lena weren't speaking over what happened, but to Hope, she didn't do anything wrong to Lena.

One day Hope saw Lena in her shirt; it was her favourite shirt. She told Lena to take it off, but she wouldn't. Finally, Hope told her, "If you don't take off my shirt, I'm going to beat you." Hope went back inside and went through some of Lena's clothes at her aunt's house. Lena used to do laundry there, so Hope picked up one of her shirts and wore it to work. While Hope was at her job, the phone rang. It was the police on the phone. "Hello, am I speaking with Hope?" "Yes," she said. He said, "a complaint has been made about you threatening a lady named Lena." Hope explained what happened, and the police officer said, "I'm just going to give you a warning; threatening someone is against the law." Hope said, "thank you, I understand," and he said, "good day to you, Ma'am." Hope hung up the phone. She was even angrier with Lena. She thought, "was Lena trying to get me sent back to my country?" Hope couldn't believe Lena would do such a thing after going through so much together. Hope thought, "I'll never trust her again."

One day Hope visited Jessie, and Jessie told her about a friend she knew in the building. Jessie said, "let's go by him and hang out." When they got there, Hope saw another guy there. She said hello and sat down. Jessie's friend and the other guy wanted to know who Hope was. She said, "this is my cousin Hope." Hope said hi, and the other guy said, "my name is Wayne; nice to meet you." They laughed and talked. It was a friendly conversation, and she had a great time. When Hope and Jessie were leaving, Wayne asked for Hope's number. He asked Hope, "so can we talk sometimes?" Hope told him that she didn't have a phone, so she asked for his number. Wayne didn't believe that Hope didn't have a phone. "Are you just saying that?" Hope said, "no, I don't have a phone; my job doesn't pay me enough to get one." Wayne smiled and said, "I believe you; here's my number."

After work, Hope would call Wayne to get to know him more. Unfortunately, he was older than her. She was 18yrs old while Wayne was in his 30s. Hope didn't mind the age gap. He was a good listener and always made time for her.

Hope and Lena eventually became friends again. Wayne came to visit Hope, and she introduced Lena to Wayne. He was a friendly guy; he was a breath of fresh air. When you were around Wayne, he made you laugh. Hope and her cousins often hung out with Wayne and his friend. It gave them something to do on the weekend. Hope saw Wayne almost every day.

One day, Hope's friend Neal came to Canada to visit. They became best friends over the years, and he wanted to see Hope. She told him where she was living, and she told him that her cousin was having a party and that he should attend. Neal spent the day with Hope before the party. Hope didn't tell Wayne about the party; she just wanted them to get something to eat and have a good time. Hope took Neal to her house to get ready for the party. When they got there, she introduced Neal to Lena and Jessie.

Hope and Neal had fun dancing the night away. Wayne and one of his cousins came to the party and asked Hope, "how come you didn't tell me about the party?" Hope said, "I wasn't sure it was your kind of a party." Hope didn't want Wayne to come to the party because Neal was there. She just wanted to spend some time with her friend from back home. Hope asked Lena and Jessie, "who invited Wayne?" Lena said, "I told him about the party when he called looking for you." Hope went back and forth at the party, so Neal and Wayne didn't get mad at her. She would leave Wayne's side to make sure that Neal was ok. Jessie would check on Neal when Hope was with Wayne.

When the party was over, it was late. No buses were running, and Neal had to go home. Hope asked Wayne if he could give Neal a ride home. Hope wanted to take Neal home, but Wayne wanted Hope to go to his hotel. Wayne said, "I'll let my cousin take him home." Hope asked Lena, "can you go with Neal to make sure he gets home safe?" Lena said, "sure, why not." Hope was mad at Lena for what she had done. She wasn't sure what Lena was up to, but she knew it would soon come to light.

Hope said goodnight to Neal, and she told him that her cousin would follow him home. He was displeased. He wanted Hope to go with him, but she told him she had to go with her boyfriend. Hope called the next day to make sure Neal was ok. She knew he wasn't pleased about how the night ended. Hope wanted to spend as much time with Neal as she could while in Canada. But she had to work. Hope asked Lena to show Neal around because she wasn't working.

When Hope came home from work, every day, Lena wasn't at home. Hope called Neal, but he wasn't home either. Hope called Jessie and asked her, "do you know where Lena is?" Jessie said to Hope, "don't say anything to Lena, but she's with Neal." Hope didn't know Lena and Neal spent so much time together, which made her mad at both of them.

When Lena came to the house, Hope got jealous when she saw her neck full of hickies. Hope called Neal and asked him what went on with Lena. But he just got angry with Hope. Hope was also angry with Lena. She knew how much Hope cared for Neal, but she didn't care. Hope was so angry with Neal. She told him she never wanted to see him again. He reminded her that she had a boyfriend, so she had no reason to get jealous. Neal said to Hope, "I like being with Lena." She didn't want to hear that. Hope knew she had a boyfriend but didn't have the connection with Wayne that she had with Neal.

Hope's aunt didn't like what was going on. She called Hope's mother, Grace, to let her know what was going on. Hope called her mother, but her mother wasn't pleased with her. Grace asked, "Hope what is going on with you?" Hope said, "Nothing is going on, mom." Grace said, "I heard you up there fighting over a man." Hope said, "That's not true, mom." "I did not send you to Canada to fight for any man," said Grace, "I'm very disappointed in you, Hope." Those were words Hope never wanted to hear from her mother. Hope cried and said, "I'm sorry, mom." Grace told Hope she sent her to Canada to make something of herself, not involved in such foolishness. Hope was angry with her aunt. Her aunt was mad at her, and she was even angrier with her daughter Lena. But Hope wouldn't show her anger towards her aunt because she didn't want to get kicked out again.

As angry as Hope was with Neal, she wasn't about to let Lena take Neal away from her. Hope cared for Wayne but didn't want to lose Neal. Hope didn't have much money to see Neal, but she didn't want Lena to win him over, so she made plans to spend the Saturday together. Neal gave his address to Hope, and she took a bus to see him. She just had enough money for bus fare there and back.

Hope didn't want Neal to know that money was a problem for her. Hope went on the bus and lost her way. She didn't have a cell phone to call Neal to let him know she was lost. Hope took the wrong bus. She asked the bus driver how to get to Islington; that's where Neal was. The bus driver told her she was on the wrong bus and would have to take a different one. Hope didn't have enough money for a return fare on another bus, so the bus driver gave her a transfer so she could take the correct bus." She was so happy and didn't know what she would have done if she had spent all her bus money.

Hope finally met Neal, and they spent the day together. She told him about her getting on the wrong bus. Hope left out that she was afraid she wouldn't have had enough money to get back home. She wanted Neal to think that she had it all together, but deep inside, she didn't know how things would work out for her with no legal status in Canada. Unfortunately, Neal couldn't take Hope to his house. His aunt didn't want him to bring any friends to her house. So instead, they took a long walk in the woods.

Neal told Hope what he was like living with his aunt. He told her that he didn't have much to eat at home and that his aunt was mistreating him. Hope felt bad for Neal, but there wasn't much she could do for him. Hope had to deal with her problems. They went to a nearby park, and they sat on a bench to talk for a while before Hope had to go home. Neal kissed Hope, but she didn't like it; she thought it would have been better. Hope pulled away, but Neal pulled her closer. He said to Hope, "I want to have sex with you right here." Hope looked at Neal like he was crazy. She told him, "I didn't come to Canada to have sex in the bush."

Hope wouldn't do it. Not only did she not want to have sex in the bush, but she was dating Wayne. Hope said to Neal, "I have a boyfriend, you know that." Neal replied, "I came to Canada to be with you." He wasn't happy, but that's the way it must be. Hope was a little upset about Neal and Lena, but she wanted to enjoy the day with him. She didn't want to talk about Lena or Wayne, but Hope had to tell him she wasn't single.

When the day ended, Hope and Neal said their goodbyes. Hope wasn't ready to go, but it was getting late. She didn't want to miss her bus. Hope didn't want her aunt to be mad at her. When she got home, Lena was there. She looked at Hope and smiled. Lena knew she went to visit Neal. Hope didn't want a man to come between them, but Neal did.

Wayne called, Hope answered, and he asked, "where were you, I called, and they said you weren't home." Wayne's voice sounded like he already knew, but Hope played along with him. She told him she was out with a friend. Wayne wanted to know who the friend was, but Hope repeated, "just a friend." Wayne was mad. He hung up the phone, furious that Hope wasn't honest with him. Hope already knew that Lena told him she did it just to get back at Hope.

Hope was trying to keep her relationship with Wayne and her friendship with Neal separate, but it wasn't easy. She wanted to spend as much time as she could with Neal when she wasn't working, but Wayne wanted to see her more and more. Wayne tried everything so that Hope wouldn't spend time with Neal. The following weekend he wanted to take Hope out to eat but not say anything to Lena or Jessie.

Hope felt like Jessie was playing both sides. While at the restaurant, Wayne got a phone call, and the person was asking him where he was. By his response, it sounded like a woman. When he got off the phone, Hope asked, "who was that?" Wayne said, "it was your cousin Lena." Hope found that very weird. She asked, "why would my cousin call you to find out where you are?" Wayne replied, "I don't know; maybe she wanted to find out where you are." Hope didn't believe him. She felt like something was going on with Wayne and Lena. Hope asked, "Is there something going on between you and her?" He answered, "no, why would I do that to you?"

Hope couldn't believe what Lena was doing. She couldn't understand why she had Wayne's number to begin with. But Hope tried to play it cool and wasn't going to let Lena spoil her date with Wayne.

After the date, Hope went home. She heard Lena's voice upstairs but went into her room because she didn't want to see her. Jessie called Hope in the evening, but Hope didn't want to talk to her. She knew Jessie wanted information about her date with Wayne to tell Lena. Hope wasn't going to give them the satisfaction. Jessie and Lena had been close since they were little kids. Hope was never that close with them. She always felt like an odd one out when she was around them. Hope tried to be as close to them as they allowed her to be, but Jessie and Lena will be best friends forever.

Neal called Hope and told her that he was leaving for Saint Catherines. Hope asked sadly, "why are you leaving?" Neal told her that he had to leave because his aunt was mistreating him. He said, "my mother is in Saint Catherines, and she said that I could come and stay with her." Hope wasn't happy. She didn't get to spend as much time with him as she wanted but understood that she couldn't help him.

7.

Chapter Seven

Wayne called Hope because he wanted her to go to Karaoke. She was very excited. Hope invited Jessie, and she was happy to go along. So Wayne picked up Hope, and his cousin was going with them also. Wayne's cousin was driving, and he drove them to Jessie's house to pick her up. Wayne told Hope that he had to drop by his child's mother, Janice's house first, and Hope said, "ok." So he went into the house, and Hope, Jessie, and his cousin waited in the car.

Time went on, and he was still in Janice's house. Hope was getting angry. Wayne finally came out and said to his cousin, "Janice wants to come along." Hope exclaimed, "Say what!" He said to Hope, "you don't mind, right," and Hope said, "no, I don't." She knew she couldn't stop him anyway.

Janice got in the car, and she, Hope, and Wayne sat in the car's back seat. Hope was in the middle of Wayne and Janice. As she sat there, Wayne put his hand over to the other side, and Hope could feel Wayne's hand touching Janice. Janice didn't care that Wayne was touching her. She came in the car with an attitude that she was better than Hope and her cousin Jessie.

When they got to the Karaoke restaurant, they got a table and sat down. Wayne ordered hot wings and drinks. Hope and Jessie tried to have fun, and they went up to sing on the karaoke machine. Janice didn't say anything to Hope or Jessie. She only talked to Wayne and his cousin. Wayne could see that Hope was feeling uncomfortable by the way he was talking to Janice. Jessie saw that Hope wasn't ok with what she saw, so she took her into the bathroom. Hope broke down and cried. She didn't understand why Wayne brought Janice along. Hope asked Jessie, "Is it normal for a guy to bring his "ex" on a date with his new girlfriend?" Jessie said, "Nope, not at all." Jessie told Hope, "You should stop crying; you don't want to give her that much power."

Hope and Jessie went back to the table. Wayne asked, "what took you girls so long? We almost ate all the wings." He was trying to be funny, but Hope wasn't laughing. Wayne could see that Hope wasn't happy. He tried to comfort her, and he told her to come and sit on his lap. Hope did and gave a dirty look to Janice, and Janice wasn't happy. Hope felt good that she didn't like it.

The night was over, and Wayne dropped Hope back at her house. He said to her, "let's go into the staircase," Hope said, "for what?" He replied, "you know." She was still angry with Wayne and believed that he was still sleeping with Janice. She said to Wayne, "no, I'm tired; I just want to go home and go to bed." Hope and Wayne were together for almost a year. He never took her to his house, and she would ask him, "Why don't you ever take me to your house?" He said, "I'm living with my sister, and we don't get along at times." Hope was young, just eighteen years old. She couldn't tell when a man was lying to her. Hope believed him, and Wayne would take her to his cousin's house when he wanted sex or would do it in his car in the parking lot.

One evening when Wayne picked Hope up, he said, "I'm going to take you to my house. Hope said, "really?" She was surprised that he wanted to take her to his home. Wayne lived in a beautiful apartment building and Hope said to him, "for a guy who sells used cars, you've done well for yourself." Wayne went downstairs into the parking garage. He stopped the car, hesitated for a bit, and said, "shit I forgot my house keys at work." Hope said to Wayne, "it's ok, let's go back," Hope didn't believe him. It seemed like Wayne was playing a game on her. Would she ever go to Wayne's house? Time would tell.

Wayne knew everything that Hope was going through. He knew she didn't have legal status in Canada. He knew that Hope wasn't happy at home. He saw that she was hurting, and he dried her tears. Later that evening, Wayne called Hope. She was at home dealing with problems with Mrs. Lewis. Every time Mrs. Lewis heard the phone ring, she wanted to be the one to answer the phone. She couldn't walk very fast but was pretty quick when it came to the phone. Wayne wanted to see Hope. He had a cousin who lived in Hope's aunt's same housing complex. All Hope had to do was walk to the back of the building into the parking lot to meet him. He said to Hope, "I want you to meet a cousin of mine." So they both went to his cousin's house. He knocked, and a guy came to the door. They hugged, and Wayne said, "meet my girlfriend Hope." Hope said hello.

His family seemed like good people. They told stories about growing up and how hard Wayne used to be on them. Hope was happy to be somewhere full of laughter. Wayne said to Hope, "let's go outside." Hope said goodbye to his family went to his car, where they had sex. Wayne was acting nervous around her, but she couldn't put her finger on why he was behaving that way. Hope asked him if everything was ok. He said, yes, everything was fine. Then Wayne pulled out a ring and said to Hope, "I know everything you're going through, and I want to help you get your papers, so you don't have to look over your shoulder anymore." Hope's mouth dropped when she saw the ring. She looked at Wayne and didn't know what to say. She then said, "I'm not ready for marriage!!"

Hope didn't think Wayne was the right guy for her. She didn't care about him, just what he told her. She was just having fun with him.

Wayne wasn't expecting Hope to say no. Instead, he said to Hope, "I was only trying to help you." Hope kissed him on the cheek and said, "I know and thank you, but I'm just not ready for that." Wayne took Hope home. He was highly disappointed.

Hope called her mother the next day and told her that Wayne wanted to marry her. Hope's mother asked, "Who is Wayne?" Hope wanted her mother's advice. She forgot she never mentioned Wayne before. Hope told her, "He's a guy I'm seeing." Grace told Hope, "If he wants to help you get your papers in the country, take the help." Hope replied, "I turned him down." Grace asked, "why did you do that?" Hope said, "Mom, don't get mad, but he's a bit older than me." Grace asked how old he was. Hope told her that he was 35 years old. Grace said, "if you like him and he wants to help, you should let him."

Hope knew her mother didn't want her to come back home. She just had another baby with James, so Hope coming back would be another mouth to feed. Hope just wanted to be a teenager. She and Lena were close again. They all liked going out to parties with Lena's brother and just plain having fun.

It was Caribana and Hope, Jessie and Lena wanted to go. It was Hope's first time, and she was ready. Hope looked at her clothes, but she had nothing to wear. The pants she wanted to wear were dirty. That morning she washed them. Her aunt didn't have a dryer. She depended on the sun to dry them outside, but it was cloudy. Hope tried using an iron to dry them, but it didn't work. Hope's aunt had a tall lamp in the living room corner. She put the pants on top of the lamp so that the light from the bulb would dry them fast. She went to her room, trying to get ready for Caribana.

While in the bedroom, Hope heard the fire alarm go off. She quickly ran upstairs and saw that the living room curtain was on fire, all because she had put her pants on the lamp. Hope was panicking; she knew her aunt would be mad. She ran to the kitchen and got water to put out the fire. Unfortunately, she burned half of the curtain and her pants, and she would not have been able to wear them anymore. Hope wasn't worried about her pants, but she was afraid of what her aunt would do. She still wanted to go to Caribana, though. Lena came by to see if Hope was ready. Mrs. Lewis came and said to Lena, "Hope almost burnt the house down."

Hope, Jessie, and Lena were still going to Caribana. They were unstoppable. They called themselves the J.L.H. The bond between them was undeniable. They had lots of fun at Caribana. Hope danced like there was no tomorrow, but Hope knew that she had her aunt to answer when she got home. But for now, she was having fun.

When Hope got home, she went into the house. Her aunt, who was in the kitchen, barked, "how did this happen?" Hope didn't know what to say, but she answered, "I put my pants on the lamp." Her aunt said in her angry voice, "why would you put your pants on top of the lamp? You almost burned my house down." Hope knew what she did was wrong. She had no defence. Alexandra called Grace and told her what Hope had done. Grace was angry and told Hope to apologize.

Hope's cousin Brian came to visit his mother and grandmother. He told Hope that someone she knew was asking about her. Hope said, "who is it?" Brian said, "do you remember Anthony? You two went to school together?" Hope said, "Yes, I remember him." Brian said, "I told him that you were living with my mom, and he wants to give you his number." She asked, "Is he living in Toronto?" Brian told her that he was living in Montreal. Hope took his number. She called Anthony that night and said, "hello," and Anthony replied, "hello, who is this." Hope said, "you don't know who this is?" He said that he didn't. She laughed and said, "I was the girl you picked on in class." He said, "Is this Hope?" She smiled and said yes. They had a pleasant conversation going down memory lane. Hope even forgot Wayne was still in the picture, but not really. She wasn't interested in Wayne anymore.

Something never sat right with Wayne. He never took her to his house and always wanted sex in the park or at his friend's house. Hope didn't understand why he wanted to marry her. She felt Wayne was playing her because she was young.

Anthony came to Toronto for a visit. He and Brian were friends. He called to tell her that he was at Brian's house and spending the week with him. Hope and Anthony hugged when she visited him, and she didn't want to let him go. It had been a long time, so they sat and talked about their school days. Their time in class together. Anthony was her second love after Neal. When Hope was in class, she would dream about him. Sometimes, when she wasn't doing well with her schoolwork, Hope would daydream that he would be hers one day. Every girl wanted to be with Anthony. Hope didn't think he ever looked at her. She didn't feel she was his type. Anthony dropped out of school, and Hope never saw him again until he came to Toronto.

Even though Hope and Wayne were dating, she wanted her primary school sweetheart Anthony. After talking for hours, it was time to get ready for Brian's party that Anthony came for. Anthony asked if he could walk Hope home, and she said yes. When they got to her house, she invited him in. Mrs. Lewis asked Hope, "Who is this young man?" He introduced himself, "I'm Anthony, Brian and Hope's friend." Mrs. Lewis asked, "Who are your people?" Anthony told her who he was related to.

Hope and Anthony went back to Brian's house for the party. They danced the whole night; Anthony didn't want her to dance with anyone else. He wanted that night for him and her. Hope spent the night with Anthony. They had sex for the first time. It was everything she imagined it would be with him. They didn't sleep much.

When morning came, Hope was still there. She got up and showered, and put on one of Anthony's shirts. They stayed in bed all day and had sex, but Anthony didn't want to use a condom. Hope didn't know why she allowed him to do that, but she did. She knew he wanted to be with her. He whispered into Hope's ear, "I want you to have my baby." Hope didn't mind if it happened.

Anthony went back to Montreal, and she kept talking to him on the phone. Finally, he told her that he disliked Montreal, and Hope said, "why don't you come to Toronto?" He said he would think about it. Before the weekend, Anthony called Hope and told her that he was moving to Toronto and staying with Brian.

Hope got scared when she didn't get her period. She thought that she could be pregnant. When Hope visited Jessie and told her she might be pregnant, Jessie said, "are you sure?" Hope replied, "my period hasn't come for a few days; it was always on time and never late." In the evening, while still at Jessie's house, she went to the bathroom, and when she wiped herself, she saw blood. She wasn't happy. Hope called out to Jessie and said, "I'm not pregnant; my period just came!!" Jessie got her a sanitary pad.

Wayne called Hope, but she paid him no mind; she didn't want to tell him it was over. He eventually got the picture when she stopped taking his calls. Hope went to Brian's house to meet Anthony. When Hope saw him, all her feelings for him rushed back to her. Hope and Anthony talked and talked; one thing led to another, and they were having sex again. It felt suitable for Hope, and she didn't want it to stop. Being with him helped her forget about Wayne as if he was never there. Hope spent the weekend with Anthony and every day after work. She loved being with him. He was everything Hope wanted in a man.

However, things weren't going right with Anthony at Brian's place. He came from Montreal to Toronto with one of his friends. He was sharing storage with two other guys and paid a lot of rent.

Hope moved out of her aunt's house because she was tired of being mistreated by Mrs. Lewis. She now lived with Jessie and her cousin Marcy, and Anthony asked to stay with her. He visited Hope at her new home, and she was glad he asked her. Hope said, "yes, you can." Hope wanted to take their relationship to the next level. Anthony didn't want to go back to Brian's house. He asked Hope if she would get his clothes. She was happy to do it with Jessie's help. Jessie did not mind going. So, they went to Brian's house to pick up Anthony's stuff. Anthony wasn't sure how to tell Brian he was leaving.

It felt helpful for Hope to have a guy next to her. She was eighteen, and she felt she was ready to settle down with Anthony. She didn't want any other guy; he was the one for her.

Things were going great for Hope and Anthony, but she got pregnant. Hope was scared. She didn't know what to do. Hope had sex with her ex-boyfriend Wayne. Anthony never used a condom, and he always came inside her. But she wasn't 100% sure, and he would say the baby was his. Hope didn't think she was ready to be a mother. She thought, "I'm too young to have a child. I would be a child bringing another child into the world."

Whether Wayne or Anthony was the father, she knew that Wayne never came inside her. They always played it safe. Hope didn't tell Anthony she was pregnant. She was trying to find a way to break the news to him, but she didn't want to wait too long either. Every day she went to work, she couldn't keep anything down. Finally, her boss saw her in the bathroom vomiting and asked, "are you pregnant?" Hope told her she was.

Everything happened so fast. Hope didn't know what to do; she shared her concerns about the pregnancy with Jessie. Jessie asked her if she was sure that it was Anthony's. Hope said, "yes, I'm sure." She couldn't believe Jessie would ask her that question. Hope started questioning herself, "can Wayne be the father of my baby? It's not possible." Hope thought, "ever since Anthony and I met, he wanted me to have a baby for him, and he had unprotected sex with me."

Hope, Jessie, and Anthony went to the mall to shop at a clothing store. Hope and Jessie looked at the baby clothes while Anthony went to the men's section. Jessie said to Hope, "I'm going to tell Anthony, and I'm going to tell him he's not the father." Hope wasn't happy with Jessie because she knew about the last false alarm. Hope never told her what using Epsom salts to clean with after her period was like. Hope knew if she told Jessie, she would have shared it with Lena. Hope didn't want anyone else to know about her pregnancy scare and didn't want Jessie to think she had aborted the baby.

Hope knew she wasn't ready for a baby. She didn't know why she let Anthony come inside her all the time. Hope started to cry and say to herself, "how am I going to tell him about the baby without thinking it's not his?" Hope and Jessie stopped speaking. She didn't like what she had said to her. Every day she went to work, she didn't have to see Jessie; she went to work till 11 p.m.

Jessie wanted Hope to get jealous when she was at home on the weekends. She would invite Anthony into her bedroom to watch T.V. Hope always felt like Jessie was jealous of her relationship with Anthony. One night Hope and Anthony got into an argument because of Jessie. Hope didn't like Anthony being in Jessie's room every night, and Hope and Anthony got mad with each other. But Jessie didn't care if Hope didn't like her boyfriend alone with her in her bedroom. When Jessie came home from work, she saw Hope lying on Anthony's lap, and she wasn't happy. Hope and Anthony were speaking to each other again, and Hope could see that Jessie was not pleased when she saw them. Hope wasn't feeling well. She called her boss and told her that she was sick. Anthony asked Hope, "why aren't you going to work?" She told him she wanted to stay home with him. Hope's boss Lisa called Jessie and told her what Hope had said, and she asked if Hope was pregnant. Jessie told her that she wasn't sure. Jessie called Anthony into her room and told him what Lisa had said to her. Jessie proceeded to ask Anthony, "did Hope tell you she was pregnant?" Anthony said, "no." Jessie knew Hope was pregnant, and she wanted to tell Anthony, but she was waiting for the right moment to tell him.

When Anthony went back into the living room, Hope could see he was angry. "Are you pregnant?" he asked. Hope stumbled with her words; she replied, "who told you that?" Anthony said, "Jessie just told me that you told Lisa." Hope thought even though Jessie was mad with her, she would never tell her secret. They never tell each other's secrets, even if they are angry at each other. Hope said to Anthony, "yes, I'm pregnant, and it's yours." She started to cry and asked Anthony to forgive her for not telling him right away. Anthony didn't believe the baby was his. He knew Hope was dating Wayne when she saw him in the beginning. Hope didn't hide it from Anthony. She was always honest with him about Wayne.

Anthony told her to tell Wayne about the baby. Hope cried and said, "don't leave me, I love you!" Anthony said, "don't worry about me; take care of you and the baby." Hope didn't know what to do. She didn't want to raise a child without a father, and she didn't have enough money for an abortion. Hope called Wayne and told him she was pregnant and wanted to keep the baby. Wayne asks, "your boyfriend doesn't want the baby?" Hope answered, "no, because he thinks the baby is yours." Wayne laughed; he thought it was all a joke. Hope asked, "can you help me pay for the abortion?" Wayne said, "you should have stayed with me instead of a guy who doesn't know how to be a man. How much do you need?" Hope told him she needed $500. Hope asked Wayne if he could give her a ride to the abortion clinic. He said, "yes, what time do you need to be picked up?" Even though Wayne lost Hope to Anthony, he still wanted to be there for her, so he took her to the clinic.

At the clinic, the doctor gave Hope a gown to put on, and she laid on the exam table crying and thought to herself, "I can't go through with this." The doctor came into the room and told her they were ready to start. He told her that they would have to do an ultrasound first. The doctor turned the screen towards Hope. He asked, "do you want to see the baby?" Hope looked at the screen and started to cry. She didn't want to go through with the abortion but didn't want to raise the baby alone. As the doctor performed the abortion, Hope said under her breathe, "Lord, please forgive me."

8.

Chapter Eight

Hope got home, and no one was there. She wondered where Anthony could be. Jessie wasn't at home either. Hope wondered if they were together. She went into the bedroom and laid down and cried. She wished she had kept the baby. Anthony came home, and he saw Hope in their bedroom crying. Hope didn't think he wanted to share the room with her anymore. He looked at her, then walked out and into Jessie's room; Hope couldn't say anything to him. She knew she had hurt him. He came to bed in the middle of the night after leaving Jessie's room. Hope asked, "can we talk?" He said, "go right ahead." Hope said to Anthony, "I love you. I never meant to hurt you." She tried to work things out. Anthony told Hope that he had spoken to Cynthia's mother and told her what she said about the false alarm with the first pregnancy. She told him Hope was right.

Anthony said, "you aborted my baby, you lied to me, I didn't believe you, and now my baby is gone." Hope said to him, "please forgive me, and I hope God will forgive me too." Hope tried everything to fix her relationship with Anthony, but he spent all his time with Jessie. They slept in the same bed, but he wouldn't sleep close to her. Finally, Jessie got a babysitting job. When she wasn't at her regular job, she slept at the other job to babysit. Hope was glad when Jessie wasn't home because she wanted to fix her relationship with Anthony.

After weeks of getting Anthony to forgive her, he was still angry that she got an abortion. It was the hardest thing Hope had ever done in her life. She tried to put it behind her, but it still hurt. Anthony loved Hope, and he wanted to be with her, but it was too painful to get over what she had done. He told her he still wanted to work on their relationship. Hope was happy to hear those words; she looked at him and cried. He smiled and wiped her tears and said, "we're going to be okay." Hope knew she must prove herself to him. She was happy to show her love to him. Hope knew it wouldn't be easy to ease his pain, but she was willing to try.

Hope and Anthony were in the living room one day, having a little time together. Jessie came home from work and saw Hope lying on Anthony's lap, and she wasn't happy to see them together. Families should want to see each other happy, but that's not how it was with Hope's family because everyone was backbiting each other. Hope and Jessie mended their friendship as time went by, and Hope and Anthony's relationship was strong. She forgave Jessie for what she had done, but she wouldn't forget it.

After the abortion, Hope didn't go back to work. However, she still had the job and was happy to return eventually. It would be hard on Anthony because he had to pay the rent by himself, but she just wanted to recover from her surgery. Even though Anthony and Hope fixed their relationship, another problem arose, but it wasn't Hope's fault this time.

One day when Hope and Jessie were home, the phone rang. She answered and said, "hello." The woman on the other end said, "can I speak to Anthony?" Hope said to Jessie, "a woman is asking for Anthony." Jessie said, "ask who she is." Hope asked, "Who are you?" The girl said, "I am Anthony's girlfriend, Jessica." Hope put the phone on speaker so Jessie could hear. Hope said to her, "what did you say?" She repeated, "I'm Anthony's girlfriend from Barbados." Hope knew the accent because her best friend Neal was from there. Hope said to Jessica, "I thought I was Anthony's girlfriend." She said, "I hear you." Hope asked, "who did he tell you he was living with?"

Jessica said, "He said he was staying with his aunt." Hope said, "Oh, I see, I'm not his aunt, and we live together."

Hope didn't know Anthony had a girlfriend in Barbados. She knew he spent time there but never talked about a girlfriend. Finally, hope said to Jessie, "and he was judging me for what I did!" Hope shook her head. When Anthony came home, she asked him about Jessica. He acted like he didn't know what Hope was talking about. She said, "your girlfriend from Barbados!" He told her that she was just a friend, but Hope didn't believe him. Hope couldn't judge him about lying when she told one of her own. Every evening after work, Anthony would stop by Brian's house. He wouldn't come home until late. Every time Hope asked him where he was, he said he was at Brian's house.

When Hope came home from work, she went into the kitchen to fix dinner when the phone rang. It was another woman calling. Hope's older cousin Lovely picked up the phone, and she heard her speaking to the woman. "Who do you want to speak to?" "Oh, Anthony's not home." Before Lovely could hang up the phone, Hope took it from her; she said, "hello, who is this?" The woman said her name was Mia. Hope said, "why are you calling Anthony?" She replied, "he is my boyfriend." Hope told Mia that she was the second person calling to say she was his girlfriend. Mia didn't know what to say, so she just said, "okay." Hope asked the question again, "who did Anthony say he lived with?" because it seemed like he was using living with his aunt Lovely to get away with cheating, while Hope's cousin Lovely is not his aunt. Mia said, "he said he was living with his aunt." Hope said, "here we go again." Mia said, "he took me to introduce me to his cousin." Hope asked, "what, cousin?" She said, "Brian." Hope told her, "He isn't Anthony's cousin; Brian is my cousin."

Hope didn't know why she stayed on the phone with her for so long, but she was happy she did. Now she knew what Anthony was doing when she wasn't around and that her cousin Brian didn't care about her. Anthony came home, and Hope was angry about what she heard again. She asked Anthony, "what's going on with you?" "A girl named Mia called for you," she continued. He acted like he didn't know what was going on. He smiled and said, "Who is Mia?" Hope said, "the same girl you took to my cousin's house and introduced her to him." She said to him, "So you're lying and saying that I'm your aunt who you live with?" He said, "I don't know what you're talking about." Hope could see this wasn't the end of his cheating ways. He got angry and left the house.

Jessie came home from work that night, and she was furious. She told Hope, "A girl called my phone for Anthony, and when I ran to answer it, the phone fell and broke." Hope asked Jessie, "what was the girl's name?" She replied, "she said her name was Mia." Hope got angry. Anthony wasn't home yet. When he got back, Hope asked him, "Why do you have women calling my cousin's phone? Now it's broken because of you."

Anthony was annoyed by Hope's question. He hit her in the face. She couldn't believe what he had done. Hope tried to fight back, but he kept hitting her harder, and she stopped fighting back. Finally, she broke free and ran out of the bedroom into the bathroom, screaming and locking the door. Anthony came to the bathroom door and yelled at her to open the door. She refused, and she cried, "please stop!" He kept yelling, "Open the door, or I'll break it down!" Hope didn't want Anthony to damage her cousin's apartment, so she said, "Okay, I'll open the door."

Still crying, she opened the door, and Anthony continued the beating. Lovely and Jessie came out of their rooms and told Anthony to leave her alone. Jessie tried to get Hope away from him, but he wouldn't let go of her. Anthony pulled Hope back into the bedroom, but he wouldn't stop hitting her. He pushed her into the bedroom corner near a window and kept hitting her in the face. Hope covered her face while he hit her in the head. Anthony then pushed Hope's head through the window while Hope screamed, "please stop!!"

Jessie ran to the bedroom and shouted, "Anthony, what have you done?" Hope was in the corner of the room, bent over crying. She took Hope to the bathroom and took the glass out of her hair. Hope did not get cut because she had hair extensions. Jessie told her, "You don't have to put up with this; leave him!" Hope said, "I love him. I don't know how." Jessie took Hope into her bedroom. Lovely told Anthony, "You didn't have to do that to her; she's not a punching bag."

When the chaos died down, Hope said to Jessie, "I hope he's thinking about what he did to me." Anthony was drunk from wherever he came from. Then there was a knock at the door. Lovely opened it. A man was at the door and said he was the building security guard. Hope and Jessie went to the door. The security guard was with a female guard. Lovely asked, "What's wrong?" The male security guard said, "we heard some noises while on patrol." Hope and her cousins knew that they were lying. They knew that one of their neighbours must have called them, but they wouldn't say. The security guards asked to come into the apartment, and Marica said, "sure." They looked around the apartment, and then they went onto the balcony where they saw the broken glass. They went into Hope and Anthony's bedroom. The male guard said to Anthony. "Hello, sir, what happened here?" He said it was just an accident. He asked, "what kind of accident was it?" The guards could see when Hope came to the door that she had been crying. Anthony told the guards his hand hit the glass. The female guard asked, "Do you share this room?" Hope said, "We both share it."

The male guard asked Anthony to walk to the living room while the female guard stayed and talked to Hope. She took out her notepad and asked Hope, "can you tell me what happened?" Hope told her, "We got into an argument, and his hand hit the window by accident." As the guard kept writing in her notebook, she asked, "What was the argument about? Why did he get so angry that he broke the glass?" Hope explained that it was about a girl that called him on her cousin's phone, and she dropped and broke her phone when she ran to answer the call. The guard asked, "Anthony doesn't have his phone?" Hope said, "no, he doesn't." She could see the guard didn't believe her story, but she wasn't going to say anything else.

The other guard returned to the room with Anthony and asked, "Is everything okay now?" Anthony pulled Hope close, smiling and said, "Everything is good." Hope lied to the guards because she didn't want Anthony to get in trouble. She thought if she had told the truth, the guards would have called the police. They left, and Anthony said, "the guards are acting like they're the police." Jessie and Marica were angry and walked away. Hope was afraid to sleep in the same bed as Anthony. She slept at the end of the bed while he slept in the corner, leaving a space between them. While Hope was sleeping, he came over to Hope's side of the bed and started touching her, but she didn't want him to. Anthony wanted to have sex, and Hope was afraid he would hit her again if she didn't let him. Hope couldn't hold back her tears. He looked at Hope and said, "I'm sorry, I'll never do it again." She just kept on crying.

One evening when Anthony was away, Mia called for him again. Hope asked, "why are you still calling? I told you I'm his girlfriend." Mia replied, "Anthony told me he doesn't have a girlfriend." Hope hung up the phone. She didn't want to talk to her.

Hope and Jessie were bored at home, so they decided to go to the mall. It was within walking distance from their home. While walking around, Hope and Jessie saw Anthony on a payphone. Hope could see he was smiling and looking like he was having a pleasant conversation. However, he didn't see them. He was too busy talking on the phone to notice that Hope was there. Hope walked up to him. He was surprised to see her at the mall. She just stood there; she didn't say anything at first. She wanted to see how he would react to her being there while he was on the phone.

Anthony didn't know what to say because he was on the phone with another woman. Hope asked, "who are you talking to?" Anthony didn't answer. He told the woman he would call her back. Hope said, "So this is what you do when women can't call the house phone, you come here and call them?" Hope and Jessie just walked away. He didn't come home after the mall. Finally, hope couldn't take it anymore. Jessie had a friend who was having a party. She said to Hope, "let's go out tonight." At first, Hope didn't want to go because of what happened with Anthony at the mall.

Jessie convinced Hope to go to the party. They got dressed and took pictures before they left the house. They got to the party, and lots of people were there, and they had lots of fun. But Hope was still angry with Anthony. He wasn't home and didn't have a cell phone, so she couldn't call him to let him know she was going out. Hope just wanted to have fun and forget about Anthony and his violent and cheating ways. But to Hope's surprise, Anthony came to the same party with his friend Mark. He wasn't expecting Hope to be at the party. She could see Anthony wasn't happy that she was there, so he and his friend left. Hope didn't care if he was angry; she just wanted to have a good time.

When Hope and Jessie got home, she thought Anthony had come back, but she didn't see nor hear him. She went into the bedroom thinking he may be sleeping, but he wasn't there, and his clothes were gone. Hope called his friend Mark and asked, "Is Anthony there?" He said he wasn't. She asked if he knew where he was. "All his clothes are gone," she said. Mark replied, "After we left the party, he went home." Hope could tell that Mark was lying.

Hope laid in their bed and cried herself to sleep. She couldn't believe Anthony had left. She thought it was all a dream the following day, but he was gone. She didn't want to leave her room. Jessie came in and asked, "Are you okay?" Hope cried and said, "I wasn't expecting him to leave." Jessie told Hope she needed to eat something, but she didn't want to with all the crazy thoughts running through her head. Hope wanted to kill herself. She had some pain medication which she now pulled close to her, and she put on her favourite song, "You belong to me" by Mariah Carey. She put it on repeat as she lay there. She picked up the bottle of pills, put a bunch in her hand and swallowed them with water. Hope didn't think she could live without Anthony; then, she realized that the pills hadn't done anything but knock her out when she awoke. She didn't take enough to cause her harm. Next, Hope took a blade and slit her wrist. She didn't want to live anymore. But she didn't cut her wrist deep enough to die.

As Hope watched the bleeding, she came to her senses and thought, "it's not right; why should I kill myself while Anthony enjoys his life? I can't hurt my mother like this." She wished she had come to her senses before cutting her wrist but didn't, and now she was in pain.

Hope spent her days calling Anthony on Mark's phone, but he always said he wasn't there. Every day she finished work, she went to Brian's house where Mark was also living, but they kept saying Anthony wasn't home. His friends would call him and let him know she was waiting for him, but Anthony wouldn't return home until Hope left. Hope eventually stopped going to Brian's house looking for Anthony. She didn't want to embarrass herself anymore, so she stopped looking for him. Instead, she decided to focus on herself and her family back home.

Hope's mother, Grace's church, came to Canada for a convention. Hope saved money while doing her babysitting job to help her mother come to Canada. While Anthony and Hope were living together, it helped her save a lot of money.

After weeks of not hearing from Anthony, he came by the house. He was genuinely lovely to Hope, acting like everything was okay with them. He spent the day, and she could feel his love again. They had sex like they were still together. Anthony then said to Hope, "I'm leaving." She didn't want him to go and told him that he could spend the night." He said, "I have to go." As he left, he turned around and told Hope, "I don't have any money to pay my rent this month. Can you help me?" Hope did not want to say no because she still loved him. She told him, "I have some money saved for my mother's plane ticket; how much do you want?" He replied, "300." Hope got the money out of her safe and gave it to him.

Now Hope was a little bit short on cash, and she would have to save more money for her mother's ticket before it was too late. After Anthony left, Jessie came into the bedroom and asked her, "why did he come by?" Hope said, "I thought he wanted to see me, but he just wanted money." Jessie said, "please tell me you didn't give it to him," and Hope said, "yes, I did." She knew that Hope was saving money for her mother's ticket, and Jessie told her, "I'm going to call Grace and let her know what you've done."

Hope didn't want Jessie to call her mother, but she couldn't stop her. Jessie called Grace and told her what Hope had done. Grace told Jessie to put Hope on the phone. Grace was angry with her. She asked Hope, "how could you give Anthony your money after the way he treated you?" Hope cried and said, "Mom, I'll get the money for your ticket." Grace did not want to hear what she had to say and told her to give Jessie the phone.

Hope was angry that Jessie called her mother. She knew that giving Anthony money wasn't right. She was saving the money for her mother, so the strain of sending money every week would get better if Grace were in Canada. Hope worked hard and eventually saved enough money so her mom could go on the church trip.

Her mom brought Hope's little brother Jacob, whom she had never met. Grace gave birth to him while Hope was in Canada. George and Grace finally broke up, and she was dating another guy that Hope knew nothing about. When her mom came to Canada, Hope was happy to see her and meet her baby brother. Grace left behind Hope's sister Leah and Ricardo, Austin, and another sister who Hope also had never met. Her name is Natasha, who Grace had with George.

Austin was in high school. He and Ricardo stayed at the house while Leah was with her father's sister. Natasha was staying with Hope's cousin Lisa. Things were going well with Hope and her mother. She was happy that Grace was there with her. Hope and Anthony were back together, and he slept over at times. But since her mother arrived, she gave the room to her mother and Jacob, while Hope slept in the living room on a blow-up mattress.

Even though Hope and Anthony were back together, he didn't live there. When Anthony didn't sleep at Hope's place, she would sleep at his house. Grace heard everything Jessie and Marica had to say about Hope and Anthony. Hope never told her mother what was going on with her relationship with Anthony. Every time Hope went to Anthony's house, she would come home the next day. Grace was angry with her. Lovely and Grace were always on the balcony talking about some mess.

But one day, everything hit the fan. Grace and Lovely didn't see eye to eye, and Lovely complained that Grace was talking about everything that went on in the house. Lovely loved her privacy. Jessie complained about the same thing, but Hope didn't know what to do. She was stuck in the middle of everything. Hope tried to speak with Grace and told her she would have to act differently now that she was there. Hope said to her mom, "you're not living back home; it's different here." It didn't go well; Grace didn't want to hear it. She told Hope, "I'm the mother; you're the child. Don't tell me what to do!"

Everyone in the house wasn't speaking to each other. Hope slept at Anthony's more often. She didn't know that her mother and cousin kissed and made up. When Hope came home from Anthony's house, everything had changed. Grace got angry at Hope and told her, "Every time you go to work, you don't call or say you're not coming home!" Hope didn't care, she thought, "I pay my rent, I'm not a child anymore, so if I don't want to call or say anything, I can do just that." She would never tell her mom that aloud, though. Grace would beat the socks off her even if she were grown up.

That night it was quiet. Everyone was in their rooms, and Hope was in the living room lying on the sofa. She fell off to sleep while resting. Soon after, she felt someone rubbing their hands down her legs, and she pushed them away. Hope opened her eyes and was about to yell, "what the hell!" but no one was there. She looked in the kitchen and the dining area and didn't see anyone. She thought, "hmmm, who could it have been?" She thought that she was dreaming. *But time would tell!*

In time Jessie started dating Dave. He was a cool guy with long Rasta hair. He seemed like the right guy for Jessie. But, every time Anthony came around, he and Dave hung out. At times they would go to parties together. Jessie hated it; she knew what Anthony and his friends were like.

One hot night Anthony came over to sleep. They put the portable air conditioner (AC) on to cool the living room down. While Hope lays in Anthony's arms, they hear a glass fall in the kitchen. She got up to check it out but found no broken glass. Hope thought, "are we both hearing things?" She went back to lie down, but the AC turned off. Anthony told Hope not to be scared that everything was fine. Hope could see that Anthony was scared, but he pretended that he wasn't because he didn't want Hope to be afraid. The AC came back on, but they knew that they had put it on auto. Hope started to panic, and Anthony said, "let's try to get some sleep." Hope agreed, but the AC turned off again. It seemed like someone was playing a trick on them. Anthony told Hope to close her eyes and go to sleep, but the AC turned on again. Hope said, "Oh hell no! I'm not sleeping out here." Hope got up and ran to Grace's bedroom, and when she looked behind her, Anthony was right there. She jumped on the bed where her mother and Jacob were sleeping.

Grace was scared. She said, "why are you guys so frightened?" Hope told her mother that something was in the living room. Grace being a spiritual woman, knew what was happening. In Grace's room, there were crosses all over the bedroom wall. It was like she was protecting herself from evil spirits. She told Hope and Anthony they could sleep in her room that night.

The window in the bedroom that Anthony pushed Hope's head through never got fixed. Hope didn't want to sleep at the end of the bed, so she told Anthony he had to sleep there.

9.

Chapter Nine

While everyone was trying to get some sleep, Grace woke Hope and Anthony up and said, "look under the door; something's walking up and down. Hope looked under the door. She could see a shadow moving up and down, but there was no noise. It wasn't Jessie or Lovely because they were sleeping. Hope thought it must be a spirit. Hope said to Grace, "now I know who touched me in my sleep."

Many days passed when Hope and Jessie found out they were pregnant. They both told Anthony and Dave. They were excited about the news. Anthony and Hope knew what they went through with the last pregnancy, and Hope was happy that God blessed her once more. ope thought things were going great with her and Anthony. He seemed happy about the baby. One day when Hope came home from work, she visited Anthony at his house like she always did. Hope saw his friends on the balcony. She didn't like his friends because they encouraged him to get involved with girls. Hope knocked on the door, and his friend Mark answered. She asked, "Is Anthony home?" He said he wasn't but told Hope she could come in and wait for him. When she went inside, she saw a female in Anthony's shirt, one she bought for him.

Hope thought, "should I beat this girl down? But again, she probably doesn't know who I am." The girl's name was Stacy. She was laughing and talking with Mark. Hope watched as he talked and laughed with her. Mark didn't care that Hope was there. She saw Mark on his phone and knew he was calling Anthony to let him know she was there. Hope waited and waited, but Anthony didn't show up. Finally, hope left and went to her aunt's house. Grace was there, and Hope proceeded to tell her mother and her cousin what had happened. They asked her what she did. Hope said, "Nothing," as she bowed her head down. Grace said, "Let's go back there, you saw a woman wearing your man's shirt, and you did nothing; I want to see the girl you're afraid of."

Hope and Grace went to Anthony's place. They saw Anthony going into the building, and Grace called out. He looked back and smiled. Then Hope ran to Anthony, and he ran away and laughed like it was a joke. Hope cried and yelled at him, "Why are you doing this to me?" Anthony kept saying sorry. Hope didn't want to stress herself too much because she was pregnant. Grace was angry with Hope. She asked her, "why are you letting yourself get down?" Hope did not want to listen to her mother. She just wanted to know why Anthony would hurt her like that. Later, Hope found out that Stacy knew her and lived with Brian's ex-girlfriend Tasha, who lived two floors above Hope and her cousins. Hope found out that Anthony would visit Stacy before he came to her house. Hope, Jessie, and Tasha were friends, but she never mentioned that Stacy and Anthony saw each other.

Now that Hope knew Stacy and Anthony were together, she went to Tasha's house to confront her. Stacy was at home. Hope asked her, "do you know that Anthony and I are together?" Stacy said no. Tasha decided to expose Stay, and she exclaimed, "yes, you know, I told you!" Tasha didn't want to lose Hope and Jessie's friendship. The girls started to argue with each other, Hope came to fight, but Tasha was doing it for her. Stacy left the house. Tasha said to Hope, "I didn't know that they were fooling around at first, but when I found out, I told her to leave Anthony alone; I thought she did." Hope told Tasha to call Stacy on the phone. "I want to talk to her," she demanded. Tasha called Stacy, and she picked up. Hope said, "I don't want to fight with you, but I want the truth." Hope asked, "did

Anthony tell you that we're together?" She explained, "Anthony told me that you two were not together, and I'm not going to leave him." Hope wanted to beat her ass now. Hope told her, "He'll never leave me for you." Stacy hung up.

Anthony came to the house. Hope told him what Stacy said to her, and he told her, "What she said isn't true." Anthony spilled everything about her to Hope. He admitted, "yes, we had sex; I left in the morning. I don't know why she was in my shirt." Hope thought, "Is that supposed to make me feel better?" Hope loved him and forgave him only because of their unborn child. Hope's boss Jean found out that she was pregnant for the second time. She told Hope, "You can't take care of my kids the way you should while you're pregnant." Hope didn't care that she found out. Hope was tired of the money she was paid and never got any extra overtime. Hope asked Grace if she would like to work for Jean.
Anthony came around more often after Hope found out about him and Stacy. He was trying to make it up to her. Anthony told Hope that he would help out more often now that she wasn't working. Hope became more worried about having a baby with no legal status in Canada. Being with Anthony was like riding on a rollercoaster. Things never stayed stable for too long.

Hope just wanted to focus on her unborn child. She signed up at a free clinic, so she didn't have to pay for a doctor's visit. Hope now heard that Anthony and Mark's ex-girlfriend Christine spent a lot of time together when he wasn't at her house. One day he came to visit her, and he had a phone. Hope asked, "Whose phone is that?" He told her the phone was Christine's. For once, he didn't lie to her. She asked him, "what is going on with the two of you?" Anthony told Hope he wanted her to help him to get his papers. He didn't have legal status in the country either. He said to Hope, "I'm going to marry her so she can help me, but I still want us to be together." Hope looked at him with tears in her eyes, and she said, "I won't be with you once you marry someone else. That will be the end for us.

I won't be with a married man." Anthony tried to convince Hope it was to get his immigration papers. Hope looked at him and thought, "why the hell did he pick his friend's ex?" Hope said to him, "from all the women in Canada, why her?"

Christine was a fast girl. She dated Brian before she dated Mark, Brian's friend, now she wanted to marry Anthony. They say you can't turn a whore into a homemaker. But she wasn't going to be his housewife. It was just business, according to Anthony. Hope couldn't take the stress while pregnant. So she told Anthony to leave. Hope now had to figure out how she would take care of her baby on her own. Hope wasn't surprised when things didn't work out with Christine. She never intended to marry Anthony. She was on social assistance and wouldn't come off it for him or anyone else. She could not be on social assistance while trying to sponsor someone. It was all in Anthony's head.

Grace and the rest of her family were not getting along. So finally, lovely decided she would move out and give up the apartment. She said it was haunted. "It is as if the glass is heard breaking in the kitchen, and there's no one there nor glass on the floor." She said that, when it was just her, Hope and Jessie, the house was more peaceful, but with Grace living there caused too many problems in the home.
Grace wasn't talking to Hope, and Hope let her know that she didn't like the way she was acting in the house. She didn't like telling her friends what was going on in the house. It wasn't right. Grace got up in Hope's face and grabbed her shirt, and said to Hope, "I'm your mother, and you won't talk to me like that." Hope tried to pull away from her. Grace opened her hand to slap Hope, but Hope told her to go. She looked at Hope and remembered that Hope was pregnant, and she let her go. When Hope came home from work, she gave Grace her baby-sitting job the next day. When her mother came home from work, she wouldn't talk to Hope. She stayed a while at Aunt Alexandra's house and returned later that evening.

Hope and Anthony sat down and talked about what Lovely had said that night. Now that Hope was pregnant, Anthony said they should rent a place together. Hope and Anthony spoke to Grace about their plan to rent a place somewhere for all of them. Grace said she would come up with half the rent, while Anthony would come up with the other half for an apartment with the same company. Grace decided to build a life in Canada, she knew it would be hard leaving her other children back home, but it was a sacrifice she had to make for a better life for her and her children. She knew that her children back home were in good hands, with families, until she could get them to come to Canada to be with her. So she sent money back home to take care of them.

Anthony found a two-bedroom apartment. Lovely and Jessie both found their apartments. Jessie didn't like that her apartment was so far away from family, but it was all she could find at that time. It was now a moving day, and everyone was getting their things together. Grace came home from work but didn't say anything to Hope or Anthony. She knew it was time to go, but she wasn't packing. Instead, Grace went outside with Hope's brother Jacob. Anthony started taking Hope's belongings over to the other side of the building. When Anthony came back for more stuff, he told Hope that mom was downstairs crying. He said, "your mother said you didn't tell her we were leaving." Hope was confused why she would say that. Grace knew the moving date; she came home every day but never talked about it.

Hope saw Grace downstairs in the building but didn't say anything. Everyone was moving, but Grace wasn't doing anything. Finally, Jessie came to Hope and said, "I asked your mom if she's not moving." Jessie informed Hope that her mom said she wasn't moving with Hope and Anthony. Jessie said to Hope, "say something to her." Hope told her, "I'm not saying anything to her; mom said she wasn't coming with us, so I have nothing to say." Anthony said to Hope,

"Grace said she wasn't going to live with us anymore, she already rented a place with one of Alexandra's friends, Mrs. P." She was hurt; Grace knew how Mrs. P treated people poorly, yet she chose to live with her rather than with Hope. Grace never told Anthony or Hope that she wouldn't live with them until moving day.

Hope was happy that she and Anthony were living together again. But she was sad that she would have to bring a baby into the world while she had no legal status in the country. Hope worried about the hospital bills and how they would get paid. She wasn't working, and Anthony's job could only cover the rent and food. Since Grace decided not to live with them, they were left alone paying for a two-bedroom apartment.

Hope decided the best thing to do was apply for refugee status. Unfortunately, Jessie didn't have legal status either. She told Hope about a lawyer helping her get her status legally in the country, and then Hope called the lawyer for a consultation. She told the lawyer her history from back home and her history of residing in Canada. He told her that he could help her get her temporary status. She got it and was happy she didn't have to keep looking over her shoulder, at least for now. Unfortunately, Hope couldn't get a job because she was too far behind in her pregnancy, so she sought social assistance.

Hope was still angry with her mother for leaving them to struggle to keep the two-bedroom apartment. Anthony would come home from work angry. Hope thought she had done something wrong. He said, "I met your mother and let her know that we would give the half of her money back, but she told me she didn't want it back because we needed it more than she did." Hope wasn't sure if she should be understanding or mad. She couldn't see any reason for him to act crazy. She thought to herself, "we do need the money." She didn't know what to say to him. He was already angry, and she didn't want him to get mad at her as well. Now that Hope was getting social assistance, Anthony told her they would split the bills between them.

Hope thought that his womanizing behaviour would stop now that they were living together and having a baby. She was wrong. Since he didn't have any status and Hope had temporary status from immigration, Anthony asked her to get a cell phone for him in her name. Every weekend Anthony went out with his friends, he didn't have a phone. When he was gone, there was no way of reaching him if something went wrong. Anthony didn't let Hope use the phone when he was home unless he was beside her. Hope wanted to get two phones, but he said they didn't need two. He always acted like he had something to hide. There was a password on the phone, and though they shared the phone, Hope didn't have the password; she couldn't use it as often as she wanted to.

Anthony always locked himself in the bedroom while he talked to other women. Hope spent most of the time outside in the living room on the floor crying. They just moved into the apartment and didn't have enough money to buy a couch, even though they were preparing for their unborn child. One day Hope asked Anthony to use the phone. Renee was on the display while she was on a call, but Hope didn't pick up. Renee kept calling, so Hope finally answered. She asked to speak to Anthony, and Hope asked, "who are you?" She said, "I didn't call for you; I called for Anthony." Hope got mad, "You're calling for my man," she said. Renee started arguing with Hope, acting as if Hope had taken her man. Hope hung up the phone and forgot she was on another call. Renee called back and went back to cussing Hope. "Do you know we're having a baby?" She didn't care, and she told Hope everything Anthony said about her.

Hope wasn't going to take it anymore. She went to Anthony in the bedroom and demanded, "what the hell did you say about me to that bitch that called your phone that I bought?" He said nothing. He took the phone and went into the hallway of the apartment. Hope could hear him from inside talking to Renee. It sounded like she was arguing with him, and Anthony didn't care what he was doing to Hope.

Hope loved when Jessie came to visit, and Anthony was gone. She lived far away and complained how she lived too far from everyone and had no friends there. Jessie asked, "since you and Anthony have an extra room, could I move in with you guys?" Hope didn't want to live with anyone. Since she came to Canada, she was always living with people. As much as Hope loved her cousin, she was happy living by herself. She said to Jessie, "I'll speak to Anthony and see what he says." Later she spoke with him that evening, and he said yes. Hope wished he'd said no. She didn't want to repeat what went on with Jessie when they were living together.

The pregnancy wasn't going well for Hope. She was sick constantly, and Anthony wouldn't help most of the time. He would rather hang out with his boys. Hope had to cook, clean, and wash their clothes, and her belly was getting bigger. She didn't have the strength to carry the laundry hamper down to the basement, but she had to try. Anthony was no help.

Jessie moved in the following week. It was bittersweet for Hope. She was happy she had someone to talk to since she didn't have a phone. However, things went well with Jessie living with Hope and Anthony. Hope didn't feel alone anymore, and Jessie's boyfriend Dave visited her now and then. Anthony and Dave became friends. Anthony introduced him to his boys, and they had a good time when they went out.

As expected, things just couldn't seem to work out for Jessie and Hope living together. Jessie didn't help as much as Hope would like in the apartment. Hope wasn't mad about doing all the cleaning but was angry about cooking for Jessie while making dinner for her and Anthony. Hope had noticed that when it came to doing work around the apartment, Jessie was always sick, but when Dave came around, she cooked for him. She wouldn't cook for everyone like Hope did for her. Hope started to wish that Jessie had never moved in. Hope told Anthony that she didn't want her living there anymore. Anthony didn't want to listen to her. He was glad that Dave went out with him every weekend, and he didn't have to hear Hope complain about being alone because Jessie was there with her.

Every weekend Anthony went out. There were always different women. They always called his phone, and he didn't care how much he was hurting Hope. Hope was doing Anthony's hair; he had dreadlocks. While working on his hair, a girl called his phone. He told Hope, "I'll be back." Hope knew it was a woman. He went into the other room to talk to her. Dave looked at Hope. He knew it wasn't right what Anthony was doing. The boys were going out that night, and the girl called to see the plan for the night. Anthony finished his call, and he came back for Hope to do his hair. Hope said to him, "I will not finish your hair; go let that girl do it for you."
Hope believed him when he said he was going out with his boys. She said, "you get me to put clothes out for you to be with another woman." Anthony didn't like what Hope said to him. Hope got angry and told him, "You're not going anywhere with that girl!" They started arguing, but Hope didn't get too close to him so that he couldn't hit her. Anthony was in the bedroom, and he came and stood outside the room. She could see him from where she was standing. Anthony picked up his Rolland bottle and threw it at her. Hope got out of the way, and the bottle almost hit her in the face. The Rolland was a rigid bottle. It broke when it hit the wall. He didn't care if the bottle hit Hope or hurt the baby. He then left the house with Dave.

Hope got a call from her mother on Jessie's phone. Hope and Grace hadn't spoken for a while, and she was surprised that she called. Grace told Hope that Anthony told her to come and get her out of his house. Hope said to her mother, "It's my house too; I help pay the bills!" Anthony called Jessie and told her to kick Hope out of the house. Anthony didn't care that he was forcing Hope and her unborn child on the street. She cried when Jessie told her what

Anthony said. Hope thought Anthony was giving Jessie power over her in her own home. Hope said, "what else can go wrong, Father God?"

Grace came looking for Hope that night. But, unfortunately, Hope didn't let her know what happened when she spoke to her on the phone.

When Anthony came home, Grace got angry and argued with Hope and him simultaneously. She saw the hole the bottle left when he threw it at Hope. Grace asked Hope, "I want to know why you're with a man that beats you every chance he gets, even when you're pregnant?" Hope didn't answer. Grace told Anthony she wasn't taking Hope with her. She said, "if you kill her, you have to eat her if you don't want to bury her." She then left the house. Hope couldn't believe her mother said that. Even though she wasn't getting along with her mother, she couldn't see how hurt she was by her situation.

Hope and Anthony didn't speak for weeks. Hope made sure dinner was ready when he came home from work, and she made sure she did his laundry on the weekend. He never said anything to Hope, not even a thank you.

Eventually, Hope and Grace fixed their relationship despite everything going on in Hope's life. She knew she needed her mother more than ever. Hope didn't like being in the house. Since she and her mother talked again, she spent more time at her mother's home. Hope and Jessie didn't get along for very long as always, and Hope couldn't take it anymore because Jessie wasn't doing anything around the apartment. She was tired of cleaning up after her when they were both pregnant. Even though Hope and Anthony barely spoke, she told him, "Jessie has to leave; I can't do this anymore."

Jessie knew things with Hope weren't the same. She didn't know what was going on because Hope never shared her reasons with her. Jessie decided to get her place, and Hope was happy to leave and get her home for herself.

Hope was now close to the due date of her baby. Still, Anthony wouldn't stop partying with his boys. Girls called his phone to find out when he was leaving. Hope didn't get angry with some girls because she didn't think they knew he lived with his girlfriend. Now that Jessie wasn't living there anymore, she went to her mom's every weekend.

Hope went to her ultrasound appointment, but Anthony didn't go with her. Hope wondered if he wanted the baby as much as she did. During the ultrasound, the doctor asked Hope, "would you like to know the sex of the baby?" Hope thought for a second. She wondered if she should wait until Anthony could make it to one of her future appointments when he wasn't busy with his boys. Hope said to the doctor, "yes, I would love to know." She knew Anthony would never come to any of her appointments. The doctor said, "It's a girl." Hope was happy to hear it. She wished Anthony could share the good news instead of being with his boys. Still, Hope wasn't going to make him spoil the moment.

Sunday evening, when Hope came home from her mom's house, she saw that one of her sheets from her bed in the other room was in the laundry basket.

Hope knew she didn't take it off the bed. She looked at the sheet, and it had a white stain on it. Hope started to freak out. She wanted to break Anthony's face. Hope went outside to use the payphone across the street from her building to call Anthony. He picked up, and she asked, "what the hell went on in my house? What woman did you bring in my home to have sex with?" Anthony told Hope he would talk to her when he got home. She hung up, knowing he wouldn't tell her over the phone. When Anthony came into the house, Hope demanded, "Tell me who the woman you disrespected my home with was!" He said, "It wasn't me. It was your cousin who came by with a girl." Hope was glad it wasn't him but angrier that he let her cousin bring a woman to have sex in her house. She cussed at him and asked, "why will you let my cousin bring a woman into my house to have sex? He's a married man!"

IO.

Chapter Ten

Hope thought Anthony was going out again the following weekend while she went to her mom's house, but he showed up there. Hope was surprised, and It was March 8th, 2006. That night they had fun. But then Hope started having pain. She told Anthony she wanted to go home because her belly hurt. She thought it was from all the hot wings she ate that night.

The pain kept on coming and going. Hope walked back and forth in the living room because she couldn't sleep. Hope went into the bedroom and told Anthony, "I think the baby is coming!" He said, "the baby isn't due yet." The ultrasound indicated that Hope was having her baby on March 13th, but it was March 8th. Hope angrily told Anthony, "I need to go to the hospital now!!" Anthony called the taxi, and when they got to the hospital, the doctors hooked Hope up to a machine to check the baby. The pain wasn't as intense as when she was at home. The doctor said, "you're not ready to have the baby." "But I'm in pain, doctor," said Hope. The doctor said, "If you're in lots of pain, I could do a Cesarean section, but you and your partner have to decide." Hope wasn't going to let the doctor operate on her. She told him, "I'll go home and wait it out to see if the pain goes away." So, they went home. Hope tried to sleep, but the pain came back even stronger. Every time she tried to sleep, the pain would wake her up.

It was 5 a.m. on March 9th, and the pain was unbearable. Hope told Anthony, "I need to go back to the hospital," and he said to

Hope, "the doctor said you're not ready to give birth yet." Hope replied, "I know my body, and this baby is coming today." Anthony told her that he would get some sheets from the closet and put them on the bed if the baby came. Hope told him with the pain of distress in her voice, "you're not delivering my baby, you're not a doctor, take me to the hospital now!!" So, they went back to the hospital, and the nurse rushed Hope into the delivery room. She checked and told her, "You are at 5 centimetres; I'm going to page your doctor."

Hope just wanted the baby out. She spent nine hours in labour, then at 2:45 a.m. Hope gave birth to her baby girl. Hope and Anthony named their baby girl Renell.

Hope was happy her baby girl came into the world safe and that Anthony missed the birth of their daughter. After that day, he came to the hospital every day.

Hope spent two days in the hospital, but Anthony wasn't there to take her because he had to work the day she was going home. She thought things would finally change after returning from the hospital, but she was wrong. Hope came home to a dirty house, dishes in the sink, and laundry. Hope put the baby down and started cleaning everywhere even though she was tired and in pain. She just had a baby, and Anthony returned to his old ways. He was still going out every weekend, and women were calling again. She didn't know what to do to make him change.

Hope thought, "he doesn't love our baby nor me or else he would change." Then, one day out of the blue, he came home and told her, "If you don't get your status from immigration, I'll have to marry someone to get my papers." Hope was still waiting on immigration for an interview. She had to wait a year for an answer about the outcome of her case. Every chance Anthony got, he would tell Hope he would leave to get his permanent residency in Canada. Hope looked at him and remembered what her aunt had said to her, and it kept playing over in her head. "Don't pick up a guy who can't help you get your papers in this country." As well, when Hope's aunt heard that she was dating Anthony, she encouraged her to leave him, saying, "find someone who can help you get your status in the country."

Hope didn't want to give up Anthony and marry a man she didn't love so that she could become a permanent resident. But, Hope said, "it wouldn't be right, and I love Anthony with all my heart." So even though Anthony didn't have immigration status in Canada, Hope still stood by him. But he couldn't appreciate that, or maybe he did but didn't care.

Renell was three months old, and Hope decided to go back to the church where she and Anthony blessed their baby. That's when Jason from the church came up to them and asked, "have you two given your lives to Christ?" They said no, and he then asked, "are you married?" They said no. Then he said, "you have a baby; why don't you both get married and live a Christian life? It's the only way to live."

Hope knew Jason was right. Hope wanted to marry Anthony, but she didn't want to push it on him. in her MIND, he was her husband because they had lived together for two years. Anthony didn't think he was ready for marriage yet. On the other hand, Hope loved him and would marry him in a heartbeat. But he wasn't prepared to give up his lifestyle. He planned to leave Hope and the baby to marry someone else for his papers.

Anthony went out to party every weekend, and Hope would take Renell to her grandma's house. He wasn't spending any time with them. He acted like those women, and his friends were more important. Hope was afraid to say anything because he would hit her. She just pretended it wasn't bothering her. One night, Hope's cousin Jeremiah came by with the same woman he had sex with her bed when she was away. The girl wasn't friendly, and while there, she acted like she owned the place. Hope called Anthony into the bedroom and said to him, "Jeremiah isn't having sex in my house where my child sleeps." She got mad at him and said, "why do you keep disrespecting our home and me like this?"

Anthony pulled Jeremiah aside and told him he couldn't have sex there anymore. Jeremiah got mad. He knew it wasn't Anthony's decision. Hope didn't 'give a damn' about his feelings. He was a married man cheating behind his wife's back.

Hope wished Anthony would treat her like his girlfriend or even the mother of his child. Still, he didn't have a clue how to make a relationship work. All he was good for was lying and cheating. Hope couldn't stop crying because of Anthony. He was no help taking care of their daughter. He thought buying food for the house and paying half the bills was all he had to do.

One day Hope took Renell to the store to buy food while Anthony was out with his boys. After returning, she had her daughter cooking in the kitchen because she wouldn't sleep, and Anthony wasn't around to help. So she had to do everything herself, and as she looked at her baby girl, she started to cry. She thought, "this isn't what life was supposed to be like with Anthony."

Finally, she went to court regarding her immigration case. She was nervous because she knew what the outcome would be. Her future in Canada was in the judge's hands. Hope's lawyer saw that Hope was very anxious. He told her, "Don't worry too much; everything will work out." She smiled. The judge came in, sat down, and said to Hope, "I read your story, and I want to tell you, I believe you." Hope wasn't expecting the judge to say that. She told how her father had abused her while growing up. It was a hard time in her life to re-live, but she needed the judge to understand why she couldn't return to her home country. The judge asked Hope, "why didn't you ever seek help from the police?" Hope said, "my father was friends with the police, and I was scared of him." The judge asked, "where was your mother when all of this was happening?" Hope told her that her mother was never around when it happened.

Everything went well at the hearing. The judge granted Hope permanent status, and she was thrilled that she could now make a better life for her daughter.

Hope got back home from her hearing, and when Anthony got home from work, she shared the good news with him, and he was happier than she was. Anthony went right out to buy a calling phone card so he could call his parents and his friends to share the good news. Hope didn't call her family with the news yet, but Anthony called everyone. Anthony told Hope now that she had gotten her papers, she could help him. Hope looked at Anthony and saw he wasn't wasting time using her. She was mad. Since they started living together, all he did was hurt her and make her cry.

They went to see Hope's lawyer. Anthony never went to any of Hope's appointments with the immigration lawyer. Now he did because it benefitted him. They sat down with the lawyer, and Hope explained why she wanted to sponsor Anthony. She wasn't sure if she was making the right decision, but that's what she wanted to do for now. The lawyer put the paperwork together and told them that getting married would help Anthony get his papers faster now that they had a daughter together.

Hope was still going to church. There was no other feeling like the one Hope got than when she was in church. Anthony never went. He never saw the need to go to church. But as soon as Hope got her papers, Anthony started going to church. One Sunday evening, when they came home from church, he asked Hope, "will you marry me?" Hope wanted a better proposal. One the traditional way, but

Anthony wasn't like that. He didn't have a ring, but he told her that he would buy a ring soon.

Anthony eventually got a ring. Hope wished that she had a say on the ring she wanted, but he wanted to control everything as usual. He took the ring to church and let the Pastor bless it. Anthony proposed to Hope all over again. Everyone at the church was happy for them both. The older folks in the church loved when a young couple committed to each other. The Pastor said, "Now you can devote yourselves to God."

It was the happiest time in her life with Anthony. They started planning for the big day and hired a wedding planner. The tradition is that the groom is not supposed to see a woman's wedding dress until the wedding day. But that didn't happen in Hope's wedding plans. Hope and Anthony went together and got her dress, and it wasn't a bother to Hope that much. With everything she had gone through with Anthony, she didn't believe in bad luck.

Hope told her mother that she was going to marry Anthony. Grace wasn't pleased with the news. She told Hope, "I won't be attending the wedding." Hope also told her aunt Alexandra about the wedding. She asked her, "why are you going to marry a man who doesn't treat you well?" Hope was hurt because her mother and aunt weren't happy about marrying Anthony. She didn't know what to do. She didn't have her father around and asked her mother to walk her down the aisle. Grace called Hope's father, Princeton, in New York and let him know Hope was getting married. Hope didn't know where he was living at the time, and she didn't care about him and didn't know he was living in the U.S. Grace thought she was helping Hope, but all she did was bring back painful memories with Princeton that she wanted to forget.

Princeton called Hope and told her not to marry Anthony. "I heard all the things he's done to you," he said. Hope couldn't understand why he was trying to be 'father of the year.' Hope listened to what he had to say. She didn't say much. "I love him, and he's the father of my child," she said and hung up the phone. She thought, "who is he to give me advice after all he did to me."

Hope had made up her mind to marry Anthony, and no one was going to stop her even if her mother wouldn't walk her down the aisle.

Anthony told his family about the wedding, and they were excited. They wanted to travel from Saint Vincent and New York for the wedding. Hope started to cry to herself. It looked like it was only going to be her fiancé's family and her church family who would be at the wedding.

Jacob, a guy from the church, knew Hope's father didn't live in Canada. He never saw many of Hope's family around. He asked her if she had anyone to walk her down the aisle on her wedding day. Hope said, "no, I don't," as she hung her head down. Hope didn't want to tell him that her mother would do it for her. But he told Hope, "Don't worry; I would be honoured to do it if you would have me." Hope said, "yes!!" She was happy that she was loved by so many in the church, even if they didn't know the whole truth about her life and the abuse she faced with Anthony.

Hope and Anthony were going ahead with the wedding no matter what anyone said. So they went to get their marriage license. Despite their ups and downs, Hope knew she wanted to marry him.

It was bittersweet after Hope found out she was pregnant for the second time. She loved Anthony, but she was confused by his actions. After giving birth to their daughter Renell, Hope asked her doctor to put her on birth control. She wasn't sure if she wanted to have another child with Anthony. He told Hope to get off the pills back then because he didn't believe in birth control. She never knew he planned to get her pregnant again. But now that the baby was here, she loved it just as much as she loved her first daughter.

At times, Hope wanted to be with Anthony and marry him, and other times she wanted to leave. But she found it hard to do it because of her daughter and now her unborn child. She wanted her children to have both their parents but wondered how much more she could take.

On Sunday, Hope and Anthony went to church. It got tense before they left when a woman called Anthony's phone. They always played the happy couple at church, but they weren't. Hope put a smile on her face because Anthony wanted her to. Everyone at church called her smiley, and they didn't know that Hope was covering her pain with her smile.

After church, they went to pick up her wedding dress from the dry cleaner. On their way, Anthony met a woman, and he stood and talked to her. Hope didn't know who she was. He didn't introduce her to the lady. She walked away and stood a distance away from them. Hope wondered if she had met the woman before or ever called his phone, and she picked up the call, but nothing came to mind. After Anthony finished talking to the lady, he returned to Hope and their baby girl. Then his phone rang. It was a woman on the other line. When Anthony looked at Hope, he saw she wasn't happy about it. Regardless, he started a conversation with her. Hope didn't say anything to him and could see that she was angry. When he got off the phone, he told Hope to put a smile on her face. Hope said, "leave me alone! I'll get the dress myself."

Anthony followed Hope anyways. She said to him, "stop following me." Hope could see he was angry, but she didn't care. She felt disrespected and wanted him to feel the same way. But he just left and went home.

Hope went to get her dress. She didn't understand why Anthony kept disrespecting her. When she got home, Anthony was waiting at the door and slapped her in the face as she walked in. Hope picked up her daughter because she wasn't going to fight back. She knew it was a fight she couldn't win. Anthony demanded she put the baby down, but she refused. Hope was three months pregnant with their second child. Anthony took the baby and put her in her crib, and kept on hitting Hope in the face. He held her by the throat and forced her into the other room. Anthony wouldn't stop beating her. It didn't matter how hard Hope screamed at him to stop. Finally, she said, "I can't breathe!!" Anthony knew she couldn't breathe as he choked her while beating her in the face. Hope said to him with the bit of strength she had, "I still love you." Hope thought those would be her last words to him if she had to die. When he heard those words, he let go of her. He knew he didn't deserve to hear it. He felt ashamed. He could have killed his future and his unborn child.

Hope ran and picked up Renell and locked herself in the other room. She held her daughter and cried. With tears running down her face, she cried out, "Lord, why does he keep doing this to me?" Hope slept in the other room that same night; she was afraid for her life. She didn't know what he would do next if she said something he did not like. Late in the night, while she slept, he came into the room and woke her up. She got scared and began crying. As she covered her face, she said, "don't hit me again." Anthony said, "I'm not going to hit you. I'm sorry." Anthony started touching Hope. He came to have sex, and she didn't know how to say no. She didn't want to make him mad again, so she let him have his way with her.

The next day Hope went back to city hall to bring the missing documents to get the marriage license. Everyone looked at her swollen red face when she was on the bus. Hope could not stop the tears from falling. Hope didn't want to marry Anthony anymore, but she was too afraid to tell him. His family was arriving the following week for the wedding on the same day as his parent's anniversary, December 30th.

While Hope sat with the lady helping her with the license, she could see that she had questions about what happened to her face, but Hope kept quiet. She couldn't wait to get back home and cry. When Hope got home, she looked at herself in the bedroom mirror. Her face and one of her eyes were red. She took out her phone and took pictures of her face as she told the mirror, "This is not the life I want for my daughter."

After getting the marriage license, Hope caught Anthony on the phone with another woman that same week. She argued with him, threw his ring at him, and told him, "I'm not marrying you anymore!!" Anthony grabbed Hope and started hitting her for giving him back the engagement ring. He wanted to marry her more than she wanted to marry him, and Hope didn't know why he didn't love her as much as she loved him. Hope wanted to get away from him, but she'd have to go back to her family with her daughter if she did. Hope didn't want to hear "I told you so," so she stayed and took the abuse.

Anthony's family came to Canada for the wedding. He added a cousin to his list of bad friends. He told Hope he was going to show Jimmy around town. Hope and Anthony gave their room to his parents. They gave the other room to his sister, and they shared the living room with Jimmy. Ever since Anthony's father, James, met Hope, he liked her. He called her his daughter-in-law. His mother Cynthia didn't like that, and she told James, "she's not your daughter-in-law yet." James said, "I don't care; she's my daughter-in-law. She's with my son." Hope could sense Cynthia didn't like her.

Hope got close with her brother Ricardo's girlfriend, Michelle. Ricardo came to Canada to be with Grace and met the girl of his dreams. Michelle wasn't new to Hope. She met her while Hope was living with her aunt Alexandra. They were neighbours, but they did not like each other much. Michelle was the only person Hope could talk with. She didn't judge her, and she was the only one she spoke to about the new baby. Hope didn't know how to break the news to her mother. But, on the other hand, Michelle was always there for her when Anthony beat on her. Michelle didn't understand why Hope was marrying Anthony, but she didn't want to hurt their friendship.

Hope wanted to have bridesmaids at her wedding party but didn't have many friends. Everyone had to buy the dress of Hope's choice. Some of her family wanted to participate in the wedding but didn't have much money. So, Anthony chose Hope's bridesmaids. He picked his friends to be at her wedding. He asked Christine, who he would ask to marry to get his papers, to be a part of the wedding party. He asked another girl that Hope didn't like, and he asked his sister to be her Maid of Honor. Hope told Anthony, "I want Jessie to be a part of my wedding." Lena and Marica couldn't afford to participate in the wedding, nor could Michelle.

Hope didn't have much to say about the wedding plans; they say the wedding is about the bride, but the wedding was about Anthony in Hope's case.

The big day had finally come for Hope and Anthony to get married. The day before the wedding, Grace decided that she would walk Hope down the aisle. Hope didn't care how late she accepted. She was happy she would have her mother at her side. Likewise, Anthony was happy to surprise his parents by getting married on their anniversary.

Hope and the bridesmaids got ready at Jessie's house. Hope wasn't feeling well. She was thinking about everything she had been through with Anthony. She didn't want to go through with the wedding anymore. She just wanted to run away. She felt like she was going to collapse. Her life flashed before her eyes—everything she had been through hit her like a wrecking ball. Hope was sure Anthony would not change, and things would be the same after they got married. Everyone assumed it was because she didn't eat anything. Hope wished everyone would stop because they didn't know what was happening with her.

Despite Hope's mixed feelings about the wedding, she knew that it must go on. But everything was not that great at her wedding. The food was cold, and the wedding planner bought many dollar store items and charged a lot of money for them. As a result, Hope didn't get her first dance after the wedding when they went home and had a party. While everyone was partying, Hope and Anthony went to a hotel to spend the night together as husband and wife. The hotel was within walking distance, but they only went with money and not their ID. It was their first time going to a hotel; therefore, they never knew the requirements to rent a room.

II.

Chapter Eleven

Anthony and Hope couldn't get a room; the woman at the front desk said, "you two look very young." Anthony told her that they had just gotten married. "Congratulations, but I'll still need to see your ID," she instructed. So they left and went to another hotel a short distance away from their home. When they got there, the man at the front desk asked, "how can I help you?" Anthony said, "I would like to rent a room for a few hours," the man said, "can I see some ID?" Anthony tried to persuade the guy to rent them a room, but he said, "I'm sorry, but you need an ID to rent a room."

Hope and Anthony had been looking forward to spending their wedding night at a hotel but couldn't, so they went back home. It was a bittersweet day, but it was early morning, and Hope just wanted to go home to get some sleep after a long day.

The next day, while Anthony should be spending time with his new wife, he hung out with his friends and continued his womanizing behaviour. He went out with his cousin Jimmy and returned late that evening to get ready for a party. Hope was angry with him. James could see that Hope was upset. He said to Anthony, "why don't you take your new wife with you and spend some time with her?" Hope could see Anthony didn't want to do that, but he took her with him and his cousin to the party. Hope didn't want to go to a party but wanted to spend some time with him since they had just married.

Hope stood in a corner looking on at the party while Anthony mingled with everyone. Finally, he looked over and saw that she wasn't having a good time. So, he came and danced with her, and the night didn't turn out bad for Hope after all.

Anthony's family went back to their home, but Jimmy stayed and lived with them. Hope thought it couldn't get worse than it already was. She was now a mother of one and had one on the way. Now she had to cook, clean and wash for Jimmy because Anthony said so. Every weekend Anthony and Jimmy would leave the house. Jimmy would always leave his clothes for Hope to wash. Hope had her daughter, and her stomach was growing. She had to go downstairs in the basement of the building and never had help doing the laundry. Hope thought as she cried, "why do I have to do his cousin's laundry, and why does he treat me like this."

Hope eventually decided to go back to school three months after her son was born on June 24, 2007. They named him Zion from the Bible. Hope tried to get a babysitter before school started, and she arranged interviews to find the best person to take care of her daughter and her son while she was at school. A young lady contacted Hope about the position. She made an appointment with her for the following day. When she came for her appointment, Hope was amazed at how young, and pretty she was. When she was doing her interview, she had decided not to give her the job. After the interview, Hope said, "we'll be in touch."

Hope knew the way Anthony was with women. She didn't want him cheating with the babysitter. She didn't want to take that chance with the pretty young woman. Hope didn't want her husband around any young lady in their house. But Hope was starting school soon, and she didn't have a babysitter. So, she decided to put her children in-home daycare. Hope thought it was best, but a week after taking the children to daycare, Hope noticed

Renell came home with a rash on her skin. So she decided not to send them back.

Hope asked Michelle to babysit until she could find a babysitter. After that, she started on the medical office assistant course, and she applied for a student loan because she couldn't afford to pay for the course herself. While in school, Hope got her first loan of $10,000. She met Wendy at school, and they became friends. They both were in the same class after receiving the first half of the student loan. Wendy went to the bank, and she asked Hope to go with her. She told Hope, "I'm going to the bank to invest a portion of my money; you should come."

The bank was five minutes away from school. Hope went and sat down with Wendy and the financial advisor. She showed Wendy how much money she would save in five years if she kept it in a tax-free savings account. Hope listened, and everything sounded good. After Wendy finished with her investment, she told Hope she should do it too, but she said, "I'll have to talk to my husband first." When Hope got home, she spoke to Anthony about it. He told her to keep the money in the bank. "I'll make sure you get your bus pass to go to school," he said. Hope said okay. She thought he had her best interest at heart regarding money. Hope finally got a babysitter. This time it was an older lady in her fifties. She told her she could only pay her $200 per week, and she agreed.

Anthony paid the babysitter until Hope got the child tax payment for the children. Anthony asked Hope for her bank card because he always wanted something, and even though he was working, he never had enough money. So hope made sure he had half of the money each month for the rent. Jimmy paid his share of the rent, and they all put money together to buy food. Hope never knew how much Anthony made at work. It was always a secret.

While Hope was in school, she opened the Cam General Service placement agency. It was always her dream to help people. So when

Jimmy came to Canada and got a job through her company to work for Anthony's company, she was happy to help him. Every Friday, when Hope went to the bank to make sure Jimmy got paid, Hope learned how to deduct taxes for the government for the end of the year.

It was getting difficult for Hope to take care of the children and keep up with her schoolwork. So she added Anthony to the business account to fill in for her at the bank.

One day Hope got a notice at the house stating that they were behind on the rent. She didn't understand why. She and Jimmy gave Anthony money each month for rent. Hope thought it had to be a mistake. So, she asked Anthony, and he said he always paid the rent on time every month. Anthony was paid through the company since he was still waiting on Immigration to get his Canadian status. His boss wasn't taking out tax, so Hope used Cam General to take his tax because he was getting paid through it.

Every week money should be in the account for taxes. Hope ignored the business account because she trusted that Anthony was handling everything. He knew what would happen if the money wasn't there for the government taxes. Anthony finally got his status on his birthday, April 4, 2008. He was happy, and Hope was delighted. Now that they both had their papers. She hoped things would be better now that they had immigration status in Canada. They could save for their children's future, own their own home, and work together at Cam General Service. But all Anthony wanted to do was live his life how he saw fit. Just being out with his boys and picking up women every weekend at the club was more important than his family life with Hope. Every time Anthony wanted something from Hope, he would ask for her debit card. There was always something he wanted to buy. But because of the love Hope had for him, she gave it to him.

A month later, Hope found out they were getting evicted from their apartment. She didn't understand. She didn't know what Anthony did with her and Jimmy's money. Hope's name wasn't on the lease, so there wasn't anything she could do. Finally, she said to Anthony, "Go to the office. It must be a mistake." Anthony informed her that it wasn't a mistake. It was true.

Hope was angry. She didn't understand why he didn't think of his children before doing whatever he had done with the money. Anthony asked her to lend him money to find a new place to live. Anthony knew he couldn't pay the $8,000 he owed for rent. The management office told him that they were going to change the locks on the eviction date. He found a new place before the office locked them out. He had to come up with the first and last month's rent. Jimmy didn't have any money, so he asked Hope, "could you lend me the money to help with the rent?" Because Hope had her student loan, Anthony asked for $1,800. So Hope lent him the money.

Hope wanted to invest half of her money for a house, but Anthony didn't think she needed to do that because he thought he could spend the money whenever he felt like it. She never spent any of the money; it was always Anthony.

Hope's babysitting service moved to the new location. Now it added to the distance for Hope to get to school. She tried to keep up with her studies, the kids, and the house duties. She wished Anthony would help, but he was never around much. Jimmy tried to advise Hope not to give up on Anthony, but that was easier said than done. She had noticed that, when Jimmy got paid, he didn't give her half of the money back. But Hope didn't say anything to him. Every time Hope gave him money, she wondered why he wasn't paying her back, but Hope didn't want to ask and came off rude.

When Anthony wasn't home, Jimmy asked Hope, "did Anthony

give you the money I gave to him?" She said, "what money?" Jimmy gave Anthony the money again because he was paying rent once more. But, again, Anthony didn't put Hope on the lease. Anthony wanted to be in control of everything, including Hope's money. Hope shook her head when Anthony came home. She didn't ask him anything, and he didn't say anything to her about the money. Every time Anthony went out, he always wanted Hope's debit card. He gave $150 to take care of the home. Hope had to do laundry, buy food for the house, and pay the cable bill. Hope didn't understand why he thought that would pay for everything. He helped to pay the babysitter until Hope got the child tax money.

It was coming up to December and Hope's birthday. She thought he would use his own money and buy her a gift for her birthday. But, instead, he used Hope's money to buy her a gift. Hope took the gift with a smile. Deep inside, Hope just wanted to tell him her feelings, but she let it go. She knew nothing good would come from it.

It wasn't easy for Hope to keep up with school and take care of her children. She would try to get her studies done, but she was tired. She did it to give her children a better future. Everything she did was for them. Her children weren't going to get it from their father. Hope loved to sing. Since Anthony spent $10,000 from her student loan money in two months, she put $1500 aside from the $4,000 she got from her last payment to do a demo. Anthony didn't think it was a good idea. He told Hope, "you're wasting your money; you don't have enough talent." Hope wanted her husband's support, but all he did was put her down. He wanted to be the only one to spend her money.

Hope's brother Ricardo, and his wife Michelle, came to the house. Anthony wasn't home. They came to spend some time with her. Hope didn't have enough time to socialize between school and the kids, and they knew that Anthony was never at home. When Anthony finally came home, he said hello to Ricardo and Michelle then locked himself in the bedroom to talk to his female friends. Anthony was about to leave again when Hope told him, "you need to spend time with the children and me." He didn't want to stay. Hope said to him, "if you're not staying, I'm going to wreck your clothes and your shoes." Anthony lost it and started breaking all of Hope's valuable items in the house. He kicked and broke everything he knew meant a lot to Her.

Ricardo went to Hope and said, "stop it, let him go." He told Anthony, "you guys need to stop it!" Ricardo pulled Hope out of Anthony's way so that he could leave. Anthony got angry with Ricardo, and he went to the kitchen and pulled out a knife from the drawer. He went at Ricardo with the knife, and Ricardo ran out of the house with Anthony chasing behind him.

Hope and Michelle never saw Anthony or Ricardo come back. They thought the worst had happened. They went looking for them but couldn't find either one. Hope thought something was wrong and it would be all her fault. She prayed, "please, God let my brother be okay." Michelle started to cry. She called Grace and told her what had happened. Hope and Michelle looked around the building and saw Ricardo but not Anthony. Ricardo was angry. He saw Hope and Michelle crying. He hugged them and said, "don't cry, everything is okay." Hope told Ricardo to go home before Anthony came back. Ricardo didn't want to leave Hope alone. Hope cried to her brother and said, "please go home. I'll be fine."

Michelle asked Hope to come with them to their mother's house. But Hope couldn't deal with her family and with what just happened. So she went back into the house to be with her children. She was scared that Anthony would hurt her if he came back and found her alone. When Hope heard the door open, her heart began to beat fast. Anthony went into the room, came back with clothes in a bag, and left. He didn't say anything to Hope or his children.

When Jimmy came home, he saw the house in a mess, with broken glass everywhere. So he asked, "what happened?" As Hope cleaned up, she said, "your cousin broke all my stuff." Jimmy said, "oh my God, why?" He didn't like what he saw.

Hope hoped that Anthony would come back home the next day when he calmed down, but he didn't. So every day Jimmy came home from work, she asked about Anthony since they both worked at the same company. Jimmy said, "I told him to come home, but he won't listen to me." So every morning, Hope gave Jimmy Anthony's lunch to take to work for him. Hope wanted him to know she wasn't mad at him anymore.

Hope found out that Anthony was staying with a girl he was sleeping with. She cried and thought, "why do I love this guy so much? Why can't I find the strength to leave him?" After everything he was doing to Hope, she never went to bed angry with him. She loved him with all her heart and soul, but she never got back the same love from him. Hope thought, "why doesn't he leave me if he doesn't love me? Why hurt his kids and me? It's not fair."

He came home after a few days but didn't go to Hope. She cooked and left food for him. She got up at 4 a.m. to make sure he had his breakfast before leaving for work at 5 a.m., but he still gave Hope the cold shoulder. She never asked him where he was, and she didn't let him know she knew where he was. She didn't want to get into another argument with him. She was glad he came home, and the kids got to see their father.

After things died down, Anthony and Hope decided to bring his mother back to Canada to help with the children. They thought it was best if his mother came so that they could save some money. They couldn't afford to keep paying a babysitter anymore because money was running low.

Cynthia came, and things were going well with her and Hope at first. But then she started to change. Hope had to spend a lot of money buying food. Cynthia cooked different meats in one pot, but Hope didn't say anything. Every week Anthony got paid, he gave Cynthia money, but sometimes he didn't give Hope any, even though she had to buy food and find money to do laundry. Finally, Anthony told Hope, "since my mother babysits the kids while you're in school, you have to give her money when you get the child tax for the kids." Hope thought, "why should I have to pay her? She's the children's grandmother, and she lives at the house for free; she's cooking so many different meats in one pot, and I have to find the money for it." Hope didn't think that his mother should get money from her. He gave her money every paycheck. Hope couldn't get mad or say anything to him, so she agreed. She thought, "at the end of the day, it's his mother."

Hope now wished that she had kept the babysitter. She was a lovely old lady and took good care of her children while Hope was in school. She knew that Anthony's mother was never going to like her. Since the first time Cynthia came to Canada for their wedding, Hope knew, by the way, she talked to her; she didn't think she liked her. Now that she has come back, Hope still thinks she doesn't like her. Anytime Cynthia saw Hope get up, she would go and cook. Every time Hope cleaned the house, she would clean it over again. Hope couldn't say anything because she lived in his son's house. She wanted to leave but didn't have anywhere to go.

Hope had applied for government housing before she moved from the old house. She was on a waiting list and prayed that something would come up soon to live in her own home. She was almost finished with school. She was happy that all the stress of school and home didn't stop her. Hope was close to the end. She never got help from Anthony, but she has almost made it.

With everything going on in Hope's life, she used her love of music to escape. Even though Anthony told her it was a waste of time, she didn't listen to him. Instead, she found herself a producer to work with her on her demo. Michelle went with her to sit with the producer. He asked Hope to sing for him. At first, she was shy because she had never sung in front of a professional before. However, Michelle was the only one who believed in her and her music. The producer told Hope, "you sound like Keyshia Cole." Hope loved her music, so it was an honour to hear that she sounded like her.

The producer gave Hope three tracks to take home to work on. He charged her $1500 to do her demo, and she was excited about it. When Hope got home, she worked on her first song. With everything Anthony put her through, the first song came easy. She finished it in one day. She wrote:

Everyone tells me you're going to go, but I tell myself no because we are good, but baby, I was wrong about everything, I was wrong about you and me again, everyone sees what you're going to do, but I was too blind to see what was true but baby now I see for myself you're no good.

You never took the time out to think of all the love we share. You hurt me so many times; it seems like you're never going to let me go. You couldn't even say you're sorry to put me in so much pain, and you never meant to hurt me. Is that too much to ask.

Yesterday you said you love me, and I tell myself I love you too, then you turn around and do me wrong, but still, I don't know how to let you go because I love you, I need you.

I used to think it was not easy to take my love away from you, but you make it easy with all the lies you tell; thinking back, you weren't there for me when I needed you mostly now, baby, I'm moving on because nothing is here for me.

Oh yeah, yeah, yeah, oh yeah, yeah, yeah.

—

Hope was excited to go to the studio to record her first song because it meant something to her. It was from a heart full of pain. Three days later, she went to pick up her first single. She was happy to take it home for everyone to listen. Jimmy and Cynthia loved the song, but Anthony didn't say anything. She thought, "Maybe Anthony thought the song was for him." She said, "then he was right."

Hope started to work on her other song. She remembered growing up and seeing what her mother went through with her father. She said, "I'm going to write a song for my mom." Hope knew that she put her mother through a lot, and it was an excellent way to tell her how sorry she was. She wrote:

Mama, I'm sorry, Mama, I'm sorry.

I know I hurt you; I didn't mean to; all you do is love, and all I do is hurt you. Mama, there's something you need to know. I was hurting too when daddy walked out on us.

I heard her at night crying; I heard her at night praying. I asked myself why she was hurting so much. I never understood until now. All that she did was for me, all I ever did was hurt her, but there is something I think you should know; oh yeah.

Mama, I'm sorry, Mama, I'm sorry.

I know I hurt you; I didn't mean to; all you do is love, and all I do is hurt you. Mama, there's something you need to know; I was hurting too when daddy walked out on us; oh yeah.

You fight so hard to take care of me and my brothers, while daddy is living the life, the kind of life we can't live; you put up with me the most because I was troubled the most, while daddy took care of another family.

Thank you for not giving up on me; I love you.

It didn't matter what Hope and her mother went through. She knew she loved her mother. Hope tried to spend some time loving what she did and loving herself. She realized that Anthony wouldn't change. He disrespected her in front of her mother, and she wouldn't say anything. Cynthia didn't care what Anthony was putting her through. He will forever be her son.

While Hope was at her placement, someone from "Housing" called her. They said they had a place for her. Hope was so excited and made time to view the house. She took Michelle with her to see the house. Anthony was just too busy with his friends to care what was going on in Hope's life. On the weekend, Hope and Michelle went to look at the house. The superintendent showed her inside. The house was small, and she didn't like it because she was used to a lot more space.

The superintendent told her, "you don't have to choose this one if you don't like it," Hope whispers to Michelle, "he senses I don't like it." Hope knew she had three chances to choose a house, but at the same time, she didn't want to say no. She just wanted to get away from her husband and his mother.

Anthony told Hope they would be living together, but he couldn't give up his lifestyle. Finally, hope couldn't take it anymore. She wasn't sure if she wanted him to come with them. Hope was tired of the abuse. She wanted to start her life afresh without any heartache or pain.

It was Caribana weekend. Anthony was going out that night. When he left the house, Hope put the TV on the lobby channel to see downstairs. She saw him talking to a girl who lived in the building, and she saw him taking her number. She got into his cousin Mike's car with Anthony. Hope called his phone, but he wouldn't pick up. Mike came from New York for Caribana, and he was wild, just like Anthony. Her husband had no one in his life to point him in the right direction.

Hope decided she would move out the following weekend, so she went and bought her household items. However, she didn't want to take anything from her current apartment.

12.

Chapter Twelve

Anthony rented a truck to bring Hope and the kids to their new place. She had the feeling that he couldn't wait to get her out of the house fast enough. Mike used his car and took Hope and the kids. When they got to the new place, Anthony took out Hope's belongings from the truck and put them in the house. He didn't put the bed together for Hope and the children.

Hope hadn't bought any pots for the house, and she and the kids had nothing to eat. Anthony didn't buy any food before he left, and she didn't know what she would give the kids to eat. She refused to call their father. She sat on the floor and thought, "what kind of a husband does this to his wife and children? Has he no love for us?" She put some sugar in water and mixed it for the children to drink before bed. Hope had no furniture, just her clothes and some dishes. She prayed, "Lord, I don't know where you're taking me, but I'll follow your lead."

It was a month since Hope moved into her new home with her children, but they hadn't seen their father or heard from him since they moved in. She went to church and then took the kids to his house to see their father after church. He wasn't home. His mother called him and told him Hope and the kids were there. Anthony didn't come home. Hope was angry that whatever he was doing was more important than seeing his children after so long.

Anthony finally came home. One look at him, and Hope missed

him. She wanted him so bad and could see how much the kids missed him, so they stayed the night. That night Hope and Anthony talked about their family. She told him to come and live with them, but he didn't want to go. He said, "We fight too much. It's not a good idea." Hope cried, begging him to come, but he kept on saying they were better off apart. Hope loved and missed Anthony, but he didn't listen to what she had to say. She went home sad the next day. Hope didn't like staying in the house alone with the children, so Ricardo and Michelle told her to spend time with them.

After graduating from school, Hope wasn't working. Instead, she spent her time raising her children. She started going by her brother's house more often because she was in a new place and had no friends. Anthony still wasn't talking to her. Anthony didn't come to the house, not even for a weekend. Sometimes Hope would spend the week at Ricardo and Michelle's place. Anthony was so close but seemed so far away.

When Hope was sitting by Ricardo, and her relationship flashed, she called Anthony. Hope talked to him about her feelings, and then he asked Hope to come over to his house and that the children could come the next day. They spent the night together, and his phone rang while he was sleeping. Hope checked his cell phone, and it was Stephanie texting him, "I miss you." Hope was shocked after having such a good night with him. She texted her back, pretending to be Anthony. She wanted to know what Anthony and Stephanie talked about. Hope sent her a dirty text, and Stephanie replied, thinking Anthony was texting her.

Anthony, once again, hurts Hope. She went through his contact list and took all the women's numbers. The next day while he was at work, Hope called the girls. One of them was from Montreal. Her name was Sierra. Hope asked her, "how do you know Anthony? She responded, "Who is Anthony?" Hope said, "do you know Joel? She answered, "yes, I know him," Hope said, "Anthony is my husband.

How do you know him?" She said, "I met him at a party when I was in Toronto." Sierra then said, "I have a boyfriend; we're just friends." Hope asked her, "did you know Joel has a wife and kids?" She said to Hope, "Joel told me he has a baby mother." Hope said, "if you guys are just friends, why did he hide from you that he had a wife?" She told Hope, "it doesn't matter to me; we're not together." Hope knew Sierra was lying about everything.

Sierra called Anthony right after she ended the call with Hope. Anthony was on his way home from work and called Hope, asking her, "who did you call?" Hope said, "I don't know what you're talking about." He always played games with Hope, so she decided to play the same game with him. Anthony said to her, "before I get home, make sure you're gone." Hope told Cynthia what happened with Sierra and what Anthony said to her. She told Hope not to leave. "Don't mind him, stay."

At 6 pm, Anthony came home. It was raining outside, but he told Hope to leave. Hope didn't drive, and she'd have to take the bus. Hope said, "it's raining and cold outside; I can't take the kids in the rain!" His mother couldn't do anything. Anthony didn't tell her to leave the kids. He didn't care that he was kicking his kids out of the house into the rain. Her home was an hour and a half bus ride from Anthony's place. Hope called her brother and asked him to give her a ride, but Hope called a taxi and went to her brother's house. It was cheaper than taking a cab to her place. That day Hope decided she would shed no more tears for Anthony. She wasn't doing this with him anymore. She changed her number and started living her life without him. The children missed and cried for him, but he didn't care about them. Hope thought, "if he loved them, he would come and seed them." But he never did.

It had been a month since Hope heard from Anthony. Jimmy had a girlfriend, and she and Hope became friends. Anthony knew they were friends. He called Grace and Ricardo for Hope's number, but they wouldn't give it to him. Hope wanted to call him when the kids cried for him, but she wasn't giving in to her love for him. She cried herself to sleep every night, but she must remain strong for her kids.

One morning around 6:30 am, when Anthony usually went to work, Hope was up. She had the feeling something was wrong but couldn't put her finger on it. She started thinking that something was wrong with him so she picked up her phone to call him but couldn't do it. She didn't want him to hang up on her. As she lay there with that feeling, her phone rang. It was Anthony; he asked Hope to talk to the kids. Hope told him they were sleeping. He asked her to wake them up. Hope awoke the kids and put them on the phone, but they were so tired that they didn't say much to him. She got on the phone and told him the kids were tired and to call them back tomorrow.

Just when Hope asked him how he got her number, Anthony started crying. She asked him what was wrong. He cried even more. He said to Hope, "I miss my kids and my family, and I'm sorry for everything. Can I come by?" Hope felt sorry for him and cried on the phone with him. She believed he was sorry. She told him he could come. He took a taxi, and when Hope opened the door, Anthony hugged her so tight she could feel that he still loved her. Anthony went into the room and hugged the kids while they slept. After that, they both lay in the bed with the children, and it felt like a family again. Then, Anthony took Hope's hand and took her outside into the living room. As they sat there talking, Hope asked him, "how did you get my number?" He told her Jimmy gave it to him.

When Anthony talked to Hope, he said all the things she wanted to hear. He was still crying, and she told him, "don't cry, everything will be okay, I forgive you." When he put his hand into Hope's hair, she started to get goosebumps. She didn't want him to stop as he caressed her body. The morning came, and the kids woke up. They were happy to see their father, and they jumped up and hugged him.

Hope saw how much they missed their father. Anthony spent the day with them. "It was a great day," she told him. When he left, he kissed them and said his goodbyes.

Later Hope got a call from Anthony, thinking he called to let her know he had reached home safe, but she was wrong. He asked Hope, "did you go through my phone while I was asleep?" Hope replied, "that was the last thing on my mind." "Did I make a mistake with you again," he asked again, "did you go through my phone?" Hope said, "no, I didn't." Anthony told her to bring the kids over and spend time with him. Hope was happy he asked but was nervous that something might happen again. He might tell her to leave his house. She wasn't sure if she wanted to take the chance of feeling embarrassed once again.

Hope agreed, and she and the kids went to Anthony's house. Things were going okay but not great. He was still going on with his womanizing behaviour. Hope didn't want to say much because she wanted her family back together, but she couldn't take being disrespected by him. She couldn't act like things were all right when they weren't. They started getting into fights more and more. Anthony wanted to go out with his friends, and Hope would block the door to stop him from leaving. She didn't understand why he wanted her and the kids to spend time with him if he wasn't around. Hope spent the week at his house and then left.

With everything going on between her and Anthony, she decided to give Pastor Wright a call. Even though Hope was going to church, no one knew that she and Anthony weren't together. The Pastor couldn't believe what he was hearing. He asked, "how long have you been apart?" Hope replied, "for a long time." He didn't know what to say. He was still in shock and said, "Let me pray for you and your marriage." He told Hope after he finished praying, "this is the devil's work; I'm going to help you and Anthony get back together, you two are young, and you need guidance." Pastor Wright planned a day for him and Hope to see Anthony. Hope didn't say anything to Anthony, so he was surprised to see them at his door. Hope knew if she told him they were coming, he would have left the house.

Pastor Wright sat Hope and Anthony together along with his mother. He reminded them why they got married in the first place. The meeting went well, Hope thought. She thought her Pastor would get through to him before he left. She hoped Anthony would tell her to spend the night and talk more about what they could do going forward, but he didn't. Instead, he said to Hope, "see you around." Anthony did not want to fix their marriage.

A week later, Anthony was lonely, and he told Hope, "I miss my family; I want to come home." So, Hope let him move into her place with his mother. The kids were happy that he was home, and Hope was delighted. She hoped he really missed them and was home for good this time. Things were good for a month after Anthony moved in with Hope and the kids, but then women kept calling his phone. In addition, he kept spending a lot of time with his friends on the weekends when he should have been spending it with them.

Every night Hope felt lonely, even when he was at home. His body was there, but his mind was somewhere else. Hope discussed with him what he was doing. Anthony said to Hope with frustration, "my body is here, but my mind is somewhere else." He proved her right. It didn't hurt too much when she thought about it. But hearing the words from Anthony's mouth hurt her more. She was hoping that her feelings were wrong.

Hope found out that Anthony moved in with her because the building owner raised the rent at the end of the year. Hope thought back on when he cried on the phone and was nice to her. She thought he genuinely missed them, but Anthony couldn't afford to pay his rent any longer. Hope was hurt when Jimmy's girlfriend told her what was going on. She went to see Anthony about what she found out, and he got angry with Hope because she found out. She cried, and she said to Anthony, "I feel used. How could you do this to me?" Anthony didn't care that he hurt Hope. He said to her, "it was a tape recorder I was playing; I can play it again. Do you want to hear it?" As tears ran down Hope's face, she thought all she did was love him and just wanted him to love her back.

Hope and Anthony were living in Brampton, and Anthony worked in Toronto. It was hard on him since his trip to his job was an hour and a half on the bus. Anthony and Hope decided they should get a car. Even though she had just found out what he was up to, she still loved and wanted him. He financed a Honda Civic, and Hope thought he would give her one of the keys when he got the car, but instead, he gave one to Jimmy. She noticed that Anthony argued with her more often to leave the house, and she wouldn't see him for days.

Hope became friends with one of her bridesmaids, Rachel, when she married. While home caring for her children, Rachel called and asked, "where is your husband?" Hope replied, "he's at work, I assume." But, she told her, "I just saw him driving with my friend Destiny, with her foot on the dashboard." Hope didn't want to believe it but didn't think her friend would lie to her. Instead, Rachel said Anthony was surprised to see her.

Anthony knew Rachel would tell Hope what she had seen, so he decided not to come home. Rachel gave Destiny's number to Hope. She didn't know what would happen but wanted to hear what the girl had to say. Hope called and asked Destiny If she knew her husband, Anthony. Destiny said no, but Hope remembered he didn't give these girls his real name. Hope asked, "do you know Joel?" She said, "yes." Destiny was angry that Hope had called her phone. She told her that "Joel said you guys were over." Hope told her, "are you that foolish to believe such a thing?" "We're still together," said

Hope. Destiny told Hope, "I don't care what you say. I'm not going anywhere."

Cynthia heard Hope on the phone arguing. She came to Hope and asked, "what's going on here?" Hope told her what happened, so Cynthia got on the phone and said to Destiny, "my son will never leave his wife for you. My son is lying to you." For the first time, Hope felt that Cynthia cared about her. Cynthia gave the phone back to Hope. Destiny apologized to Hope, telling Hope everything that happened between them. Destiny said to Hope, "He sleeps at my house when he doesn't come home."

When Hope got off the phone, she called Michelle and started crying. She was stressed out and hadn't eaten anything all day. Michelle tried to comfort her as she continued crying. Michelle told Hope to ignore what Destiny had to say and that she needed to be strong for her children. While Michelle was talking to her, Hope passed out on the floor. Hope's daughter came into the room and saw her mom lying on the floor. Renell called her mom, but she didn't answer. Finally, Renell picked up the phone, and Michelle called for help. Michelle told Renell to take the phone to her grandma. Cynthia came into the room and saw Hope lying on the floor. She yelled to Michelle, "Hope's not breathing!" Michelle told Cynthia to call the ambulance. Hope finally woke up and saw Cynthia standing over her and Renell crying. Cynthia told Hope that she called for an ambulance. Hope cried and said she didn't want to go to the hospital, but they encouraged her to get checked out when the ambulance came.

While Hope was at the hospital, she waited to see a doctor. She tried to remember the last time she was happy with Anthony. As she cried, she thought, "all I'm getting from Anthony is heartache and pain." She felt so alone. Grace, Ricardo, and Michelle came to the hospital to see Hope. Michelle hugged Hope tight and told her, "don't you ever scare me like that again!"

Hope was delighted she had people in her life who cared about her. They told her they were trying to call Anthony, but he didn't pick up. They left messages, but he didn't answer or return their calls. Finally, after Hope was there for an hour, Anthony brought her some food. Hope looked at him. She wasn't sure if she should be angry with him. After three days, she just needed her husband.

Hope left the hospital with her family, and they went to her house. Anthony took Hope home and went underground to park. He wanted her to get out of the car, and Hope asked him, "are you not coming in?" He said he was going back to Toronto. Hope said, "I just came out of the hospital; why can't you stay?" Hope didn't understand why he had to go back to Toronto in the middle of the night. "I am not coming out of this car until you come inside," she said. "Is that girl more important than your family? Is she worth breaking up your family for?" Anthony got angry and told her, "if you don't get out of my car, I'll take you to Destiny's house so I can tell you in front of your face that we are not together." He drove out of the underground parking lot. Hope thought he meant what he said, and she told him, "you're going to shame me like that after all I've done for you?"

Anthony took Hope to the front of the house. Grace and the rest of the family were worried that Anthony and Hope might be arguing, and they came out of the house. Hope told her that Anthony was going back to Toronto to be with Destiny. Grace got angry with Hope and said to her, "you just came out of the hospital; stop stressing yourself." "Do you want to go back to the hospital? Let him go wherever he wants to go," said Grace. Hope wouldn't listen to Grace, and Grace went back inside very angry. Finally, Hope said to Anthony, "I'm tired of this; if you don't want me, let me go."

Grace went outside again and told Anthony to come inside so that Hope would also come inside. He went inside as Grace requested.

While there, Grace and Cynthia talked to them both to fix their marriage. Hope's family went home, and Anthony stayed. They talked that night to try and fix the problems in their marriage. Hope told Anthony that they needed to start doing things differently for their children. Anthony said to Hope, "things are going to be different for both of us going forward." They placed their hands on the Bible and swore that they would both change.

It had been a long time since Hope could trust and believe Anthony. He swore on the Bible, but he could still be lying. The following day Anthony went to work. Hope wondered if he would come back. Cynthia cooked dinner, but he didn't show up. Hope called his phone, but he didn't answer. Then she called Destiny to see if he was at her house. She said he wasn't there. Hope thought, "he swears on the Bible, but he played me, and he's playing God."

Every day Hope woke up, she called Anthony, but he wouldn't pick up. Cynthia couldn't handle what was going on. She sat at the table, looked out the window and cried. Hope didn't know what to do but comfort her. Anthony finally came home after four days. Hope argued with him about what would have happened if something was wrong with the kids, and she called him, and he didn't pick up. Finally, Anthony replied, "I'm not an ambulance!"

Hope thought he would stay this time, but he just came by for clean clothes. He slept the night and the next day, but then he was gone again. She wondered how she could win her husband back. She searched for an answer but didn't know what to do. She tried everything to make him love her, but nothing seemed to be working. Anthony started sleeping at home more often, and Hope thought that something must have been going on with him and Destiny.

Destiny called Hope every time Anthony came around. It was Valentine's Day, and he bought her a box of chocolates. Hope felt special and loved it. She knew he didn't have a lot of money, but it was the thought that counted. Destiny called Hope and told her that Anthony had bought her a cologne set and given her $100. Hope started to cry. She couldn't believe what he had done. She knew the game Destiny was playing. She acted like Hope and her were friends, but she just wanted to break Anthony and her up. Hope got off the phone and cried. She thought, "he gave me a cheap-ass box of $7.00 chocolates and went all out for her, it looks like she is the wife and I'm the side girl."

Hope was angry with Anthony. She told him she knew what he had done. He said, "I borrowed money from her; I was just paying her back piece by piece." Anthony was lying to Hope. That night He told her that he was going to a party with his friends. Hope helped him pick out his clothes while he was in the bedroom. She got on the phone with Destiny and told her, "I want you to listen to how he brings down women he was with." Hope hid the phone in her bra and went into the bathroom while he was showering.

Anthony was happy, he had a good day with Hope with no fighting, or maybe he was happy he was going out with Destiny. Hope couldn't tell. Anthony told her, "I'll never leave you for any woman. Those women were bitches." Hope said to him, "you were going to leave me for Destiny?" He said, "never, why would I leave you for her?" He continued, "I don't want Destiny, you're my wife, and I love you." When he came out of the shower, he saw someone was on the phone. He asked Hope, "who's on the phone?" Hope tried to think of a way to get out of answering him. She said, "it's Michelle on the phone. I called her by mistake." He said, "Michelle, I love my wife; no woman can take her place." Hope laughed and said, "Michelle, let me call you back." She got off the phone before he knew it wasn't Michelle.

Anthony left to be with Destiny and came home at 2 am. He held Hope close and made love to her, acting like he didn't just come from seeing another woman.

13.

Chapter Thirteen

Destiny called Hope the next day. She told her what went down that night. She said Anthony was mad at her because she was dancing with other guys. She was also angry with Anthony because she heard him say while on the phone with Hope, but she needed a ride to the party. Destiny said, "He left me at the party and went into his car and waited until the party was over because he was jealous." Hope said under her breath, "that's why he came home and made crazy love to me."

Destiny got tired of breaking up Hope and Anthony, and it wasn't working. So the next day, when Anthony was on his way home from work, Destiny called him, and at the same time, called Hope to include her in a three-way call with him. Anthony didn't know Hope was on the other line. Destiny said to Anthony, "can you bring me some food?" He asked her what she wanted, and she said, "rice, peas and chicken." Destiny told Hope, "when he gets here, I'll call you back." When Anthony was at the door, Destiny called Hope and told her she would hide the phone to hear. Hope listened to their conversation. After he gave Destiny the food, he went into her bedroom, and she said to him, "take your clothes and leave my house," throwing his clothes through the door.

Hope couldn't hear what Anthony said, but it seemed like he picked up his clothes and went back to her room. Destiny kept saying to him, "take your clothes out of my house!" Hope didn't want to hear any more. She didn't like the way Destiny was treating him, so she hung up the phone.

When Anthony came home, his food was on the table. While he ate, Hope stayed silent. He asked her why she was so quiet. Hope told him, "I don't want you here." She said, "I heard how Destiny was treating you, so why shouldn't I treat you the same way." Anthony looked at Hope, wondering how she knew that. She said, "I'm here treating you like a king while you mistreat me, and you're out there treating those other women like queens. How unfair is that?" Anthony got mad and told Hope, "I'm going back to Toronto to get my things." Hope knew how Anthony got when he was angry. "Don't go back to Destiny's house; wait till tomorrow," Hope begged, but he wouldn't listen.

Hope got a phone call from Destiny. She was crying and said to Hope, "I'm going to call the police on your husband." Hope thought, "Now he is my husband?" Destiny told her that Anthony held her by the throat. When Anthony returned home, Hope said, "what did you do?" He wouldn't answer, and he went to bed.

The police called Hope, they asked to speak with Anthony, but she told him he wasn't at home. Hope got angry with Anthony, and she said, "turn yourself into the police before they come here where my children are." Anthony thought about what he should do. He decided to go to the police. Hope called a taxi for him, but the police stopped the cab while it pulled out the driveway, and they arrested him. Anthony thought he could go around and do it to other women because he beat Hope.

The following day, Anthony returned home. He only spent a few hours at the police station. Hope was happy that he was home. She asked him again, "What happened last night at Destiny's house?" He said, "I went to get my clothes from her house, but she didn't want to give them to me." Hope said, "did you get into a fight with her, she said you choked her, and she has asthma." He admitted that he did choke her, but it was not like what she said. He explained that he just held her neck so she would let go of his clothes bag.

Hope knew how Destiny was treating Anthony, and she knew that Destiny did it so that she could get back at him in hopes that Hope would walk away from him. But Destiny got played by her own game. She thought she was winning, but Hope knew her game. Hope just played the game better than her. Anthony's lawyer wanted Hope to write a letter on his behalf. He treated her wrong throughout their whole relationship like she didn't matter. Now he was in trouble, and Hope was all that mattered. Hope wrote the letter. She was mad at Anthony for putting her and the children through this mess. Hope didn't want him to go to jail, but it pained her that she was being a fool for him.

Anthony was stressed out about going to court. He was ordered to stay away from Destiny, but he still contacted her. Hope was angry when she found out and thought, "I shouldn't have helped his ass in court." Anthony quit his job because he said the stress was too much for him. So now, he only gave Hope $150 a week to take care of the home. Hope knew it wasn't enough, but she took it and shut her mouth. Hope wasn't working, and all the bills were on her, including Anthony's car and insurance; she had to take care of the family all on her own. She was stressed, wondering how she would take care of her family because Anthony wasn't doing it. So now Hope depended on her kid's child tax credit and her GST every three months to take care of all of them, including his mother.

Anthony got up every day and left the house to be with his friends and look for other women. Hope tried to keep it together for her children, but it was hard. Finally, she cried out, "I can't do it alone!" Hope needed Anthony, but he was never there, and when he was, he wasn't there. Anthony asked Hope to borrow money from her mother to get gas for his car and buy food. She didn't want to do it but thought it was the only way to keep him happy.

Every day he left home, he said to Hope, "I'm going to look for work." It had been three months, and Anthony still didn't have a job. Things were getting harder and harder on Hope. Cynthia spent most of her time at her friend's house because she couldn't handle the arguments between her son and Hope any longer.

Hope didn't have any food in the house. So she sent the children to her mother's house because they could get something to eat. She didn't want her family to know what was going on, so she would make up some excuse for why the kids were there. Anthony told Hope she should go back to school, but she didn't want to because she already had one student loan with the government; she didn't want another one. But she went back to school. Not because she wanted to, but because Anthony wanted money. First, she had to do a test to get into college because she didn't have a high school diploma. Fortunately, she passed and would start school in a month.

Hope was waiting for her GST cheque to come, and she wondered what she would eat when it came. She checked her bank account and saw that $150 was in there. She was so happy but didn't spend the money because she wanted to wait for Anthony to come home. She smiled and told him, "I got my GST." Anthony was happy because he didn't have any money to give her. He said, "let's go get something to eat." They went to a Chinese restaurant in Toronto and shared a food bowl. They didn't want to spend all the money. They needed the rest for gas, food, and laundry.

After that time, they were broke again. Hope was waiting on the child tax credit to pay the bills, including the car insurance and car payment. Hope said to herself, "We have so little money, but I have to make it work." The money was gone before she could save any in her bank account. Hope always made sure Anthony had gas for his car even though he was always gone. When Hope had paid everything, there was nothing left most of the time. Hope couldn't pay all the bills. She had to leave some for the next month to pay Anthony's bills. Hope never knew how to tell him how she felt. She was scared that Anthony would get mad and hit her or she wouldn't see him.

The stress started to get even worse for Hope. Finally, she couldn't take it anymore. They began to fight more, and Hope retorted to Anthony, "you're not being the man of the house." Hope always had to fix anything that broke in the house. The couch was no good, so she had to throw it out. Now they had to sit on the floor. She felt so ashamed she didn't want to invite anyone over to their place.

Anthony had to go back to court. The date was getting close. Things weren't going well with his case, and he started spending more time at home. But Hope loved seeing Anthony at home. He spent time with the family, taking the kids to the park. Hope and Anthony didn't have any money to take them to the movies, so they had a movie night at home instead.

While Hope was cooking, Anthony came in and hugged her. He told Hope how much he loved her. Hope had been waiting for this kind of love from him for three years but lamented, "but all good things must come to an end."
One day they went to visit their friend Jen. She went to braid Jen's sister Natalie's hair. While there, Anthony's phone kept ringing. The calls showed up as unknown. Hope asked him, "why aren't you answering your phone?" He told her that he didn't want to, then Anthony left and said he was going for a drive till Hope was finished.

While on their way home, Anthony's phone kept ringing. She asked him who was calling all the time. He said, "Destiny is the one calling my phone." Hope asked, "why is she still calling you?" Hope wondered why he wasn't staying away from her. Anthony turned to Hope and said, "I still want to be with her; I want to be with both of you."

Well, it was a long drive home. The pair argued with the kids in the backseat. Finally, Hope cried and said to him, "after all that girl has done, you still want to be with her?" Anthony dropped Hope and the kids home and drove away. Hope knew he went to be with Destiny, but she could do nothing. When he returned home, she asked him if he had visited Destiny. Anthony said no, but Hope didn't believe him. Anthony still wasn't working. There wasn't much in the house to feed the kids. Hope saved all her pennies since she was in her teens, so she took them to the bank to see how much money she had. Hope got $30 for them, but it still wasn't enough for her to feed the children. Anthony told her he would borrow some money from his friend Wayne. He came back with $200, but Hope didn't believe a friend of his would lend him so much money. Nothing added up when it came to Anthony and money.

One night Hope had sex with him to tire him out. While he slept, she went into his car, snooping around to see what she could find out. She couldn't understand why he was so comfortable not working to take care of his children and now borrowed money from his friends. Hope was shocked by what she found in his car. There were welfare pay stubs. She checked the dates. He never told her he had been getting money from the welfare office for three months. Hope thought, "I have no money, and I'm taking care of him, his mother and our kids, and he was getting money." She couldn't believe it. Hope put the stub back where she found them. She played it cool and didn't say anything to Anthony. She didn't know if she could be quiet about it but had to try for now.

Hope called Michelle crying, telling her what she had seen. Michelle couldn't believe he did that to Hope. Hope didn't know how she would have handled it without her sister-in-law by her side, through all her ups and downs with Anthony. Michelle was the only one she could trust. They did everything together, and Anthony didn't like her. He thought Michelle knew too much of what was going on in their home. When Michelle and Ricardo came around, Anthony would talk to them and pretend that he liked them. Deep down, he hadn't let go of what happened between Ricardo and him in the past.

Michelle decided to go to school with Hope as well. Hope asked Anthony to go back to school, but he didn't want to. Hope said to Anthony, "you're not working, so both of us should go back to school together." He said no. Anthony didn't mind that Hope went to school because he could get money. But she didn't want to give him any money because she knew he was getting welfare. Hope and Michelle were studying the same course to become personal support workers when they started school. Hope was happy she had her best friend with her. Hope had to go into the school to sign the paperwork to get her student loan. Anthony was happy to take her and knew when the money was coming.

On the way to the school, a police officer followed his car. They weren't sure why they were following him. When they reached the school parking lot, the officer got out of his car and walked up to Anthony's car window. The officer asked to see some ID. Anthony asked him, "what's the problem, officer?" The officer said, "you know you're not supposed to be around this girl." The officer thought Hope was Destiny. Hope told the officer that she was his wife, not Destiny. The officer told Anthony, "we have a restraining order against you, so you have to stay away from that girl."

Anthony was embarrassed about what happened with the officer. Hope said to him, "and you still want to be with her even though you have a restraining order against you." Hope shook her head and walked to the school.
Anthony didn't know Hope knew about the welfare he was getting. Hope was fed up with pretending she didn't know. Hope found his social worker's number and called her. Hope had to leave a voice message with her name and number to call her back. When

the worker called back, she told her about Anthony and sponsored Anthony. She wanted to know what would happen if he took money from them and if she would have to pay it back. The social worker said she would because she was responsible for him." The worker asked Hope if they were still married. Hope said, "yes, we are, and we live together." The worker asked for her address. Hope gave it to her, and she gave Hope the address she had on file for him. Hope told her, "I know that's not the address Anthony uses. I saw all the pay stubs, but we live together." The worker asked for a copy of their marriage license and any mail with his name coming to the address. Hope said, "yes, I'll send it to you."

The next day, while Hope was on her lunch break at school, she faxed the information to the worker. She knew she couldn't do it if Anthony were around without him asking questions. But Hope didn't care if Anthony found out. Anthony was a liar and a deceiver. The worker called later that day, but Hope was in class. When Hope got home, she heard Anthony and the social worker on her voicemail on a three-way call that she was supposed to be on that day. Instead, she heard the social worker ask Anthony where he lived and lived with his wife. Anthony told her they weren't together, and the worker accused him of not being honest on his application and that he would have to pay back the $2,000 he got from them. Anthony insisted that they were not living together, but the worker told him, "your wife has proved that you are both living together." Anthony still couldn't tell the truth about where he was living, and the worker said to him, "you won't be able to get help from us again in the future."

Hope wasn't worried about how Anthony would react to her anymore. She was tired of Anthony using and abusing her and acting as he cared for her or their children. Hope called the social worker the next day, and the social worker asked her, "are you both living together?" Hope said, "yes, we are living together." She asked Hope how long they had been married, and she said three years. Then, she asked if Hope would be the one to pay the money back. "Don't worry about that; he'll be the one paying it back," Hope replied.

Anthony made sure Hope wouldn't find out about his welfare. His checks went to his old address, but he wasn't smart enough to take them out of his car. Hope's church sister, Kelly, lived at Anthony's apartment with her family after moving and living with Hope. She was also receiving assistance. Anthony didn't know about it, but his social worker found out about Kelly, so she asked if Anthony was living there. She told the worker that Anthony wasn't living there. It was just for her and her family, so she confirmed that Hope was telling the truth.

While Hope was in school, she wanted Cynthia to babysit the kids since she lived there. But Hope was shocked when she told her she wouldn't be living there anymore. "I'm going to stay with Jimmy and help him and his girlfriend with their new baby," she said. Hope couldn't believe she chose to babysit someone else's child and not her grandkids. So, Cynthia moved out, leaving Hope to find herself a babysitter. But, before she left, she told Hope, "I don't like the arguments with you and my son."

Cynthia saw how her son was treating Hope. She was there through everything but never had much to say. Finally, Hope didn't have Cynthia living with her anymore. Now when she needed her help with the kids, she left.
Hope spoke with her mother, Grace, and told her that she might forget about school because she didn't have a babysitter. Grace told her she would take care of them while at school. Hope and Grace didn't have the best relationship, but Grace was there for her. Hope was happy that she didn't have to worry about a babysitter, but the kids would have to spend the week with Grace, and she would see them on the weekends. Hope dropped the kids off every Sunday and picked them up on Friday. She missed her children, but it was the best she could do. She wanted to pay Grace to watch

the kids, but Grace told her, "these are my grandkids; I won't take money from you." Hope didn't want to leave the kids there or help her mother. Grace wasn't working and didn't have much money to care for herself, let alone her brothers and sisters. Because Grace wouldn't take any money from Hope, she bought rice and a box of chickens for her, things she knew Grace needed. It was her way of saying thank you.

Ricardo ended up missing payments on his car, so they repossessed it. He asked Anthony to take him to get his car back from the car company. Anthony took Ricardo to the company, but they got pulled over by the police on the way back. The officer came up to the car and asked to see his driver's license. Anthony gave it to him and asked, "what's the problem, officer?" He told him that he had made an illegal turn. Anthony started arguing with the officer, who told him that his license plate sticker was expired. The officer didn't like Anthony's tone of voice, he asked to see his insurance, but he had none. He gave him a fine of five thousand dollars. The officer told Anthony he couldn't drive his car and that it would have to be towed and he would have to go to court to pay the fines.

Ricardo never got his car back because he didn't have enough money to get it back. As a result, Anthony couldn't drive his car back home. Anthony called Hope to let her know what happened and that he needed her help to pay for the tow truck. Like always, Hope came to the rescue. She was always there to get Anthony out of trouble. Ricardo felt terrible for what happened to Anthony. He said, "if it weren't for me asking you to take me to get my car, this would never have happened." However, Hope thought Ricardo shouldn't blame himself because it would have eventually happened. It was only a matter of time.

Anthony and Hope made sure their kids got to Grace's house so that Hope could go to school. But now, Hope could only spend time with her kids when she went to Grace's because Anthony couldn't drive his car. Hope went to Grace's house on Saturdays to spend time with her children and leave in the evening. She couldn't take them home because it would be hard to bring them back and go to school on Monday. Now that Anthony didn't have a car, he spent most of his time home. He called his friends to get his car back on the road, but no one could help. All the money he got from social assistants was gone because he spent partying with his friends and women.

While visiting the kids at Grace's house, Hope and Anthony rode the bus to get there. He told her, "you're the only one that's always there for me; you never let me down." Hope knew what he said was just for the moment. When he got his car back, he would return to his old ways with his friends. Hope didn't help Anthony get his car back on the road right away. She liked having him home every night. She had to take the bus to school now, but she didn't mind doing it once she saw her husband was home more often. Things were going great for a while. Hope's student loan came in, and she paid Anthony's outstanding car payment, insurance, and the fee to renew the license plate. Every month Anthony came to Hope for money to make his car payment. Everything was always on Hope when they went out with the family.

Eventually, as Hope predicted, Anthony returned to his old ways, leaving Hope and the kids again. He was always gone every opportunity to spend time with the kids. He preferred being with his friends. Anthony would take Hope's credit and debit cards, and there was nothing she could do about it.

14.

Chapter Fourteen

Hope wanted to know where Anthony always went. So, she started a search to find the truth. He saved women's phone numbers under men's names to fool her. Hope decided to call all the numbers on his phone to uncover his deception. If a man answered, she hung up without saying anything. She found three female numbers from guys named Anthony. Their names were Ashley, Nickie and Natalie. She spoke with Ashley and asked if she knew Anthony and like every female said, they didn't know him, but they knew Joel. She said she met Anthony and his friends at the club, and they exchanged numbers and spoke on the phone every day. Hope asked if she knew that he had a wife and children, and she said Anthony never mentioned it. Hope asked Ashley if she ever saw the car seat in his car. Hope didn't know if they ever met after the party, but she assumed they did. Ashley said every time they saw each other; she never saw a car seat. Anthony put the car seat into the trunk of his car, and Hope said bye to Ashley and hung up, feeling sad. She said, "not only me he disowned but our children too, how could he!"

Hope didn't want to hear anything from the other girls because she already knew what they would say to her. Finally, Anthony came home and saw Hope looking sad; he asked her what was wrong, she didn't want to get into any more fights with him over another woman again, she smiled, and she said, "everything is okay, I'm just a little tired."

One day Anthony opened up to Hope. He told her that he almost cheated on her. Hope asked, "what do you mean?" He said, "after partying with my friends, I met a girl; we went to a hotel, and just when we were going to have sex, a bad smell was coming from her vagina so that I couldn't go through with it." Hope looked at Anthony like he was crazy. She said, "who paid for the hotel room?" He told her, "I did, but I let her sleep the night there, and I came home to you."

Anthony continued with another story, "one night I met a girl at a party, and we became friends. She invited me to her house, so I went. We wanted to have sex, but my penis wouldn't get hard for her; I didn't know what was happening, so I left and came home to you." Hope remembered the night he was talking about. She said, "is that the night you came home and made love to me?" He said, "yes." She asked him, "why are you telling me all of this?" He told her he wanted to change. Hope didn't understand why he told her those things because it broke her heart.

Hope knew Anthony would never change and that she would have to find a way to live with it for her children's sake. She didn't want them to grow up without a father as she did, so she put up with Anthony's cheating ways.

Hope had a friend named Rebecca. She moved to Canada and was living with some friends. She had problems living there. One day Rebecca called Hope, letting her know that things weren't going well. Even though Hope was going through her trials with Anthony, it felt good to help someone else.

Hope told Rebecca, "I'm here anytime you need me." She called Hope one night and was crying. She told Hope that the lady she was staying with kicked her out. Hope felt sorry for her. However, she knew Rebecca didn't have any family living in Canada, so Hope invited her to stay with her. Rebecca moved in with Hope, and things went great. Hope didn't ask for rent, she just wanted Rebecca to take care of herself, and her friend was pleased to hear that. Anthony didn't have a problem with Rebecca living with them. Hope didn't mind because she knew that, as much as Anthony loved women, Rebecca wouldn't mess around with Anthony. But, of course, Hope and Anthony were still getting into fights. He wouldn't stop his partying ways and focus on her and the kids. At this point, Hope didn't know what was left for her to do.

One day Anthony was going out with his friends, and Hope told him that he wasn't going anywhere. She blocked the door so that he couldn't leave. Anthony insisted he was going out with his friends. Hope cried, pleading with him, "please spend some time with your family; we miss you." Anthony didn't care. Hope wouldn't get out of the way. Finally, she told him, "if you go out with your friends, leave my keys." She didn't know what else to say. Hope was shocked she said that, but Anthony left her no choice. Anthony got angry that Hope wouldn't move, so he pulled Hope into their bedroom and started beating her. He grabbed her by the throat and started choking her. Renell came into the room screaming, but Anthony wouldn't stop. Rebecca came into the room begging Anthony to stop, but he wouldn't. "You're going to kill her!" she screamed. Hope said, "I still love you." He let her go and left to meet his friends. Renell ran into Hope's arms as she cried. Her daughter wiped her tears and said to Hope, "don't cry, mommy, it's okay." Hope's son, James, hugged her, but he was too young to understand what was going on.

As months went by, Rebecca was dating Randy, a friend of Anthony's who visited her every weekend. Hope knew him when he moved to Canada, but they never talked much. Now that he was coming around more often, Hope opened up to him, hoping he could be the voice of reason to her husband. Unfortunately, Hope knew she couldn't go to any of Anthony's friends to talk to them about him. They would cover up all his lies and womanizing.

Thanks to Anthony, all of Hope's money from her student loan was gone. One day she sat down and talked with Rebecca telling her, "now that my financial status has changed, I would like your help with one of the bills." Rebecca was okay with the proposal Hope gave. She told her, "I'll pay the hydro bill." Hope was nervous asking her, but it turned out fine. But a few weeks later, Rebecca decided things were going well with Randy and her and would move in with him. Hope felt hurt. She helped Rebecca when she needed her, and now she was leaving. But as much as Hope was going through problems with Anthony, she wouldn't turn her back on her friend Rebecca.

Hope didn't show Rebecca how much she felt betrayed by her. Rebecca gave Hope an envelope and inside it was $400. She thanked her and said, "all the best to you and Randy." Hope knew that it was a temporary arrangement with Rebecca living with her, but she didn't think she would leave her when she needed her the most. So, Hope focused on finishing school while Anthony kept living his life the way he wanted to, having no job and hanging with his friends.

While Anthony was sleeping, Hope went through his phone to see what he was up to. She found a number that wasn't on his phone before. The next day Hope went to school and thought about who it could be, hoping it wasn't another girl's number. Hope thought about calling the number, but she didn't want to get Anthony mad. She couldn't help feeling that he was up to something again. Hope called the number, and a girl answered. Hope's heart skipped a beat. A girl's heart was supposed to skip a beat for a boy they loved. In Hope's case, her heart skipped because a girl answering the phone wasn't a good thing.

"Hello, who am I speaking to?" The girl on the other end said rudely, "you called my phone; who are you?" "I am Anthony's wife," she said, "I found your number in his phone." Hope didn't want to be rude because she knew she wouldn't get anything from the girl if she started to attack her. "Do you know my husband," she asked. The girl said, "yes, I know Anthony." Hope asked her how they knew each other. She told Hope, "we've been dating for a year." Hope couldn't believe what she was hearing. Hope said, "this can't be true." Hope asked, "how do I know you're telling the truth? Why don't I know about you as I do with the other girls he's been with?" She told Hope they met at a party and have been going out ever since. Hope asked, "what other things have you two done together?" She told Hope, "he took me to hotels." Hope asked, "with what money?" She told Hope, "I can tell you what Anthony has in his wallet, he has a TD and a Visa card, a CIBC card and his ID. Hope said, "those are all my cards he's spending on you." Hope didn't want to hear any more, but she did, even if it hurt.

When the conversation ended, Hope said, "thank you for letting me know what was going on with you and my husband." Hope got off the phone, and she was hurt. After everything she had gone through with Anthony, she thought he would never love her. Hope couldn't function, and she cried the rest of the day. She was happy the kids were at her mother's house so they couldn't see her cry. She couldn't cook or clean up around the house. She just spent the day in her room crying.

When Anthony came home, Hope was angry. "Why do you keep hurting me this way," she yelled. He looked at her with an annoyed look on his face. "What did I do now?" he said. She told him what the girl had said to her, and he acted like he didn't know what she was talking about. "I want you to leave my house," she demanded. Hope couldn't believe she said that to the man she loved. Anthony went into the bedroom and took his clothes out of the closet. He was mad. "All day, you don't clean up around the house, but you have time to be on the phone calling people," he said. Hope got angrier because he was justifying what he had done once again. Finally, she told him, "since you can't treat me right, let me help you pack your clothes and leave my house!"

Anthony didn't fight to stay. Hope's money was all gone because of him. There was no reason for him to stay any longer. In his eyes, Hope didn't have anything else to give. Thus Hope and Anthony separated. Before he left, he said, "I can't live with you anymore; we fight too much, I'm not happy with you anymore." Hope glared at him while he put all the blame on her. "I do everything for you, I put you first in everything, and you still never loved me the same way," she cried. Hope hadn't been happy for years but stuck with him because of their kids. She tried to make it work, but he was never there for her like he should have been. Hope said to Anthony, "I fight women for you, I fight just to be with you, and you still couldn't love me right." He just stood there as she cried. Hope could see there was no love in his eyes for her.

Hope was now left to raise two babies on her own. She must now find her way. All her money was gone, and so was Anthony's love for her. He used to drop Hope off at school, but now that they weren't together, he dropped her off whenever he felt like it. Anytime the two got angry with each other, he would let Hope take the bus. But when the month came, she still paid his bills from their kid's child tax credit. However, one month Hope decided she no longer wanted to be used by Anthony, so she stopped paying his bills. This left Hope to hurt all over again. Now she had no way of getting to school. Because she had no money, she dropped out of school.

It wasn't a hard decision for Hope to drop out of school because she didn't like what she was studying anymore. Anthony was why she went back to school to get a student loan to pay his bills and spend money on women.
Hope's mistake when they were together was that she did not have a backup plan. She knew he would leave someday, but she prayed and hoped she was wrong. Sadly, her fear came true. Hope thought, "he kept telling me that he was in love with me, so how can he walk out of his family when we need him the most? If that was love, I don't want to be loved like that again."

Ever since Hope and Anthony separated, she tried hard to get him back, but he always made it clear he didn't want her back. Every time she saw Anthony, he was with a different woman. Anthony lived life with Hope's cousin, who helped break up their marriage.

Hope knew everyone should think for themselves and that no one should make you do anything you don't want to do, but Anthony was a follower, never a leader. Since Hope's cousin's marriage failed, he didn't want any of his friend's marriages to work. So he tried to break up her marriage, and he succeeded. Finally, Hope's cousin Brian said, "my marriage already fell apart; I don't care about anyone's marriage." Hope thought, "why would your own family want to hurt you like that, he knew we have kids together, and they are just babies; they need their father, and it hurts my kids. I'll never forgive him for that."

Hope and Jessie put together a birthday party for both of their birthdays. Her birthday was December 3rd, and Jessie's was on the 6th. She was having fun, trying to forget about her problems with Anthony, even if just for that day. Anthony came with another woman. Hope told herself, "I'm not going to let him see how angry I am or to see that I'm jealous." So she pretended he wasn't there. She danced with one of her friends while Anthony danced with the girl. He couldn't keep his eyes off Hope.

When Hope went into the kitchen to get a drink, Anthony came behind her. Hope and her friends were taking pictures when Anthony came up to her and said, "Hi." She said hi to him and continued taking pictures. Hope's friends pushed her and Anthony to take a picture together, and he didn't mind, and neither did Hope. They were in the kitchen laughing and talking like they were still friends.

Anthony's new girl saw them holding each other, she got mad and left. Hope didn't care that she got angry. All her friends laughed and said, "wifey run things in here." Hope was happy about what had happened. The girl came to her party with Anthony, and when the girl saw Hope, knowing she was his wife, she could have left, but she stayed. Hope said, "she got what she deserved." Everyone laughed when Anthony went after her. they told Hope, "you're the man's wife." Hope said, "hell, yes." Hope didn't care that he went after his date. She just kept on having fun. It was her birthday, and she wasn't going to let anyone or anything mess up her day.

The next day, Hope felt good. She replayed what happened at the party, but her phone rang as she was about to go to bed. It was Anthony. He said, "goodnight, how are you and the kids?" Hope said, "I'm doing pretty good, and the kids are sleeping. How are you doing?" He said he was doing good and that he was thinking about her. He asked her if she had a guy in her life, and Hope wondered if Anthony was losing it. He knew she wouldn't have any guy in her life because she still loved him. But here he was playing foolish games. Hope answered him and said, "No." She asked him, "what about the woman you brought to my party? Is she okay?" She said, "I didn't mean for her to get angry with you." Hope knew it was just a lie. She loved that the girl was mad at him and hoped they would break up so she could get her husband back. He said, "we're good now, and she just left," Hope said, "Your woman just left. Why are you calling me?" "I still love you and miss you," he said. Hope still loved him but didn't want to say it back.

Anthony asked if they could work things out. Those were the words Hope had wanted to hear for a long time. Hope said, "how can you want to work things out and still be with someone else?" He told her he didn't love her.
Anthony told her about the woman he was sleeping with because he wanted to be honest with her.

.Hope told Anthony they could work things out, and then he confessed that there was a woman who was having his baby but hoped that wouldn't change things between them. Hope was in shock and didn't know what to say. She was silent on the phone for a while, then said to him, "we'll still be together." But, Anthony told Hope, "there were two other ladies that I got pregnant, but one of them lost the baby, and the other one got an abortion because she was married." Hope asked, "Who was this married lady, and why would she cheat on her husband with a married man?" He said, "the lady was at Jimmy's wedding." Her name was Celie." Hope remembered seeing her at the wedding, and she said, "I know her, and she knew you were married." But that didn't stop her from getting with Anthony.

Celie wasn't happy that Anthony and Hope were back together, but she didn't have a choice but to accept it. Since Hope and Anthony got back together, it was a problem for Hope with Celie. She would pick fights with Hope all the time. Anthony found a new place to live even though they were back together. Hope and the kids went to Anthony's house every weekend to spend the weekend. While Hope was at his place, Celie called because she knew Hope was there. Most times, he wouldn't answer. When he did, Hope could hear Celie asking him why he didn't answer his phone and who was there with him. Celie acted like she was the one Anthony was married to, and Hope didn't like it. Celie knew Anthony was spending time with his family, but it seemed like it didn't bother her. Hope told Anthony, "she needs to know what time it is." She acted like Anthony's wife, and Hope was his side chick. Hope looked at Anthony and thought, "I don't even have that much power like she has over Anthony."

He promised he would always be honest with Hope. Anthony would show her his phone to show her he was telling the truth. Hope was pleased he wanted his family back. Hope and Anthony had been back together for a month, and things were going well. When they weren't together, they talked on the phone. Hope never knew he was still playing her and had two women visiting his house. It was Valentine's, and she couldn't spend it with Anthony because it was a school day for the kids. Hope asked Anthony, "I wish I could spend the day with you." He said, "me too." Hope wanted to know what he was doing. He told her he was just relaxing then said he was going outside, but he would be back. They said their goodbyes.

Anthony called Hope that night. He told her, "I'm with the girl I brought to your party. Hope got angry. She couldn't spend Valentine's Day with him, but another woman could. He wanted her to be okay with it. She remembered why they separated in the first place. He told her that he was sorry, and like always, Hope forgave him.

Anthony told Hope to bring the kids to spend the weekend with him. Hope said yes, and he assured her he wasn't going out with his boys. But, she didn't believe him. Anthony took a shower to get ready for his night out with his friends, so Hope looked through his phone, but he caught her and wasn't happy. Hope asked him, "why are you mad when you told me I could go through your phone because you didn't have anything to hide?" He told her it was only okay when he was with her.

Anthony went out. Hope stayed up waiting for him, but he didn't return, so she went to bed. When she awoke in the morning, Anthony wasn't there. She cried, knowing he was going to hurt her all over again. Hope called Emily, who came to her party with Anthony. Hope asked to speak to Anthony when she answered, but she told her he was sleeping. Hope started crying, "this guy brought me to his house to let me sleep alone while he is with another woman." Hope called Michelle and her brother to pick her and the kids up to take them home. She didn't want to be there when Anthony got home. She didn't want to hear his excuse for what he did.

When Hope got home, Anthony called. She let it go to voicemail. He left a message that said, "Hey, don't worry about me, I'm okay, I'll be home soon." He thought she was still at his house, and he didn't know that Emily had told Hope he was there. When he got home and saw that Hope and the kids weren't there, he called her, but Hope wouldn't take his calls. Hope felt ashamed about what he had done.

Anthony kept calling all day, and Hope finally answered. He wanted to know why she wasn't taking his calls. She told him she didn't want to. Anthony said he was sorry he didn't come home because he was too drunk. Hope asked him where he slept. He said, "I slept at Emily's house, but nothing happened." Hope said, "Is that supposed to make me feel better that you slept at your ex-girlfriend's house?" He said, "baby, I'm sorry." Finally, Hope couldn't continue the conversation and told him she had to go.

Later that day, she talked with Emily, and she told her that Anthony was still trying to get with her, but she said she kept telling him to stay with his wife. Emily gave Hope some advice about Anthony, but Hope thought, "really, she's sleeping with my husband and wants to give me advice?" Nevertheless, Hope went along with it because she wanted to know what was happening between them. She knew how a woman falls for a guy and wanted to get this other woman out of her guy's life.

Hope decided to break up with Anthony again, but he told her it was over before she did it. She had let him back into her life only to hear those words again after two months of being together. Hope tried hard to get over Anthony, but her heart still belonged to her husband. She couldn't get close to another guy.

Hope tried to work on her marriage that whole year, but Anthony wasn't interested. She tried to work things out, but he was too busy chasing other girls.

15.

Chapter Fifteen

One day Anthony came by the house. Hope was happy he did to try to work on their marriage. She told him how much she loved him and didn't understand why he kept hurting her. Finally, he told her, "I can't go anywhere in life with you." She was shocked, and it broke her heart even more.

Anthony told Hope, "you're not working or doing anything with your life." Hope shot back, "I spent my whole married life putting you first! I went back to school to get an education and had my children. What more do you want from me?" She didn't understand what he was talking about. She told Anthony, "I used to work in Toronto in the evening and came home late at night. You were driving and never once came to get me at work. I prayed every night that I would get home safe to you and our children," as the tears rolled down her face. Hope said to Anthony, "you'll never understand my pain."

Every night when she finished work at 10 pm, she prayed that the bus wouldn't stop running. She had to take three buses to get home, and the last bus home stopped running at midnight. Anthony came home and slept, saying he had to work the next day. As Hope went down memory lane with him, she said, "when I look at you, I don't see a husband. I see a heartless man who doesn't care if there's anything wrong with me while I'm out working late at night." Anthony didn't want to listen. He knew what she was saying was the truth but was too selfish to care.

Hope told Anthony that he never gave her money to pay the bills every time she got a job. "I have to do it myself, and when I'm not working, you only gave me $150 a week. I had to buy food for the house; I had to do laundry and take care of our kids. Is that fair to me?" But, she said, "maybe you're right; we'd be better off apart."

Hope was hurt by Anthony and what he had said to her, and she wasn't sure if she would get another chance to let him know how she felt. So, therefore, she let everything out.
Hope asked, "why would a man think they don't have to support their family?" I was trying to make a life for us," she cried.

She had her own business, and Anthony was the reason she had to close it down before it got far. Now he told her that she wasn't going anywhere in life and that he couldn't be with her. Hope said, "I should be the one who says those words to you." After hearing how she felt, Anthony didn't know what to say except, "I have to go now." Hope felt good saying those things to him. She tried to make their marriage work, but he never understood what it took to keep a good woman. Hope stayed with Anthony because she loved him. She kept telling herself he would change. She kept making excuses when he beat her and cheated on her even though it hurt their kids. Hope dropped out of school because of Anthony. She didn't have money to get to school, and the stress of Anthony didn't help.

Now she had no job and two kids to look after. So when she asked him for money for his children, sometimes he gave and other times, he didn't. One day Anthony told Hope that he had stopped working, but she didn't believe him. So, she called Jimmy and asked him if Anthony had quit his job. Jimmy said no, and that he was still working. She didn't understand why Anthony would say such a thing not to put food on the table for his kids. Hope felt hurt. She thought, "forget about me; he's made it clear he doesn't want anything to do with me, but why doesn't he want to take care of his children?"

It was so sad to hear when a father didn't want to be there for his children. She prayed that God would make way for her and her children to survive. The only way Anthony would give her money was when she would have sex with him. When she didn't, he would give her nothing. So she had to sell herself to her husband, just for food. As Hope lay there while Anthony was having sex with her, she thought, "A husband is supposed to take care of his family and make sure they don't need anything."

Anthony stayed at a shelter instead of home, fixing his marriage. He just wasn't a man yet. He was a little boy who was running scared. Hope became close to Anthony's cousin Jen. She was a lovely lady she could trust, so she opened up to her. Jen thought everything was good with Anthony and Hope. She was understanding and felt Hope's pain.

Once Anthony wasn't living with her anymore, he wouldn't help the kids. The cable bill was due, and Hope didn't have money to pay it. She asked Anthony to help because it was the only thing that entertained the kids, but he said he had no money. When it came to his family, he never had.

Hope called Jen and asked her to speak to Anthony to help her with the kids. Jen asked, "what's wrong? What did he do?" Hope told her that she asked Anthony to help pay the cable bill, but he wouldn't. Jen asked, "how much is the bill?" Hope told her it was $700. Jen didn't ask why it was so high, and she offered to lend her the money to pay the bill. Hope was surprised and asked, "how are we going to do this?" Jen said, "I'm going to give you my credit card information, so call the cable company and pay the bill." Hope couldn't believe she would take such a risk to help her but was happy she had a friend like Jen.

Anthony took a girl to Jen's house, and Hope wasn't happy when she heard about it. Jen said to one girl, "Did Anthony tell you he has a wife?" The girl said she knew. Jen called Hope the next day and told her what had happened. Hope didn't like what she heard, but there was nothing she could do but cry. Anthony knew Jen would tell Hope, but it seemed like that's what he was hoping to happen.

Anthony didn't want Hope, but he went to her to get him out of trouble. He went to Montreal without telling Hope. She found out when he called her from there. He asked her how she and the kids were doing. "We are doing fine," she said. Then he asked if she had any money because he needed help. Hope asked him, "Why do you need my help?" He said, "I got into an accident with my car. It's at the mechanic." She asked him how much it would cost to get it fixed. He told her $400. Hope told him that she didn't have any money. Then he asked her, "Can you borrow the money from your mother?" She said, "I'll get back to you."

Hope knew that Anthony was using her again, so she didn't return his call. However, that evening Hope spoke with Jimmy's wife, Kimberly. She told her that Anthony had called and asked for money. She said to Hope, "I know; he called Cynthia and told her what happened." Kimberly also told Hope that, when Cynthia got off the phone with Anthony, she said, "thank God Anthony had some money he was hiding from Hope so he could get his car fixed." Hope was hurt that Cynthia felt that way. She never asked Anthony for anything but to take care of his children. Hope told Kimberly, "That's not right, I let this woman into my house, and that's how she feels?" Hope knew she had done everything possible for her family, even for Cynthia, so she couldn't understand why she didn't like her.

It was summer vacation, and the kids were out of school. Hope and the kids were spending the summer with Grace. Anthony spent most of his time at Hope's cousin Brian's house. He only lived 5 minutes away from Grace, but he wouldn't come and see the kids. Hope begged him to visit, but he said he was too busy. So, she stopped calling him and focused on taking care of her children and getting another job. She was happy that her mother was there to help with the children while she looked for a job to get back on her feet.

Sadly, Hope got the news that her aunt Alexandra died from cancer on November 25th, five days before her birthday. Even though her relationship with her aunt got strange after marrying Anthony, she loved and missed her. Hope sang at Alexandra's funeral. It was heartbreaking for her. Anthony was there, and he looked at her while she passed by him. The kids were happy to see him and ran to him. But, he didn't say a word to Hope. Anthony didn't care to ask how she or the kids were doing after losing their aunt.

Two weeks after the passing of her aunt, Hope got a job with an insurance company. She showed up every day at work while studying to get her insurance license. She went out to get clients even on the coldest days, looking for clients and building her team. After so long, Anthony heard that Hope was working and wanted to see her. It had been almost a year since they broke up. He asked if she was at her mother's place. Hope said, "yes, what's wrong?" Right now, Hope didn't care, but she didn't want to come off as rude to the father of her children. They talked for a while, and Anthony said to Hope, "I'm sorry for everything I have done to you." Once again, she thought he was playing his same old games. Hope wanted to believe him but didn't know-how. Finally, he told her he had a new place and wanted her to come and see it. She asked, "have you taken your girls there yet?" He said, "no, you're the only one who knows about it." Anthony asked Hope to meet him downstairs. Hope told him she would call a taxi. He again assured her that no one knew about his new place and that she was the first to know. When Hope got there, she asked him, "Is this supposed to change the way I feel about our situation?" He looked at her and smiled. Hope went inside, and It wasn't much to see. He had a small bedroom with no bed. The living room had a wooden chair the last owner left behind. Anthony said to Hope, "it's not much, but it's somewhere I can call mine." Hope thought, "he left his family to live like this?"

Hope and Anthony spent the whole night talking. As they lay on the floor, he cried and told her, "I don't know why I do the things I do, but I know I love you, and I want things to work." Hope wiped his tears but couldn't stop crying. She remembered he had done this before. Start crying, saying he missed them and wanted to fix things. Everything Anthony was saying, she heard it before. Anthony loved playing this game with Hope's heart and didn't care how much he hurt her. Hope wanted to tell him to get out of her life, but instead, she told him she would take him back. They stayed up till 5 am until he had left to work that morning.

It felt right when they made love that morning, and all the bad things just went away. Hope loved every minute of it. There was no bed, so they made love on the floor. Hope didn't care, she was with her husband again, and that's all that mattered. She loved him and wanted to be a family with him and their children. She told him she was sorry too and needed to work harder on their marriage, and he agreed.

Anthony left Hope at his home while he went to work. He told her he got his job back at his old workplace. She was happy for him and could see he was trying as he said. Hope cleaned up around his house. A Walmart was close by, so she walked there and bought a blow-up bed for him. It wasn't much, but she wanted him to feel comfortable until he could do better. When Anthony came home, he was surprised, not for cleaning up because he knew Hope didn't like a dirty home but because she went out and got him a bed. "I love you so much," he said. Hope said, "I love you too." She spent the day at his house, and he asked her to spend another night with him. She wanted to but received a call later that evening from her mother, who was unhappy with her staying at Anthony's. "Come and get your children," she said with an angry voice. "After your husband mistreated you, you lay down with him?"

Hope told her, "Mom, I love him, and we're going to work on our marriage." She understood that Grace didn't want her to get hurt again by Anthony, but she wanted to see how she could give the kids the life she never had with a father at home.

After six years away from St. Vincent, Hope, Ricardo, and Michelle planned to go home for Christmas. She told Anthony about the trip, so they sat and made plans about their life and compared what they had been through to where they were now. Hope looked at Anthony while planning their future together and thinking back on how they met and how much she loved him. She remembered how Anthony used to look at her the same way he is looking at her now, the way he used to touch her, and at that moment, Hope knew she couldn't live without him. Anthony was everything to her, so she put the past behind her and moved forward. But she didn't know that moving forward meant him bringing his womanizing behaviour with him and that the two women he was dating wouldn't be in their lives anymore.

When she went to St. Vincent for Christmas, Anthony took the chance to be with Celie and Emily. It was their anniversary, but he didn't call Hope. She called him, but he didn't answer. Hope wanted to be positive, making excuses for him so she wouldn't cry. She thought, "I love him with all my heart even though he keeps hurting me. I just can't stop loving him." The next day Anthony called and told Hope that he was partying with his boys. She wasn't happy with him but didn't want it to spoil her vacation.

While back home in St. Vincent, Hope did her first music video because she wanted the little time she had in her hometown to count. She met with the director and planned the video shoot of her song, 'Moving On. She wanted the video to match the pain in the song. The director wrote a script, and they looked around the city for the perfect location. Hope met with a producer to talk about working together. They spent time creating tracks for her to take back to Canada because it was impossible to do the short time she had left in St. Vincent.

Hope loved the feeling of being back in the studio and meeting new people. They laughed and talked and were having a good time. She couldn't wait to get back home to work on her craft. Hope enjoyed spending time with her family and friends. First, she, Ricardo, and Michelle went to a show called '9 Morning', listening to artists sing Christmas carols. After that, they spent a lot of time at the beaches and the beautiful rainforest. Their friends loved taking them around to enjoy the country after being away for so long. Michelle loved every minute of it because she wasn't from there, and she loved the cultural differences. As much as Hope missed her children, she was not ready to go home, but the time had come, and she would never forget the love everyone had shown her.

When Hope returned from her vacation, Anthony was at home with the kids. When she came in, Anthony held and kissed her. "I'm so happy you are home," he said. Hope wished that Anthony would move in when she got back home, but that was just wishful thinking. He spent the week with them because he was on vacation. Hope got sick when she returned, and Anthony took care of the kids, showing how much he loved her. He told Hope, "there's no other woman out there for me but you." Hope believed him. She couldn't believe this was happening to her. She had the life she always wanted with him. While he was at her house, Emily called him. He told her, "I'm with my wife right now." She hung up. Then Celie called. She asked, "where are you?" Anthony said, "I'm with my wife."

Celie got angry, and Anthony told her, "I'm back with my wife!" She didn't like what Anthony said. She tried hard to get him away from Hope even though she was still married and living with her husband. But Celie didn't care because she wanted Anthony. Hope decided she wasn't going to let go of her husband. She would fight for Anthony and thought, "let the fight begin!" Celie sent messages on Facebook, cursing Hope. She kept calling and texting Anthony's phone, arguing with him. She just wouldn't let go of him. Finally, Anthony told Hope nothing was going on between Celie and him. Hope wanted to believe him because she wanted their marriage to work.

Sadly, Anthony couldn't stick with one woman for too long. He started to get bored and felt foolish around his friends because they had more than one woman while he was only with Hope. Celie and Emily started coming over to his house again. Celie bought things for his apartment and him. She thought the only way to get Anthony back was that she had to buy his love, and Anthony didn't mind it one bit. When Anthony came to Hope's place, she checked his phone. She felt something wasn't right and that he was up to his old tricks again. Hope saw that when she called him on their anniversary, he didn't answer because he was with Celie. She cried. It was a slap in her face, and once again, Anthony brought tears to her eyes.

Hope and Celie were arguing all the time. She told Hope everything she had done with Anthony and that he said she was too controlling and that he didn't want her. Hope didn't want to back down when it came to keeping her husband but realized it might not be worth it because of what Anthony said about her to Celie. Hope wanted to give up her fight for Anthony. But she didn't know what she was fighting for anymore. She felt Anthony wasn't giving her a reason to fight for him.

Hope would let go of Anthony and let him be with the two women. They seemed to be more important to him than his family after they had been back together after just three months. Hope was always fighting for Anthony's love but never got it. He didn't want to fight to keep his family together, and he was selfish, never giving what his kids and Hope needed. She cried, thinking, "the kids need a father who was going to be there when they called for him; I need a strong man by my side, not a weak man; when things got hard, Anthony would run away like a little boy."

Hope started to reflect on her life more and more. As she sat there crying, she thought, "all my life, people came into my life and left. Is there something wrong with me?" She got angrier when she thought about what he had put her through. She didn't know how much more she could take. She had given up so much just to be with him. Unfortunately, she never had a backup plan to protect herself from Anthony. She didn't think she needed to, even though the signs were everywhere. She hoped he would change, but he never did. Anthony didn't love her and his children enough to change.

Hope remembered their wedding day when Anthony told her he invited a girl who would later try to break up their relationship. She thought then, "if she comes to our wedding, I'm going to have a flashback about the night when Anthony pushed my head into a glass window because of her." Hope wondered why she wanted to come to her wedding. The bride was supposed to be happy on her wedding day, and Anthony did that for her. She felt it was bad enough that Anthony asked a girl Hope didn't like to be a guest at their wedding, and another girl he had sex with was one of their bridesmaids. He took away the joy of being a happy bride from her.

Every wife should be happy with their husband, but Hope wasn't, and she couldn't see a reason to be. As she continued to reflect on her life with Anthony, she thought that maybe they were not meant to be together. Every time Hope walked in the street, she would see the other women Anthony had sex with while they were together. She would hold her head down because of the shame she felt. It was becoming too much for her. She thought she should be the one to hold her head up high, but she never could.

Hope had put herself into a corner, questioning herself and asking, "why doesn't Anthony love me the way I love him?" She always thought she would leave him but never found the strength to walk away. He kept saying he would change, and deep inside, she wanted to believe her heart because she loved him. She kept making excuses for him because she didn't want to leave. She spent so much time alone in her bed, and every time another woman made him mad, he would come home and take it out on her with a beating. As terrified as Hope was, she fought back, trying to stop him. Hope would let him be other times because she knew she couldn't win.

Hope had a smile on her face every day to hide her pain inside. Her friends knew something was wrong, and the family started questioning her about what was going on. But Hope didn't want them to tell her to leave Anthony. It hurt, even more when her kids would wipe the tears from her face and say, "don't cry, mommy, it will be ok." When Hope looked at her brother and his wife Michelle and saw the love they shared, she felt jealous and asked herself, "why can't my husband love me like that?"

Thus, after three years of marriage, Hope and Anthony finally broke up. She kept waiting for him to change and come home, but he never did. Finally, after reflecting on her life, she realized that she had waited long enough.

To celebrate her newfound freedom, she started partying with her cousin and Michelle. It was time she got over her husband, and even though it felt good in the part, she still asked herself, "why am I here?" Partying is not for me," she said. Hope knew she didn't belong there. She was a wife and mother, after all. Hope stopped going to church as often as she used to. She started questioning God, blaming him for her failed marriage. Hope stopped praying because she thought it was in vain. She had often prayed, asking God to save her marriage, but he didn't. So, now she turned to partying.

Hope just wanted to feel something. She wanted attention from guys when she was partying. They told Hope how beautiful and sexy she was. Hope loved to hear it because she never heard it from her husband. Hope never felt that Anthony loved her or even liked her, and to hear these men telling her she was sexy felt good. She wished her husband could have said it to her. Even though these other men said it, it wasn't enough to give them her number or anything else. They weren't her husband.

One night, Hope went to her friend Nicole's party, where she met Rohan. She saw him looking at her from across the room. Hope asked Nicole who he was. Nicole told her he was a friend of hers and was just playing with Hope. However, Hope found him cute and very attractive. Rohan came over to talk with her, and he said, "Hi, my name is Rohan. What's yours?" Hope looked at him and smiled. "My name is Hope; I saw you trying to get my attention," she replied.

After the party was over, Rohan offered to drop Hope and her cousin home. On the way to her mother's house, Rohan tried to know Hope better. As much as he was cute, Hope was still in love with her husband and wanted him back.

16.

Chapter Sixteen

Hope would have done anything to get Anthony back, but he was with someone new every time she saw him. He would look at her like she was a stranger, and her tears would flow. Finally, Anthony told her to find a guy to love her because he couldn't be the way she wanted him to be.

Rohan dropped Hope off, and he asked her for her number. She asked him why, and he told her that he wanted to get to know her better. Hope smiled, but she was just playing "hard to get." She gave him her number, and he called her the next day. He was a smooth talker; he knew everything to say to get a girl, and Hope liked that about him.

After three months of talking to Rohan, it was pleasing to Hope. They spent every day together after he finished work. They went out to eat, and they enjoyed each other's company. He showed her how a man should treat a woman. Hope decided to give him a chance; he showed her lots of love and care. She wished that she would have gotten that from her husband.

Things were going well with Hope and Rohan. He always checked in on her, and she thought that was sweet of him. They went out a lot together and had fun. Hope didn't have any problems with him. Although, sometimes, she thought it was too good to be true. Rohan treated her like a woman. He appreciated her and complimented her for the little things she did for him. She liked that about him.

She never asked him for anything and just having him in her life was good enough for her. While Hope got close to Rohan, Nicole stopped talking to her. Nicole said that Rohan was her boyfriend; however, Hope didn't know they were that close. She remembered asking Nicole about Rohan, and she told her they were just friends, but it turned out they were more than friends, and Nicole didn't say that to her.

At Nicole's party, where they met, and before they started dating, Rohan was all over Hope, and Nicole did not say anything. Hope thought, "if I knew he was her guy, I would not have gotten involved with him!"
Things started to change in the new year. Rohan wasn't the guy Hope fell for. Women started calling her phone about him and telling her what he said about her.

Hope, Ricardo, and Michelle went to Montreal to visit her family. Her cousin Rochelle was getting married, and she was having a baby and bridal shower at the same time. Hope asked Rohan to take her to Montreal because she wanted to introduce him to her family. He told her he'd take her, but his car wasn't suitable for driving long distances without a tune-up. Hope told him to find out how much it would cost, and she would pay for it. The next day Rohan told her that it would cost $400. The only money was her child tax benefit, so she gave him the money. Hope thought that her family would like him by taking Rohan to Montreal. However, her family in Toronto didn't want Hope to be with him because they heard about him. When it was time to go to Montreal, Rohan told Hope he didn't have money for gas, so she gave it to him. She thought it was her job to help him because she was the woman in his life.

Rochelle gave her room to Hope, Rohan, Michelle, and Ricardo, for the weekend. When the baby shower started, Hope looked over at Rohan and saw how he looked at Rochelle's girlfriends. He acted like he and Hope were just friends. He loved the attention one girl was giving him, but Hope didn't pay it any mind. Finally, the men left the baby shower so the ladies could begin the bridal shower.

Rohan went partying with Rochelle's fiancé Jay, her brother Chase and Ricardo. They came back when the bridal shower was over, and Rochelle's girlfriends were still there. They didn't have a ride home, so Rohan offered to take the girls home because the men were going to another party. Hope wanted to go to the party, but he didn't want her to go, so she went to bed. Before Hope and Rohan headed back to Toronto, she and her family went out for dinner the next day. At the table, she saw Rohan looking at Chase's girlfriend, trying to look cool, but Hope saw right through it. She didn't say anything to him on the trip back to Toronto.

Two weeks later, Hope was to go back for Rochelle's wedding. Hope asked Rohan if he'd like to go to her wedding. He wasn't sure he wanted to go back, and he came up with many excuses. Hope knew something wasn't right with him, but she wasn't sure what it was. Finally, however, she thought, "what's in the darkness must come to light."

The day she had to go to the wedding, Rohan told her that he had no money to go back and nothing to wear to the wedding. She had already decided that she was going with her brother, and now he wanted to go. Hope said, "at the last minute, you call me saying you want to go to the wedding, and you have no money to buy anything to wear." She asked, "what am I supposed to do now?" She didn't have much money, only her child tax benefit. He knew when the kid's money came in. So, Hope gave him money to buy something to wear and money for gas. Rohan took the money with no intention of buying anything to wear. He just took clothes from his closet, and he didn't give her back the money, even though he knew she had no money left after paying her bills.

Everything was going well at the wedding. Hope and Rohan didn't sit together because she was one of the bridesmaids. Hope looked in the direction where he was sitting, but he wasn't there. She asked a friend, whom he met at the wedding, where he was, but she knew he was lying when he said he didn't know. Hope went outside to look for him and found him with Rochelle's cousin, Susan. Hope stood there. The girl looked at Hope and said to Rohan, "this is your girl?" He looks at Hope, then turns back to Susan, telling her, "she's alright." Hope wanted to cuss him out, but too many people were around. She went up to Rohan and asked, "can I talk to you?" Susan walked away. They sat in his car arguing, and Hope let him know how disrespected she felt. Although Rohan was upset, he didn't think he did anything wrong. They went back to the party as nothing had happened.

Another girl named Anna, who was checking Rohan out at Rochelle's baby shower, went up to him at the party while he and Hope were dancing. Rohan hugged her like they were longtime friends. Hope didn't know that Rohan gave her his number the first time they went to Montreal. It turned out that they talked on the phone when he came back to Toronto, which is why he hugged her that way. Anna told Rohan that Hope had called her phone when she was in Toronto at the party. Then Hope and Anna got into a fight. Anna told Rohan, "Hope called my phone asking about you." While Rohan and Hope were sitting in the car, he asked her, "did you call that girl's phone?" Hope said, "what are you talking about?" He told her what Anna had told him and he got out of the car. Anna was still in the parking lot talking to her friends. Hope got out for some fresh air, and she told Rohan that she wanted to go home, but Rohan wasn't ready to go.

She heard Anna and her friends talking about her, and she heard them say that Rohan didn't want her anymore. One of Anna's friends talked loud enough so that Hope would hear her. She started arguing with Anna, and she said to Hope, "you're with a man who doesn't want you." Rohan told the girl that they weren't together.

He stood there and didn't say anything, enjoying the fact that two women were fighting over him.

As lovely as Hope was, she forgave him. While driving back to Toronto, someone sent Hope a message on Facebook telling her to leave her man alone. Hope told Rohan about the message, but he said he didn't know anything about it. The girl's name on Facebook was Diamond, and she didn't know anything about her. Rohan told her it was her friend Nicole doing it. She believed him because she and Nicole were not talking because of Rohan.

Every time Rohan wanted to see Hope, they always went to her house. He never once asked her if she wanted to go to his house. Instead, she asked him why he never took her there, and he would come up with a new reason every time. Hope spent a lot of time at her mother's house. Every day Rohan came from work, he called her to come downstairs to her mother's apartment. Then they would go out and get something to eat. When Hope was at her mom's house one night, Rohan called, saying he wanted to see her. Hope went downstairs to meet him, and Rohan said, "let's go to your house." Hope didn't ask any questions. She already knew why he wanted her to go to her house, or so she thought. She went back to Grace's house to get the keys. Hope asked Rohan what was going on.

He told her that he had to leave his house because the owner was selling the house and he had lost his job. Rohan asked her if he could stay with her for a bit. Hope said he could, and that night they went to her house.
While they dated, Hope didn't bring Rohan around her children. But after six months of seeing him, she thought it would be okay. However, her children didn't like Rohan from when they met him. Hope's daughter Renell went into her room every time he came around. All Renell wanted was her father. Rohan tried to get them to like him, but his work cut out for him.

One day Hope went with Rohan to the agency to help him find a job. After weeks of going from one agency to the next, he finally got one. Every morning at 5:30 a.m., Hope got up to make breakfast and packed his lunch before he went to work. He called her during the day to let her know what he wanted for dinner, and Hope made sure it was ready for him. Rohan got a second job working in the evening, and he got home at 3:00 a.m. One night, he called Hope to fix him some fried chicken while sleeping. She got up and prepared it for him, but she couldn't believe that she had to fry chicken when he could have eaten something else.

Every time Rohan was home, he was always on his phone late at night and on his computer, video chatting with other women even when Hope was beside him. He had no respect for her. She would ask him who the woman he was talking to was, saying his cousin was back in his country. Hope looked at the girl and remembered seeing her naked picture on his phone and thought, "why would one of his cousins send him naked pictures?" She shook her head and said, "why did I see her naked picture on your phone?" Rohan told her she was wrong about what she saw. She said, "don't look at me like I'm crazy; I know what I saw." He said, "I don't know what you're talking about." Hope didn't say anything else because she knew she wouldn't get the truth from him.

The next day, while Rohan was painting Hope's house, he talked on the phone with a woman. In the bedroom cleaning, she heard him say to the woman that they were good together and forget about what his family was telling her. Rohan didn't know that Hope had heard him and was angry. She came out of the bathroom and didn't say anything. She left while he continued his conversation on the phone, and she went to the store. When Hope got back, he was off the phone. He told her that he was talking to one of his family members. Hope asked him why he would tell his family that they're good together. He said, "I don't know what you heard, but I didn't say that." Hope knew he was lying and told him she heard what he said. Rohan didn't like it when she said that she had heard him. He knew she thought he was lying to her, and he was right. Hope wasn't going to waste time entertaining a conversation if it wasn't going anywhere.

Rohan lived in Hope's house, and he worked but didn't give her any money to buy food. Instead, he gave her $50 to buy laundry detergent, and she had to give him back the change. Hope couldn't believe he did that, knowing she had no money for food even though she had to cook for him. Hope had to borrow money from her mother and friends to put food on the table for her children and Rohan. Hope thought, "what kind of a man is this?" Rohan reminded her of Anthony and the way he used to treat her. Rohan was working, and he always told her he had no money. His excuse was that he had to pay for his insurance and car. She didn't believe that was the only thing he was using the money for; she knew Rohan was making good money at his jobs.

Rohan's womanizing ways got worse. Every time he didn't sleep at home, he would say that he slept at his mother's house. Hope wondered if it was true and knew she had to find out. One day when Rohan came home, after not sleeping home the night before, she was on her computer chatting on Facebook with her friend Jack from St. Vincent. She left it open and went to the store because Rohan wanted chicken for lunch. While she was at the store, Rohan searched her Facebook and saw that she had talked to a guy who wasn't happy. When she got back, Rohan wouldn't talk to her. Hope knew he searched her Facebook and saw that she was talking to her friend. Hope asked him if he went on her Facebook, but he lied and said he didn't know what she was talking about. Then he told her he was leaving to go back to his mother's house. Hope said to him, "you sent me to buy chicken, and now you want to leave?" Rohan saw that she was getting angry and said he would stay. Hope wanted him to admit he had crept on her Facebook and saw her messages, but he wouldn't.

Hope finished cooking, and after Rohan was finished eating, he said that he was going back to his mother's house. Hope said, "okay, I guess when you reach your mother's house, you'll call me." He said nothing and left. Rohan later texted Hope, letting her know what he saw on Facebook. He said, "I saw you were talking to that guy." Hope got angry. She knew that he had checked, but he lied about it. She said, "and!" but he didn't respond.

Hope had met a guy named Jack a long time ago, after being introduced by a mutual friend. They had been talking for quite some time. She had liked Jack, but they couldn't be together because of the long distance. Hope told Rohan, "if that guy were here, you and I wouldn't be together because I met him first." Rohan told Hope that he was moving out and would live with his mother until he found his place. Hope said, "I thought you already moved out because you spend most nights at your mother's house, or so you've said." Rohan came for his clothes and told Hope they couldn't get along. But even though Rohan moved out, they still saw each other.

Hope decided to go back to making her music. Her friend Paul was having a concert and wanted her to do the show with him. So every Saturday, she went to the studio to rehearse. There she met Chelsea, who was also a part of the show. They became friends, and because they were living close to each other, when Rohan picked up Hope for rehearsals, she asked him to give Chelsea a ride. While Hope was rehearsing her songs, Chelsea went outside, and Rohan followed her as if he would use the bathroom. Hope didn't think anything of it, but it seemed suspicious. Hope dressed at her mother's house because it was closer to the concert. She took her bag with extra clothes to change into at the show.

When Rohan dropped her off at the concert, Hope asked him if she could leave her bag in his car, but he said no because he wasn't sure if he was coming back to the show. So Hope asked, "why aren't you coming to the show?" His uncle was in the hospital, so she took her bag. Rohan ended up going to the show that night. They forgot about their problems and had fun. Hope was happy to share her voice with everyone that came out to see her performance. After the show, they went back to her place. Hope thought Rohan would spend the night, but he didn't.

Every weekend Hope went to her mother's house. She heard more and more things about Rohan from her cousin Meesha, and she heard what Nicole said about him and other women. Grace grew tired of hearing what Nicole said about Rohan and asked her daughter, "why don't you leave Nicole alone?" Hope told her mom that they were never together; they were just friends. Hope kept asking Rohan about what Nicole was saying, and he told her it wasn't true.

Nicole told Hope's family that Rohan was married, but Hope didn't believe it. She thought, "how can he be married when he was living with me for three months?" Hope asked Rohan about what Nicole had said. He laughed and told her, "Nicole and your family are jealous because you have a man for yourself." Hope could see in Rohan's face that he was hiding something. So she called Nicole to find out the truth about Rohan and his wife. She told Hope that Rohan had a wife and found out through his cousin. Hope asked, "how could that be?" Nicole replied, "if you don't believe me, check her out on Facebook," and she gave her his wife's name. So Hope went on Facebook to see for herself. She saw the woman and him together. There were lots of pictures of them taking trips together. Hope thought, "here he is with this woman who he said wasn't his wife."

That night Hope broke down. She trusted Rohan, and he was playing her for a fool all this time. She let him in her home and around her children, and he was lying to her.

The following day Hope didn't tell her family, she just wanted to be alone, and she kept crying. Finally, her mother came into the bedroom arguing with her and asked her, "you're going to make one guy keep you down; I'm disappointed in you, dry your tears and stop crying!" But Hope's tears wouldn't stop. Hope's aunt Angel, Meesha and Michelle were all in Grace's bedroom talking to her, but it was no help because everything they were saying made her cry even more. While they were talking, Hope made plans in her head on how she would make him pay and how she would make him feel bad for how much he'd hurt her. Finally, Hope told her family she was going home and wanted to be left alone.

On her way back to her place, Hope called Rohan, but he didn't pick up. On his BBM on his Blackberry phone, he wrote on his status that he and his family were having an event. Hope thought everything made sense now that he didn't invite her. Maybe she was supposed to be his woman, but he never introduced her to his family except for his brother and cousin because they were just like him and knew what he was doing. She thought back about every family event he wouldn't take her to. Hope believed even more now that he had a wife. She sent him a picture Nicole had sent her, with him and his wife.

Rohan came over to Hope's house that same night and asked her where she got the picture. She said Nicole sent it to her, and she asked him who she was. He said, "this is an old picture of me with my old girlfriend." Hope looks at him dead in his eyes. He didn't know she had already seen his wife on Facebook. Hope told him, "I'm done with you!" Rohan proceeded to say, "everything you're hearing is not true; that's not my wife!" Once again, Hope believed him. She didn't see any wedding pictures, so maybe it was his ex-girlfriend.

Rohan asked her if she could cook because he wanted lunch for work the next day. Hope said, "no!" Rohan kept asking because he didn't have anything for lunch, but then he said he would see if his mom could cook. Hope thought, "maybe he's right if he had a wife;

why isn't she taking care of him." In time Hope met her neighbour Mo. Their kids went to the same school. They met at the bus stop waiting for the school bus. After a few days of going to the bus stop, they talked more and more, and Hope found out that she was just like her, a single mother of two with a failed marriage. The ladies opened up to each other, and their children were around the same age group. They became friends.

Mo introduced Hope to her twin sister Unique and her husband, Ken. They welcomed her with open arms and made Hope feel like part of the family. Next, Mo had a get-together and invited Hope, who brought Rohan and the kids, to her house. Unique and Ken were there while the children were playing. She introduced Rohan to everyone. He wasn't shy around them, and he fit right in. They all played games and had a good time. While all the excitement was dying down, Unique got tired, and she went to lay down.

Hope and her friends continued playing games when Unique returned from her nap and said, "who is Sam?" Everyone looked at each other. Hope and everyone else said, "we don't know that name." Unique looked at Rohan and asked, "do you know a lady named Sam?" He said no. "I just had a dream, and the name came to me," said Unique.

Hope looked over to Rohan, looking nervous, but Hope didn't know why. A few minutes later, he got a call after Unique told everyone about her dream. On the phone, it seemed like the other person on the line was angry with him by the way he was talking. "I'm busy right now; I can't make it. Let someone else give you a ride home," he said to the person on the line. When he got off the phone, she looked at him, and he could tell that Hope wanted to know who it was. He said, "Sorry everyone, it was my brother who wanted a ride home from a party."

When it was time to leave, Mo wanted Hope and Rohan to get alone. She told her to leave the children at her house until the next day. Hope was happy that the children were staying over. They went over to the house and made love. While Hope lays there in his arms, he says, "I have to go now." "I thought you were going to spend the night," Hope remarked.

Roman replied, "no, I can't, my brother still wants me to pick him up," and he left. Hope didn't want to go back to Mo's house to get the kids because she felt embarrassed, so she slept the night alone. The following weekend Mo's family was having a BBQ, and she invited Hope, but Hope went alone. While talking to Hope, Ken could hear the pain she was going through in her marriage and with her children. Ken and his family were Godly people, and he prayed for Hope and told her things she never told him.

"I want you to go on a five-day fasting and pray every day at 4 a.m., and after the five days, God is going to reveal some things to you," said Ken. Hope didn't understand what was happening, but she knew that with God, anything was possible. So, every night at 4 a.m. Hope got up and prayed. She fasted from 6 a.m. to 6 p.m. for five days, and she felt closer to God. She went to church with Mo and her family and learned more about God. She didn't want anything to distract her from her fasting, so she kept herself pure.

After the fasting, it was Rohan's birthday. As much as Hope was disappointed about what happened the night, they were supposed to spend time alone, and she took him out. They went to the mall, and she bought him a watch. It was expensive, but she thought he was worth it. Then she took him to Niagara Falls to enjoy his big day. A few days later, Hope received a call from a lady who said that she was Rohan's wife. She asked, "Do you know Rohan?" Hope told her he was her friend. Then, she asked, "how do you know Rohan?" Hope said, "who did you say you were again?" She said, "I'm his wife, Samantha." Hope responded, "you need to take this up with your husband because if you didn't call me, I would have never known he had a wife," and Hope hung up.

Hope was angry with Rohan. She thought, "why didn't I tell the woman the truth? Why did I cover for him?" Rohan made Hope believe for a year and a half that he was hers, and she believed him. She told Rohan everything she had been through with her husband, and he made her believe that he would never hurt her. Hope broke down and cried. After getting off the phone with his wife, she texted him and told him what had happened. He asked Hope, "why didn't you hang up the phone?" Hope replied, "this is not the time for you to turn things around on me." Hope asked him, "Is she your wife and don't lie to me again?" He told her, "yes, she is my ex-wife?" Hope asked, "how can she move from your ex-girlfriend to ex-wife?" He couldn't answer. Rohan then asked Hope, "what did you say to her?" Hope said, "I told her we're just friends." He told her she did the right thing. Hope stopped texting. She didn't want to read any more of his lies.

Rohan still texted her and said, "you handled it like a big woman." Hope was confused. She thought, "have you lost your mind? Leave me the hell alone!" Rohan knew Hope was angry, and he wanted her to stay with him. He said, "I never told you I was married because my marriage was over." Hope replied, "do you think anything you say at this point will fix anything with us? Now I know the truth." Rohan said, "all I can do is try."

17.

Chapter Seventeen

Hope called her cousin Rochelle in Montreal and told her what she found out about Rohan. Her cousin said, "I know he's married; my husband told me that Rohan said he was married and that his wife travels a lot." Hope was disappointed that Rochelle didn't tell her. "Why didn't you tell me?" she cried. "You believe in Rohan too much, and you wouldn't have believed I was telling the truth," Rochelle replied.

Hope trusted Rohan and believed him when he said there were no other women in his life, but he was just playing Hope for a fool. Then, finally, it hit her, and she thought, "All the time he was with her, his wife was out of town; When he was living in her house, it was because his wife had kicked him out."

After Hope had spoken to Rochelle the next day, Rohan texted her and said, "Say no!" Hope didn't understand what he meant by it, then asked, "say no about what?" Then he said, "I'm going to call you, just say no!" Rohan called Hope and asked her, "were you and I ever together?" As hurtful as it was, Hope, said, "no." Hope hung up the phone and asked herself, "did I just save his marriage?" Hope remembered Mo's brother-in-law told her to fast for five days and watch God work, and he did. God revealed Rohan's secret to her. Hope cried and said, "whoever said God isn't real is a liar."

Hope made up her mind. It was over between Rohan and her. She just couldn't see herself with a married man. She knew how it felt when a woman was with her husband. "I won't put another woman through the same thing I went through," she thought. So she went over to Mo's house to let her know that the fasting worked, and God showed her Rohan for who he was. Mo sat her down while talking to her; she couldn't believe what happened because she thought Rohan was good for Hope. After Mo heard everything, she told Hope, "maybe he and his wife aren't together; maybe it's over between them." Hope started to think that maybe Mo could be right.

Hope called Rohan and asked, "Why didn't you tell me from the start that you were married?" He said, "I didn't know how." "So, you decided you were still going to be with me?" she asked. All he could say was, "I'm sorry." She told him, "I should be the one who decides if I want to be with a married man!" All Hope got was excuses. Even though Hope was still married to Anthony, Rohan knew about him and their separation. Rohan told her, "you shouldn't get mad because you're married too." She said, "yes, I'm married, but my husband and I have been separated for three years, while you, on the other hand, were living with your wife." Hope tried to hear him out and decided to give him another chance until she found out the truth.

Hope and Rohan talked for a week after the truth came out about him. But Hope's heart felt heavy. She couldn't do it. She could feel the wife's pain. Hope felt the same pain when those women entered her marriage and broke it apart. She wasn't going to do it to another woman. Hope talked about her decision to leave Rohan with Michelle. She explained that being with him wasn't right even though his wife and he weren't together. "Remember how you felt when your husband had so many women interfering with your marriage," said Michelle. Michelle didn't know that she had stopped talking to Rohan. Hope said to her, "I broke up with him; he wasn't worth it. I am not going to lose my soul because of him."

Hope moved on with her life, focused on her children, and built a life for them. After trying to get her back, Rohan realized that she wouldn't take him back, so he stopped calling, and she never saw him again. As disappointed as Hope was, finding out about Rohan's marriage, life had to go on. She spent more time with her family, especially with Meesha and Michelle. She was enjoying being single. She was happy, and she didn't have to do anything to please anyone but herself. She and her children started going to church with Mo. Hope took the time she lost to make it up to her children by spending time with them. Hope loved the feeling she got when she was in the house of the Lord. Renell was glad that Rohan was no longer in their lives. She never thought of him, and when it was all said and done, her children's happiness was the only thing that mattered to her.

After two years without Rohan, Hope got herself a job working in a factory to take care of her children. She was happy being single, and she spent more time with family and friends. After two years of not hearing from or seeing Hope, Rohan tried to contact her through her friends. They would call and tell her that he had asked for her number. Hope told them not to give him her number. Well, Rohan got her number, and he called Hope wanting to know how everything was going with her. She didn't want to be rude, but she couldn't help but say, "here we go again. I thought this part of my life was over." He said he was trying to be nice. "My wife and I are divorced," he said, and Hope replied, "What does that have to do with me? I don't care; it's not my problem." He said to her, "I'm sorry that I lied to you, but my wife and I weren't together when we were together." Hope said, "Okay, I forgive you. What's in the past stays in the past. You are the past."

Hope didn't care how much Rohan tried to get with her. She wasn't going down that road with him again. She thought, "I've been through too much with him, and I don't care how much he tells me he loves me; I won't fall for it again." Rohan thought he was a player; he played with Hope's heart and thought he could pick up where he left off because his wife left him. Hope thought, "not anymore; I'm stronger now when it comes to him." But Rohan kept calling and texting Hope, thinking things were good between them. She wondered if he had lost his mind by wanting her to forget what had happened. When Hope brought up what he had done to her, he said, "forget about what happened. Things were always good with us." Hope said, "you must have amnesia; things were never good with us." Then, Hope thought, "he knocked his head. I'll never get back with him as long as I live!" Rohan was terrible news, and she was glad to be free of him.

Hope was three years free from Rohan and tried to get her kids to have a relationship with their father. Hope's daughter Renell was acting out in school, so she didn't waste Rohan's time. She wanted to focus on her daughter, who wasn't doing well at home or school. She was now eight years old, and all she wanted was for her father to come home. Hope tried to keep their father in their lives, but sometimes it was a waste of time. The children weren't happy when Anthony came around because he didn't stay long enough. Hope believed that every child needed their father, but Anthony grew tired of them quickly. He was always in and out of their lives. Hope tried everything to make him want to be in his children's lives, but nothing worked for very long.

When Anthony picked up the kids and took them to his house, and they got back home, Renell would always be angry, declaring that she didn't want to go back to her dad's house. Hope would always call Anthony to find out what happened, and she told him what the kids said to her. He said he did nothing wrong, and she told him she could help him make them want to come back. She told him that their daughter loves to bake. "Bake with your daughter; your son loves games, so play with him, you don't need money to have a good time with them when they're at your house, take them to the park," she advised, but she knew Anthony wouldn't do it.

As young as Renell and James were, they liked to talk about their feelings. Renell tried to talk to her dad about things, but he just shouted her down. Hope asked him why he wouldn't listen to what his daughter had to say. "She wants to talk about grown-up stuff," said Anthony. Hope said, "Renell just wants to know why mommy and daddy aren't together; Don't shout her down, just listen!"

Renell loved the attention. She was dying for her daddy's love, but when she was at his house, he gave his love and attention to another child who wasn't his. Anthony was living with a roommate and her daughter because he didn't want to live alone. "You only see your children every other weekend, and when they're around, you should be giving them all your attention." He told her that Renell was selfish. Hope replied, "really now?"

Renell could feel that something wasn't right. She said to Hope, "mummy, why doesn't daddy love me." She hugged her and cried as Renell's tears streamed down her face. "Don't cry, baby girl; your dad loves you, and no other child can take that away from you," said Hope. She tried to be important for her children but didn't understand why she kept telling them that Anthony loved them but never showed it. She wanted him to love his kids even though they weren't together.

Things were getting tough for Hope, raising her children alone. She could hardly get a job, and she decided to go for help at the welfare office to feed her children. But unfortunately, Anthony wouldn't help take care of his children. So every month, she received $700 to pay her bills and buy food. Christmas was coming, so Hope tried to get a loan so that the children would have a happy Christmas. She thought that the loan company she contacted was legit and based in New Jersey. However, the lady told her that she was qualified for $5,000 but would pay $500 before getting the money.

After leasing phones for Anthony and his cousin Jimmy, her credit was no longer good when they were together. At the time, she didn't know how important credit was in Canada until she couldn't do anything for herself without it. She had a credit score of 300, and no loan company would lend her money. So Hope searched on the internet to find a loan company in New Jersey that said any credit is approved. Some loan companies in Canada said that, but she never got approved.

Hope was happy to pay the money to buy presents for her children. The lady at the loan office gave her the name to pay the cash to through Western Union and told her that she would get the loan an hour after sending it. She went to Western Union and paid the fee. One hour later, she checked her account, but the money wasn't there. Hope called the loan company, but no one picked up. She thought the loan officer was busy, so she waited and stayed calm, then Hope rechecked her account, but the money wasn't there. She called the company again and still no answer.

"What did I just do," she thought as she dropped to her knees and cried. She used money from her child-tax to send to the loan company and used the rest to pay bills. She couldn't pay all her bills because she depended on the loan to pay them and buy food for the house. Hope called Anthony and asked him to buy a box of chicken for the children, but he told her that he didn't have any money. Hope said, "it's Christmas; I just need them to get something to eat." He again said he had no money. Hope let Renell and James spend the weekend with him. She didn't want the kids to see her crying.

When Hope picked them up, she asked, "how was your weekend with your father?" Renell said, "Mom, I don't want to go back to daddy's house." Hope asked why, and Renell replied, "Daddy wouldn't let us watch TV, and before daddy brought us home, he went to bring milk for a lady's baby." Hope was angry with Anthony. She said to him, "I asked you to buy the kids chicken, and you refused; then you took milk for another man's child, how dare you!" Anthony didn't say anything and hung up his phone. Hope's family kept telling her to take him to court, but she didn't. She said, "I don't believe the court should have to force a man to take care of his kids." But Hope was done; she had enough. "I should have listened to my family and taken him to court, but it's not too late," she thought.

Hope didn't let what Anthony did bother her until she had no money and no food in the house. She called and asked him to buy her food. As usual, he told Hope that he had no money. Hope, crying to him, said that the kids were hungry, but he didn't care. Hope knew she couldn't sit by and see her kids hungry. So, she went to the Jewelry stores to sell her wedding rings, but no one would buy ten-carat gold. Hope went back home disappointed and sad. She needed to find something for the kids to eat. She looked in the kitchen, and all she found was a little bit of flour and sugar. She couldn't make anything with that, but she had to try. She couldn't celebrate Christmas with the children. Hope called Ricardo and asked for help. He and Michelle sent her $50 to buy some food. That's when Hope decided she had enough of Anthony and would take him to court.

It was hard finding a good job. Hope hoped that if she couldn't take care of the children, Anthony would be a good father and do it for his kids. But she was wrong; Anthony was a deadbeat dad. Hope couldn't believe she chose a man who didn't want to take care of his kids. She thought, "if only I'd listened to my family, maybe I would have been better off right now." She regretted marrying Anthony. He just used her for his benefit. She thought, "that wasn't love, that was a betrayal; He didn't love me or anyone but himself, but I believe in my God, and he will see me through this."

So, Hope took Anthony to court for child and spousal support, and he was displeased. He spent all of Hope's money and left when it was all gone. He spent her money on women, and she wanted him to pay it all back. So, it was fitting to seek help from the court for her and the children. After Hope took Anthony to court, he hated her, but Hope didn't care. Yes, she loved him, but she wasn't going to put up with him anymore, 'definitely' not after he left her to take care of their kids while he played daddy to someone else's child.

On the day of the court hearing, Hope didn't have a lawyer. She didn't see the need to have one, but Anthony brought a lawyer. Anderson, Anthony's lawyer, talked to Hope. "You won't get spousal support, only child support of $500.05," he said. Hope could see he was trying to get her to believe him.

Hope had assistance from the government. She sat down with a social worker named Roxana from the welfare office, and she told Hope, "Once you're on welfare, we have to be at court as well. I've heard everything that went on in the court." Hope didn't know that she was there. Roxana asked, "who is Renell's father?" Hope told her Anthony was.

Hope remembered the first time she went on welfare. Anthony told her to tell the worker at the office that she didn't know her child's father because he didn't have any status in the country. Hope was afraid of him, so she did as he told her. She made herself look bad in front of her worker just for him. She let her worker believe she was dating two men simultaneously, and the worker thought the other guy was the father because her daughter looked like him. Anthony and Hope were not married at the time. Hope lowered herself to please him, and he still treated her like nothing. He beat her whenever he could, and now it came back to bite her at the courthouse.

Roxana said to Hope, "I'm looking at your file, and in 2006 it states that you didn't know your child's father. So, who is Renell's father?" Hope was shocked that they still had that information. She got off welfare in 2007 and never went back until 2010. She thought, "they have a saying, what's in the dark must come to light, and my past just came back to bite me in the butt." Hope told Roxan that Anthony was her daughter's father. Roxana asked, "how do you know, did you take a DNA test?" Hope said, "at the time, I wasn't sure if he was the father because I was dating him and another guy at the same time. No, I didn't take a DNA test because my daughter looks like Anthony more and more." Hope continued, "because my husband was in her life for so long, he said he didn't care if she wasn't his daughter when we were together."

The lies kept coming because Hope didn't know how to change her story from what she had already told them. She could have told the truth that it was Anthony's idea because he used to beat on her, and she had no choice but to lie for him and say those things. However, she didn't want to get in trouble and didn't want him to get in trouble because she still loved him. Finally, Roxana asked, "why didn't you update your information about Renell's father?" Hope said, "I wasn't thinking at the time; All I knew when I went back on welfare was, I needed help because my husband was not supporting his family anymore."

Hope did what was best for her and her children. She had no job or money to take care of her kids, and the bills weren't going to pay for themselves. The way Roxan was looking at her, she thought, "oh my God, I'm going to get in trouble because she doesn't believe me." Roxana told Hope, "I have to talk to your husband after I take a break." Hope pulled Anthony aside to let him know what was going on and be on the same page. He looked at her and said, "Now you want my help? You bring me to court, want money, and now you need my help?" Hope reminded him that it was his fault she was in this mess. "Because I listened to you and lied back then, this is why this is happening. It's entirely your fault," she cried. Anthony was mad and didn't want to hear that.

Roxana came back from her break, and she talked with Anthony. While they were in the room, Hope prayed that he was on the same page with her. Finally, Anderson came to her and said, "you need to take the deal. That's the best you're going to get, child support of $500.05 and no spousal support." Hope thought about the offer, and it looked like the best she would get. She had no money, and the faster this was over, the better it would be for her and the children. Hope's mind was telling her to take the deal, but her heart was telling her to say no, that's not right. She knew that Anthony had a great job and her children deserved more, and she deserved better. After all, she had done for him; she thought, "I deserve to walk away with something."

Roxana finished speaking with Anthony, and she called Hope back into the room. Hope said to Anthony's lawyer, "I'll have to think about it; I'll get back to you." However, Hope wasn't going to give him an answer right away. The lawyer went back to the judge and set another appointment. Hope went back to speak to Roxan, and she told her, "I have to report everything that took place and the way it's looking, you'll have to pay them back some money because welfare overpaid you for your daughter." Hope asked, "why will I have to pay back the money?" Roxana said, "Anthony claimed he was giving you money for the children, and we were giving you more money for Renell because her father was not in her life, but it turns out that her father was always in her life."

Hope was mad with herself for listening to Anthony back then. She should have been more assertive and stood up for herself. Instead, she let him use and abuse her because she was weak. Hope thought, "Now I have two student loan debts because of him, phone bill debts because of him, and now welfare debts because of him." Hope cried and thought, "how much more is Anthony going to take from me." Hope went to her mother's house and told the family what had happened. They advised her not to take the lawyer's deal and find herself a lawyer before going back to court. Hope didn't know how to get a lawyer because she had no money. Michelle told her,

"Get yourself a legal aid lawyer; they'll help you because you don't have any income."

Hope went back home and searched for Legal Aid. She contacted them, and they gave her an appointment to see them before she got a lawyer. Fortunately, Legal Aid approved her application and gave her a certificate number to give to her lawyer when she finds one. So, Hope found a lawyer close to home, and she went to see him with all her paperwork from the last court hearing. The lawyer took her case. His name was Steven. Hope told Steven that she wanted child support and spousal support from her husband. Steven gave her a task to do. "Go home and write down everything about your husband and what being married to him was like," he instructed. As painful as it was to bring up the past, she did it. Twice a month, Hope went to court to fight her case. Anthony didn't want to pay spousal support or the child support Hope wanted.

After getting Anthony's information and tax receipts from his lawyer, Hope's lawyer asked Anthony to pay $599 in child support and $500 in spousal support. Hope spent three months going back and forth to court. Every time she went, she took Renell and James with her. She grew tired of taking the kids to the courthouse because she didn't want to see the sad look on their faces when they saw their father walk into the courthouse. Before the hearing, Hope told Steven that she didn't want spousal support anymore. She just wanted the case to be over. Steven looked at her like she was crazy. She told him, "I'm tired of bringing my kids to the courthouse, and I just want it to be over." Steven said, "okay, I'll let the judge know."

Hope left the courthouse feeling defeated. She called Anthony and said, "you win again." Anthony said, "what did you think would happen? No judge will make me pay spousal support." Hope hung up the phone. Anthony didn't know it was her decision not to get spousal support. Hope was still on welfare, and her work told her that they had decided, and she had to pay back $6,000, with a portion coming out of her monthly payment.

Hope grew tired of feeling like she didn't control her own life. She told her caseworker she wanted to find a job to take care of her children. She knew that the money she was getting couldn't take care of her and the children. It was gone before the month was over as soon as the money came in. The worker said to her, "I can get you a volunteering job at a shelter." Hope was excited because she loved helping people. Her worker set up an appointment for her to go into the shelter. She sat in on the orientation and loved the work the shelter was doing. Even though she wasn't going to get paid, she was happy to start.

Hope went to the shelter Monday to Friday from 7 a.m. to 4 p.m. She helped feed the less fortunate breakfast, lunch, and dinner. She loved to see the looks on their faces and how polite they all were. Her children were in daycare while she was at the shelter. After she saw what people were going through, she said to herself, "my life is not all that bad." She picked herself up and held her head up. Hope no longer held her head down because of what she went through because many people were going through a lot worse. Even though Hope loved what she was doing at the shelter, she needed a job to help her pay the bills. The welfare office gave her money, but she wanted to go out and work for her own money.

18.

Chapter Eighteen

Hope called her caseworker and told her that she needed to find a job. The worker let her know she'd have to send her file to the employment department, where she would be assigned a new caseworker. The new caseworker, Penny, called Hope and told her to find a job and let her know when she found one. She was given a $150 allowance for clothes and bus fare to get to work. So, she signed up with an employment agency and got a job at a factory. Now she had to find a babysitter for the kids. She had no family around where she lived, but she did have her friend Mo. She was not working, so Hope thought she could help her out. She called Mo and asked her to babysit for her and pay her. "I can't babysit for you," she said, "you need to stay home and take care of your children; No one will do it the way you would," she advised. Hope felt hurt. She thought they were close enough friends that she would babysit her children, but she was wrong.

Hope could lose the job if she didn't find a babysitter. So she asked her neighbour Jay to babysit her kids while finding a daycare. She told Hope she'd do it. Jay wasn't her first choice, but she needed someone to take care of her children to go out to work. Hope had applied for subsidized daycare and was on the long waiting list. Hope told Jay she could only pay her $200 a week, and she said, "no problem, I'll do it for that much, but just for a little while until you find daycare for them."

Every morning at 4 a.m. Hope got up and left the house by 5 in the morning to drop off the kids next door. She had to get to her bus by 5:30 a.m. to get to work by 7. Hope wasn't a morning person, but she didn't mind. She knew she was doing this for her children. At work, she had already made an enemy. She never knew when because she hadn't said anything to anyone.

Her job was to clean medical supplies stored away for years in the hospital. She didn't like the job, but it was the only thing available. The supervisor's daughter, Beth, worked there, and she didn't like Hope. As much as Hope was doing the job, Beth wanted to get rid of her. Hope was always quiet at work. She only talks when spoken to. She ate and stayed to herself. On the coldest day, Hope proudly walked 5 minutes to work once she got off the bus. She eventually became friends with the bus driver, who took her on the second bus to work. Then, her first bus ran late one morning, and she panicked. She couldn't miss her last bus to work. Hope couldn't afford to get fired. The bus finally came, and while running to the next bus stop, Hope prayed she wouldn't miss the bus because she knew Beth wouldn't be pleased. Beth was looking for any reason at all for her mother to let Hope go. She once said as she looked at Hope, "if I don't like someone who's working here, I'll get my mother to fire that person."

When Hope got to the other bus stop, the bus was there. She ran to get on before it drove off. When she got on the bus, the driver said, "I was waiting for you; I knew you may have missed the bus and had to take the late one." Hope thought it was so lovely of him to think of her.

Hope didn't like her job, but it put food on the table, and that was all that mattered. But in the end, Beth got her fired anyway just because she could. Hope called the agency to help her find another job. She didn't want to sit home and do anything. The lady at the agency called her the next day and got her a job at a beer factory doing inventory. She was excited about her new job because it was closer to home and paid more. Now that Grace had gone back to St. Vincent, Her sister Leah had to live with her. It was another mouth to feed.

While Grace was still in Canada, she decided to apply for permanent residency, finding Sheldon the lawyer to help her. He took her case, putting her three youngest children on the application. Sheldon asked Grace to talk with Hope to speak on Grace's behalf when it's time for the hearing. She was happy to help her mother, brothers, and sister. Hope went with Grace to see Sheldon, talk about her case, and see how she could help. He advised Hope to testify about what she witnessed with her mother and father growing up because of what she went through with her father.

It was time for Grace to see the judge, and Sheldon and Hope were confident that everything would work out for her. Judge Jeffrey questioned Grace first and wanted to know why she was in Canada for so long without any status. "I was afraid that I would get sent back home," Grace said. Every question Judge Jeffrey asked Grace, he didn't believe her. She cried so that he could hear the pain in her voice. Sheldon spoke on her behalf, but the judge just didn't believe her. Finally, Judge Jeffrey asked to speak with Hope because Hope was nervous about everything she was testifying.

The judge asked Hope to tell him a little about what she went through while in St. Vincent. She let him know how abusive her father was to her and her mother, "my father molested me, and I didn't let my mother know about it," she said. Judge Jeffrey asked, "why didn't you and your mother report what was going on to the police? "We were too scared, and my father was close to the police." "I don't believe you or your mother, and if I were the one who did your case, you wouldn't get your permanent resident card," Jeffrey said. Grace and Hope said, "we're telling the truth. "But Jeffrey didn't believe them. He denied Grace's claim. Jeffrey let the lawyer and them know she would receive a letter in the mail when she would have to leave.

Hope was angry because she didn't believe Sheldon did his best to help Grace with her case by not fighting hard enough for her. He let them know they could appeal for humanitarian and compassionate reasons, but Hope believed all he wanted was more money from Grace. After the letter came, Grace was given 30 days to leave, but she had to check in with immigration every week. Hope was there every step of the way to see her mother through it. Finally, the time had come for Grace and her sister and brothers to leave. Leah was not on her application, and she asked Hope for her to live with her. Leah wasn't on the application because she was the last to come to Canada. Hope was going through a lot with Anthony not being there for their children. Hope didn't mind taking Leah in. She loved her sister; she helped raise her back home and Canada and always looked for her. She gave her Renell's room, and Renell now shared it with James. She didn't like it, but it was okay. Hope knew they never wanted to sleep alone and always ended up sleeping in the same bed.

It was the first day on the job, and Hope felt the tension in the air. She tried to be friendly with a co-worker named Jaslene. They worked together and shared the same desk. However, Hope could tell that Jaslene didn't like her presence. Hope was filling in for Jaslene's friend, who was on vacation. She travelled to her home country, the Philippines; Jaslene's friend was a Canadian but visited her parents. Jaslene faked a smile, but Hope could see through it; she knew the game and faked a smile right back.

At the job, Hope met a truck driver named Rick. She didn't like him at first, but he was into her. She had to be nice to him because it was her job. Every time he came with a shipment, she had to do the inventory before he left. Rick seemed nice, but she wasn't interested in meeting new people. She was just getting over Rohan, who she thought was the right man for her after her husband. "I can't believe it took eight (8) months to get over that loser," Hope thought. But unfortunately, she found it hard to get over. They dated for a year and a half, and he didn't tell her that he was married.

Rick came off like a sweet guy, but Hope didn't pay him any mind. Jaslene told Hope that he was a nice guy, but she didn't care; she wanted to focus on her kids and sister. Rick came to her workplace every day and asked her out for coffee. She always said no to him, but he wouldn't give up. In time Hope started to look at him differently. She loved a guy who fought for what he wanted. One day, when he came to drop off the daily merchandise, Hope was doing his paperwork. Just like that, he asked for her number, and she gave it to him. Hope didn't know why she did it, but she did.

Rick called Hope three times that night, but she didn't pick up. The following day, when he came to work to drop off the products, he asked, "why didn't you answer my call?" "I was sleeping when you called," she replied, but that was a lie. She didn't know what to say and still wasn't interested in him. He kept calling, but Hope still wouldn't answer his calls. Finally, when Rick came to her job, he stopped asking her out for coffee. He was mad that she didn't take his calls. Jaslene saw that Rick was angry with Hope, and she asked her, "why isn't Rick speaking to you anymore?" Hope replied, "because I don't take his calls."

One night Hope was bored at home. So, she picked up the phone and called Rick. The conversation went well, and they started talking every night. Still, Hope wouldn't go out with him for coffee; she just wasn't ready. Finally, Hope came home from work one day, and her friend Mo asked to come over to her house to hang out. Her sister Unique, her husband Ken and their children, came with her; they all stayed outside to play. Suddenly James came into the house holding his hand, looking bad, but Hope didn't know why. "What's the matter?" asked Hope, but he didn't answer. Suddenly Mo's son came in and yelled, "James fell off the tree he was climbing!" Hope looked at James' hand and saw that his bone was sticking out. She started to panic and cried, "what happened to your hand?" "I fell out of the tree, and my hand hurts," he cried.

Mo and Unique tried to comfort James while Hope was on the phone with Anthony. She told him that James had broken his hand and she was taking him to the hospital. "How did you make that happen?" he growled with an angry voice. Anthony wasn't happy with Hope, which wasn't making the situation any better. Hope hung up, and soon the ambulance took them to the hospital. Mo let Hope know that she'd be at the house with Renell.

On the way to the hospital, James showed no fear. The paramedic was amazed at his bravery. While waiting to see the doctor, Anthony showed up at the hospital. Hope was surprised that he came after how he acted on the phone. Mo and the children eventually met them at the hospital. It took a long time to register for an X-ray before James could see the doctor. Then, James' hand suddenly hurt, and he started crying. Hope tried to comfort him, but it wasn't working. Anthony also tried to comfort him as well.

At 3:30 a.m., they left the hospital. The doctor had to put on a temporary cast and wanted James to return the next day, to put on the permanent one. James wanted to go home with Anthony. He was happy to take James and Renell with him, and he offered to take James back to the doctor because Hope had to work the next day. Hope gave Anthony James' health card and left. After she got home from work, Anthony dropped the kids home.

Hope and Rick were now talking for over two months; they were calling and texting each other a lot more. Hope finally invited him to her house, but Rick wanted her to come to his home first. She didn't want to because she didn't know him that well. At the same time, she wasn't sure if she should invite him to her house, but that's a chance she took. She thought to herself, "Hope, what are you doing? What if he's a bad guy, and you are bringing him to where your kids live." She started to second guess herself, but she told Rick to come to her house after 9 p.m., when the kids would already be in bed.

Rick was on his way, and while waiting, the doorbell rang. She ran to the door, and it was Anthony. She was shocked to see him. "I came to drop off James' health card," said Anthony. At the same time, Rick pulled up in the driveway. She hoped Rick would come after Anthony left, but it would be awkward now. While standing in front of the door with Anthony, Rick said hello to Hope and went into the house. She felt terrible; she never thought Anthony would see her with another guy. Anthony said, "I don't know what happened to us and why we're apart." Hope said, "we're apart because you never forgave me for having an abortion and mistreated me by cheating with women and beating on me."

Hope could see that Anthony wasn't ready to leave because he thought he could stay over. Hope wished she never invited Rick over because she didn't want her husband to leave. But after they finished talking about what went wrong in their marriage, he left. Hope paused for a minute before she went inside. She felt terrible for what Anthony had walked into. She went inside and invited Rick into her bedroom. She didn't want the kids to wake up and see him. He was a gentleman. He didn't push himself on her, but after eight months of not being with a guy, Hope wanted him badly, and Rick didn't disappoint. It was excellent from start to finish. It seemed like he was trying to get Hope to forget about her husband.

As time went by, things went well. That was until Rick told Hope about a friend of his named Jackie. He told her they were friends with benefits, and he didn't love her. But starting from that night and sometimes during the night, Hope got calls from a lady with an unknown number calling her a "bitch" then she hung up. She thought, "who is calling me names? I'm not with any woman's man."

Hope didn't know anyone who would play games with her. So she never thought about Rick's friend Jackie.

One day a man called Hope said, "hi, I've noticed that you are calling my man's phone," he said to Hope. "Who is your man?" she asked, "You know who man I'm talking about," he replied. Hope said, "I'm not talking to any gay guy, so you'd better tell me who you're talking about." "Leave my man alone!" the guy replied. "Enough of this; tell me who your man is, or I'm going to hang up my phone." He kept on saying that she already knew. Hope said, "okay, goodbye," and she laughed.

When Hope got off the phone, she couldn't believe what had just happened. She thought, "someone is playing a sick game with me; it's got to be Rick; maybe he's gay." Hope was worried because she had sex with him. She put her hand on her head and prayed, "Lord, help me, what have I done?" She called Rick after she got off the phone, and she told him what had happened. She asked him if he knew any gay guys. He said he didn't. Rick got upset, "you think I'm gay?" he asked. "I was just asking a question," Hope replied. They both laughed and thought it could be his friend Jackie. He let her know what Jackie was capable of.

Rick wanted Hope to go to the club with him. He introduced Jackie to her by picking Hope up at her house. Jackie seemed like a nice person the first time Hope met her. She welcomed Hope like a friend she hadn't seen in a long time. Hope, Rick, Jackie, and her friend Natasha, went out to have a good time. After the club closed, they went to Rick's place. While at his house, they laughed and talked. Hope recognized Jackie's voice as the woman calling her and calling her "bitch." The same woman put a guy on the phone to make it seem like Rick was gay before they met, but Hope played it cool.

Hope, Rick and Jackie would spend time together on some weekends. The kids would go to their dad's house sometimes, or they stayed at home with Leah, and every time Jackie wanted Rick and Hope to have a threesome with her. Finally, Hope started to get sick of it. She wanted it to stop. She thought, "what did I get myself into? My fantasy was to do a threesome but not like this." But Hope gave in to her one night after the club. She spent the night at Rick's house. They both touched each other while Rick kissed them. Hope could tell that Jackie was into women. She wasn't happy with herself the next day and wished it had never happened.

Jackie wanted to be Hope's friend because she wanted to know what Rick and Hope were up to when she wasn't around. Jackie added her on Facebook to keep an eye on her. She called Hope on the phone every day so that Hope wouldn't be on the phone with Rick as much. Deep down inside, Hope knew that she used to call her phone before they met. Hope was on to her but didn't say anything. Every time Jackie called Hope, she said, "I don't know what's going on; I just can't stop thinking of you." Hope didn't know what to say. She didn't know Jackie was into women like that, but she confirmed what she was thinking. She made Hope feel uncomfortable, so Hope called Rick and told him how Jackie made her feel. They decided that Jackie wasn't going to get close to her again.

The next day Hope called Jackie and told her how she was handling things and uncomfortable. Jackie got angry and swore at her. Hope didn't care; she just wanted her to stop. The more lies Jackie told, the angrier Hope got because she knew that it was Jackie who had called her phone and texted Rick's phone, pretending to be Hope's guy. But after Hope and Jackie met, all the calling and texting stopped. Hope stopped talking to Jackie, and Jackie got angry. She went on to Hope's Facebook page and messaged her for the world to see. She wanted Hope's friends and family to think that Hope was with her guy. Hope deleted her message. She didn't want to fight with her on social media.

Now that Hope and Jackie no longer spoke, the unknown calls and text messages started again. Jackie texted Rick's phone and repeated everything Hope and Rick texted on their phone. She hacked into his phone to spy on him. Jackie got mad one night because Rick came to Hope's house. He stayed the night, and he went home the following day. When he went to his car, there was a line on the driver's side of his car. It looked like someone used their keys on his vehicle. They knew it was Jackie, but they had no proof. Rick told Jackie what happened to the car, and she acted surprised. She knew she did it, but Rick couldn't tell her she did it because he genuinely didn't have any proof.

When Rick was driving Hope home from his house, he stopped at a red light one night. At the entrance to an apartment building close to his house, a bright light shone at his car. Rick looked to see where the light was coming from, and it was Jackie. She came to his apartment to see who he had brought to his house. She knew Hope would be there that night because she wanted to come over, and Rick told her that Hope would be there. After that, Jackie followed Rick everywhere he went. Now she goes to his parking lot, waiting to see what or who he brings back to his place.

Whenever Jackie called Rick, and he didn't answer her calls, she made calls pretending to be someone else and called Hope a "bitch", thinking that she was with him. Hope was performing at a show with her cousin Brian; Jackie and Rick were supposed to come to the show, but this was before Hope ended her friendship with Jackie. On the day of the show, Hope called Rick but couldn't reach him. That night he called her and said that he wanted Jackie to attend with him. She didn't mind because she would meet Jen at her house, and they lived 5 minutes from each other. She didn't care to know why he didn't pick up her calls; she already knew he was with Jackie all day.

While at Jen's house, she called Rick to see if he was ready. Hope let him know that she was at Jen's house next door. He told her that he would wait for her in the parking lot at the store close to Jen's house. Hope and Jen went to meet him there. While they were in his car to go to the show, Rick exclaimed, "what the hell?" Hope didn't know what was going on. Rick said, "I'll be back." He came out of the car, and Hope and Jen heard him screaming, "move your car!" Hope thought it was someone parking wrong, so she stayed in the car. While Hope was in the car talking to Jen, she looked at the back of the car, and she realized that it was Jackie blocking Rick's car. Jen wanted to know what was going on.

Hope said to Jen, "they'll figure out what is going on with them." Jackie was angry that she wasn't going to the show with Rick. Suddenly Hope felt someone hit her in her forehead, and she cried, "what the hell!" She looked up and saw that it was Jackie. Quickly, Rick came and pulled Jackie away from Hope. Jen looked at Hope's face and cried, "your face is bleeding!" Hope looked in the mirror and saw that Jackie had cut her. She started crying after she saw what Jackie had done to her face.

Rick and Jackie were arguing, then Jen came out of the car angrily. Hope was still sitting in the car. She just wanted to leave, but Jackie tried to open the car door to hit her again. This time Hope got out of the car. She wasn't going to let Jackie think she was afraid of her. "Hope, how could you do this to me? Did you really do this to me," Jackie asked her? Hope looked at her like, "what the hell did I do to you?" Jackie wanted to fight with her. Hope got angry because Jackie cut her on her face, which was not enough for Jackie. People gathered in the parking lot, begging for Jackie to stop, but she wouldn't. Hope grabbed her by her shirt, she didn't know where she got the strength, but she put Jackie on the ground.

Rick and Jen tried to get Hope off Jackie, but Jackie held on to her braids and pulled on them. Hope held her by the throat while she pinned her to the ground. Rick didn't know what to do, so he called the police, and they came. Hope got angrier because she lost some of her hair from fighting with Jackie. She wanted to beat her some more, but the police arrived. The police talked with Rick, Hope and Jackie separately. They also talked to some of the witnesses. The police told Hope she could press charges if she wanted, but she said no. So Hope, Rick, and Jen got back into the car and continued on their way to the show.

Hope felt embarrassed and ashamed. She didn't want to perform anymore. She just wanted to go home. Her family asked what happened to her face, making her angrier and more ashamed. Hope couldn't believe what had happened with Jackie. She went into the bathroom and cried and couldn't stop. Hope knew she didn't do anything but stop being friends with Jackie, but in Jackie's head, Hope took her man from her.

Jackie and Rick were friends with benefits before Hope came along. They both brought their friends into their threesomes, according to Rick. That night Jackie thought, when she saw Rick with Hope and Jen, they were going to do just that. That night Hope knew she had to stop talking to Rick. She could have lost her life because of him, but because he showed her so much care and how sorry he was for what happened, she didn't know how to break it off with him.

Hope didn't know that Jackie was a psychopath. Rick told her that "they were just friends." Jackie told her they were just friends, then she turned around and said Rick was her man. Hope thought, "which is it? Make up your mind, people."

The following day Hope woke up to nasty messages on Facebook and name-calling so that everyone on her Facebook could see. Jackie let Hope know that she would call Children's Aid on her. Hope blocked her on Facebook, but Jackie found ways to get at her to make Hope's life a living hell. Her daughter called Hope, swearing at her. Jackie created a fake Facebook profile to see what Hope and Rick were doing, and she attacked her. Hope put her Facebook account private so Jackie couldn't see anything she posted. It still didn't stop her from acting crazy. Hope just wanted Jackie to stop. She had so many things going on with her and Renell.

Children's Aid was coming to her house about Renell. Hope spoke with her one morning before she went to school, and she was being rude to her. Hope was stressed out because she had no help with the kids, and their father didn't seem to care. So, she took Renell's belt and hit her. It didn't leave any bruises. Hope just wanted her to listen. Renell went to school angry and told her teacher that her mother beat her and hurt her legs. Hope went to the bus stop that night, but Renell wasn't on the bus. She called the school, and they told her they called the police because of what Renell had told them. Hope was angry with the principal, and she said, "why didn't someone call me and tell me that my child was in the care of the police?" The principal said, "it was our job to report any kind of abuse."

Hope hung up and called a taxi, then called Anthony to tell him what was happening. Anthony was angrier with her than worried she might lose their daughter. Hope knew she must do this on her own. So she went to the police station and let them know who she was. Officer Matt took her into the room where Renell was. The officer questioned Hope about what had happened with Renell. She let the officer know that she didn't hit Renell with a stiff belt but a soft baby belt. He told Hope, "Once you use a belt or anything else, it's considered a weapon." Hope didn't know that because she got beaten with worse than a belt. She didn't know any better.

Hope didn't know that the officer had spoken with Renell. "I spoke with her, and she is brilliant for her age; you'll have to be careful with her," he said. However, she knew what the officer said was true; Renell wasn't an average child. She was mature for her age. Officer

Matt told Hope that she could take her home, and he told her that she was getting off with a warning.

Leah and James were at home. Hope thanked God that her son was not at the police station with Renell. She had asked Leah to get Renell from school. On her way home with Renell, she got a call from Jackie calling her a 'Bitch'. Hope couldn't take Jackie anymore, she just wanted her to go away, but she wouldn't. Jackie knew what Hope was going through with Renell. Hope had opened up to her when they were friends. Jackie knew that Hope's daughter had challenges with her anger towards her brother and her friends and that she got into fights. Jackie showed as if she was caring, but she was just getting information to use on Hope deep inside. She knew that Children's Aid would now visit Hope once a month to help her with Renell.

Jackie called Children's Aid and told them that Renell was in a gang. The following week, a lovely man from Children's Aid visited Hope. He said to her, "We got an anonymous call saying that Renell was in a gang." Hope knew who it was. She said, "I'm not sure who would say something like that; it's not true." The social worker believed her and said, "I don't believe she's in a gang. I just wanted to let you know." Hope cried. She didn't know what to do anymore. Renell got into fights with her friends in the community and followed the wrong crowd. "Don't cry, Miss, you're a great mom. When you feel down, look at James, it says it all," Michael, the social worker said to Hope.

That same week Hope spoke with Renell again about her behaviour. Hope didn't hit Renell, but she told the school that her mother had hit her again. Once again, Hope went to get her and James from the bus, and they weren't on it. She called the school, and she found out that Children's Aid had picked them up. Hope was told that Renell said she hit her again. Hope couldn't believe she did it again, and again it wasn't true. She took a taxi to the police station once again. Hope told the officer that she didn't hit her this time either. The officer wasn't sure if she believed her. "This is your last warning. If your children come back here, you'll lose them." She could not believe what Renell was putting her through.

Now Hope was scared to talk to Renell when she did anything wrong. Michael, the social worker, visited them and let her know that he would bring in a therapist to help her with Renell. Cindy, the therapist, came once a month and talked with Renell, firstly by herself and then Hope and her together. Hope spoke about her fear of talking to Renell when she did anything wrong. Cindy advised Hope not to give Renell that power over her, or she'll get away with everything.

Hope noticed Renell doing things for attention. She decided to spend more time with the kids instead of leaving Leah to take care of them when she went to help Rick with his business when she wasn't working. But Rick made Hope's life more depressing than it was already. He always wanted to make his problems her problems. When Rick was sad, she would have to be unhappy as well. Rick always acted needy like a bit of a child. Hope had been trying to get away from him for weeks because she couldn't do it anymore. "You would think a forty-nine-year-old man would be more grown than this," she thought. Hope lost weight because she was stressing out and not eating correctly, and they were always on the road. She went from 130lb to 100lb. It was all about his world. "You have to come into my world," he would say to Hope. "What about my world," she would ask. He said to Hope, "my world is full of excitement, and I don't want to be responsible for anyone's feelings." She looked at him differently and knew she must leave him. Hope could see that Rick never cared about her that much when he said things like that to her.

"I don't want to be with one woman," Rick said one day. Hope asked, "does that mean that I shouldn't say I have a boyfriend?" He said, "I want you to tell every guy that you have a boyfriend because I want you for myself." Hope replied, "I can't have any other guy, but you can have more than one woman. Are you serious right now?" He said, "yes, I am serious." Rick knew Hope wasn't the kind of woman who would sleep with more than one guy. So Rick would make plans with Hope and other women at the same time. If the other woman said yes, he forgot all about Hope. He thought Hope didn't know what was going on. She felt depressed that she was with a guy who didn't want to be with just her.

Hope played dumb with Rick and studied him and the game he was playing. He also thought she was dumb because she never said much. She used to believe everything he said to her, but not anymore. Rick wanted Hope always to know how he felt when he wanted sex or just wanted to be left alone. "How immature, he is acting like a little kid," she thought, "I already have three kids to raise. I can't raise another one that's a grown man." It's okay for him to be on the phone anytime he wants and with whomever he wants. But, when it came to Hope, she wasn't allowed. While she was in bed with him, other women would call him. He would tell them, "I'm in a meeting; I'll call you back." He kept pushing her away from him but never realized how far or he didn't care. Finally, she turned to him and said, "do I look like one of your employees?"

But who is Hope kidding? After everything he was doing, why would she think she could get him for herself?

19.

Chapter Nineteen

Deep inside, Hope didn't want to be with Rick anymore. She wanted her husband back because she still loved him. She didn't think that would ever change. Rick was just there to keep Hope's mind off her problems, but now it seemed like it was a waste of her time. She was with Rick but wasn't in love with him. Hope liked that he loved to go out and have fun, and every day he went to different places. Hope loved that, but she still hoped that Anthony would return to her and his family.

Rick thought sex was everything and that he was good in bed. Hope made him believe he was that good because it was always about him. She wanted to let him know that he could improve a little, but she knew he would get angry, so she let him believe whatever he wanted to. Rick thought women kept coming back to him because he was that good, but that's not all Hope wanted from a guy. She wanted someone to love her, hold her at night and be there for her. Hope needed a shoulder to cry on. "I'm not asking for much, but I can't get it from him or my husband," she thought.

Rick made it clear that he couldn't love her, and Hope asked herself if she was wasting her time. She felt like a robot when she was with Rick. Anything he asked of her, she did it for him. Now Hope could see why the other women were just with him for its fun but didn't want to be with him. Finally, Hope thought, "Lord knows I want to do it, but it isn't worth it. It isn't worth me being a fool."

Sleeping at Rick's house was a nightmare. He expected Hope to be awake when he was in pain, so she could take care of him. It was okay at first when she used to massage his back and feet, but now he woke her up in the middle of the night to do it. He said to Hope, "you're sleeping like a rock when I try to wake you." Hope thought, "no, honey, it's just that I choose not to listen to you at times." Finally, she got sick and tired of it all because sex wasn't acceptable anymore.

She had no desire for him. He treated Hope like his daughter as if he knew what was best for her. She felt stupid when she was around him. "This is no way for a woman to feel when you're around your man," She thought. She knew there was somewhere she needed to be, but she didn't know where. Hope thought, "they say when you leave your ex, the other guy is supposed to make you forget about your ex." With Rick, she missed her ex-husband more than anything. Lately, every time Hope had sex with Rick, she thought about Anthony. It was the only way Hope could take her mind off sex with him. She just wanted him to finish what he was doing. She knew it wasn't right, but she couldn't help herself.

When it came to Hope and her music, Rick wanted to act supportive, but only if he could tell her what she should do. Hope wanted to control her music and life, but he wanted to be in control. So she performed in her first music video called "Let's Go ."She loved how the director produced the video, but Rick didn't. Hope thought, "maybe because he wasn't in the video; He thinks he has a better idea for the video." Rick wanted to have dancing girls wearing schoolgirl costumes in the video. It showed her how much he loved young girls.

Rick told Hope that he would produce an event to showcase her talent. Hope thought it was nice of him to do that for her. She had ideas for what direction she wanted to see the show go. Hope wanted to hire a promoter for the show, but Rick thought it was a waste of money. She chose the date she wanted for the show, but he thought it should happen on her country's Independence Day. Hope didn't want to do the event on that day because there were always a lot of parties taking place, and people went to the one they thought would be the best. Rick wanted Hope to do her music video at the show. He said to her, "I'll rent a stage where you can perform while the director captures the moment." Hope thought he had a good idea for once. She called the director and told him of the video reshot's.

Rick said that he was going to print tickets for the show. They had a month to put things together, but Rick wasted time. Three weeks before the show, Rick printed the tickets and gave them to his co-workers, and he asked them to spread the word to anyone who didn't have tickets.

Hope let her friends and family know about Rick's show for her. She gave them the date of the show, but no one thought it was a good idea to do the show on that day because the big promoters were doing theirs. But Hope couldn't do anything; it was already too late. Rick had already rented the hall and bought the drinks for the show.

Hope had a cousin named Sista, who was a dancer in Montreal. She asked her to get her group to perform in the music video and the show. So, Hope sent the song to her to rehearse for the video. She also asked her friend Nick, and his producer Norman, to be part of the show and use his studio to rehearse. So, every Saturday for a month, they went to his studio to rehearse. Sometimes Norman was at the studio, and sometimes Hope, Nick and Rick would show up, and he wasn't there.

Things started to look like they weren't going to work out the way Hope wanted. "I think you should put off the show," said Nick. Hope thought about it for a second and responded, "I think it's too late, it's just a week away, and Rick won't go for it." The week before the show, Sista and her crew came from Montreal. Hope hoped that she wouldn't have to buy their clothes but wear what they wanted as long as fit for the video. However, Rick had other plans. He wanted Hope and the girls to wear schoolgirl uniforms. Rick and Hope took them to a flea market to buy clothes, and he picked out the styles for them. Rick told Hope to know that he would pay for the clothes. Hope was relieved because she didn't have enough money. While going to the cash desk, he saw some jackets, and he thought it would look nice on Hope and the girls. Unfortunately, the clothes totalled more than Rick wanted to spend at the cash desk. He wanted to spend $60, and he was over by $100, so Hope had to pay the rest. She wasn't happy, but she paid the money without showing it.

After shopping, Rick invited the girls to his home to show what they had rehearsed. The girls showed what they came up with. Rick loved it. Then he wanted Hope to do her songs and dance, but she didn't want to. Next, Rick wanted her to do a show, and he asked Sista to help her come up with something. She showed him how she would perform, but Rick didn't think it was good enough. Next, he wanted Hope to do a lap dance while he sat in the chair at the show. She didn't think that suited her personality, but Rick thought otherwise.

It was showtime, but Rick didn't have the stage he said he would rent. Now Hope didn't have a proper setting to perform on. He didn't get many responses from his friends or co-workers to come to the show. Rick knew Hope didn't have many friends to invite to the show, but he didn't want Hope to worry. He said he would get it done, but he failed on his promise.

Norman was late for the show, and when he got there, he had a problem with his equipment. "What else could go wrong," she cried. Hope was devastated. On the day of the show, Hope's director was disappointed. It wasn't what they were expecting. She promised them it would be a sound stage and lots of people there. She felt embarrassed. Her friends and family came out to show their support, but there were not enough people to fill a room. "You could count everyone in the room and see every angle in the room. When it came to Rick's friends, there were only two. She wanted her first show to be great, but it was not good that night because Rick didn't listen to her. The party was over before it started.

Hope tried to put life into the party and did her best to perform well. She did her first song, "Let's Go," for her music video while the director was filming. Rick was in the video. Hope didn't want him in it, but he would feel left out. He thought he should be in everything Hope did. As soon as the song was over, the director left. Hope performed a cover called, "No No No, You Don't Love Me, and I Know Not ."With that song came the lap dance. Hope wasn't feeling the song, but she tried her best to go through it. While dancing, Rick took one of her legs and put it on his shoulder, knowing she was wearing a skirt. She was shocked; she was not expecting him to do such a thing. Her cousin Meesha came and threw $5 on her. Hope just wanted it to be over.

After the show, Rick made less money than he expected to, at the bar and at the door. Whatever money he made, he didn't give any to Hope. He thought, since he was the one who bought the drinks and paid for the tickets, he should keep everything. She just kept her mouth shut and let it go.

Due to what Hope went through, and seeing what her mother Grace went through, how she never had enough to feed her and her brothers, and now that she was grown up, she wanted to help people, especially in her hometown. So Hope registered a charitable foundation, and Rick thought he knew what was best for it. Hope was trying to give her children everything she never had growing up, but Rick thought he knew what was best for them. Any time Hope and Rick got into an argument, he told Hope that he didn't care about her children because they weren't his, but he had a lot to say about how she raised her children. Hope thought to herself, "why am I with another loser, a guy who talks like that about my kids?" Rick only wanted Hope, not her children. He was just using her for sex, telling her she made him feel young.

Rick had a job to do, and he asked Hope to go with him. The school was out, and Hope's cousin Meesha wanted the kids and her sister Leah to come to her house to spend the week. She was happy that she didn't have to worry about them while going on the job with him. Hope tried to look past the things Rick did, to see the good in him, but sometimes it was hard. She didn't love him. On the road, everything was going fine until one of his pickups went wrong, and he took it out on Hope. She tried not to say anything that would get Rick angry because she wanted him to get the donation. Unfortunately, she had to do a pickup for her foundation that same day.

Rick knew he had to pick up the gifts for Hope because she reminded him in the morning. As the day went by, Rick got angry with someone at his job. When it was time for him to get the stuff for her, he said, "I can't do it for you today." She was disappointed, but she tried not to show it. Hope texted the lady and told her she couldn't make it. The lady texted her back and said to her, "I had plans with my husband because it was our anniversary, and I broke it off because you said you were coming by." Hope felt terrible. She turned towards Rick and said, "the lady texted me." Before she told him what she said, he shouted at her and said, "And?" Hope shut her mouth and didn't bother telling him.

Rick got angry with Hope for no reason. Every time he had a problem with someone, he took it out on her. Rick didn't talk to her on the way home, so she wouldn't bother him. Hope loved to talk to herself, thinking, "I'm going to let him calm down and won't say anything to him." It was a long journey on the road with him. Finally, they went to buy dinner and went back to his place. Hope asked him, "Are you ready for your dinner?" He said, "No." They were in the living room watching TV, but he still wasn't talking to her. Finally, she went to take a shower and went to lay down because she was tired. It was a long day. Hope woke up about 11 pm, and Rick was still watching TV. He still wasn't talking. She ate her dinner then went back to bed. A little later, he came to bed.

Hope always slept with her back towards Rick. He would turn around and hold her when he felt like it. He told her he loved his own space while sleeping. Even if Hope wanted to hold him while they slept, she let Rick make the first move. But he didn't because he was still mad at her that night. The following day Rick didn't wake her up to work with him. "He thought I was tired and wanted to sleep in." Hope thought. She got up and called Rick that morning. She had to, or he would get angry at her if she didn't. "Why didn't you wake me up?" she asked, "why?" He didn't reply, then Hope asked, "do you want me to cook for you before you come home from work?" He said, "no."

Rick was on the phone arguing with Hope, and he told her that she didn't talk to him and didn't touch him during the night. "You turned your back on me," he said. Rick had been with Hope for six months, and he knew that's how she slept, but he just wanted to pick a fight. He told Hope, "there is a spare key; take it and go home." Hope tried to figure out what she did wrong. Why was he so angry at her for no reason? She thought, "I didn't do anything wrong, he wasn't talking to me, and he said I was mad at him."

Even though Rick didn't do what he was supposed to do for her, Hope didn't let it bother her. She didn't leave right away. She called Rick an hour later to let him know she was staying until he came home. He got angrier and said, "leave my place now, don't make me come home and meet you there." Hope felt hurt. She promised herself she wouldn't step foot into Rick's house anymore. But that didn't last because Rick was the only guy Hope knew who had a truck, and she needed him to get the donation for her. She also had to do a job with him the next day.

Rick called Hope to help him with the job, and she went. After they were finished, she wanted to go home, but he took her back to his house. Hope was crying inside; and wanted to go home but didn't know how to say it. She was usually scared that he wouldn't get her donation if she told him she wanted to leave. So, Hope tried to take a nap before they got the donation so he wouldn't see how angry she was.

Rick got the donation for her and dropped it off at her house; then he took her back to his house. Even though the kids were with Meesha, Hope didn't want to return to Rick's house. Unfortunately, the job they were doing together had to be done again, so Hope didn't have any choice but to go back to his house. The next day Hope tried to get her clothes dirty so Rick would take her home after work. So, she asked him to take her home because of the clothes and work to do at home. "I was hoping to take you back to my house, but I'll drop you home before I go home," he said. Hope felt good.

He wouldn't pay her for all the work she was doing for him. He let her know how much money he was making and never thought that Hope was a single mother and needed to take care of her children. Rick was selfish when it came to his money.

Rick usually called Hope, but that night he didn't. So Hope didn't call him. She was tired of listening to him talking about himself. It's always about him. "He makes my ears bleed when he talks about himself," she thought. For once, she wanted Rick to take her more seriously, but that never happened. Rick was too selfish.

Rick tried to hit on Hope's friends. He would ask her to do a threesome with her friends. Hope said okay just to shut him up. She did a threesome with him, so he thought it was also okay for him to do it with her friends. Hope went to her cousin's baby shower with Jen and her friend Nisha. After the baby shower, Rick wanted Hope to go to the strip club with her friends. The night was young, and she wanted to have some fun with her two girlfriends, so they went. At the strip club, Rick liked the attention he got. Everyone thought he had three girls. A stripper came up to Hope in the club and asked, "are you new?" Hope said, "Say what?" She asked again, "are you one of the girls?" Hope said with a smile, "no, I'm not." She said to Hope, "you should come and try out; Mondays are amateur nights." Hope didn't know what to say but, "sure I'll come out." Hope knew she was just lying to the girl.

After the club, Rick dropped Jen home, and Hope and Nisha returned to his house. He said he was too tired to drive her home because she lived far away. Nisha was supposed to go back to Hope's house to stay the night, but they slept at his house that night. Hope and Nisha slept in the same bed with Rick. He couldn't be a gentleman and give them the room for themselves. Hope was in the middle between Rick and Nisha. While she slept, she could feel Rick's hand touching Nisha. Hope knew that Rick was aware that it wasn't her he was touching because he passed over her to touch Nisha. He kept doing the same thing, touching Nisha's private parts.

Hope believed Nisha knew he was touching her because she positioned herself for him to do it. But she acted like she was turning in her sleep. It seemed like Nisha and Rick wanted a threesome to happen. First, Rick touched Hope, then Nisha. Hope got angry, got out of bed, and went to the living room. From where she was sitting, she could see Rick holding Nisha. He knew Hope was no longer in bed, so he stopped touching Nisha. After Rick dropped Nisha home and took Hope to her place, she talked about what he had done. Rick acted like he didn't know what he was doing and didn't think he did it. Finally, he said, "if I did that, I was sleeping." He had an answer for everything, and she hated that Rick thought he was smarter than everyone.

She went to work with him the next day while Leah's kids were at home. The good part about working for yourself and being a truck driver is taking whoever you want with you. She spent half the day on his job before Rick dropped her home. He asked Hope to create a template for his business and a logo. Things were going great because she didn't hear from Rick for the rest of the day when she got home. Night came, and she still hadn't heard from him. So, at 8 pm she called him to find out why she didn't hear from him. The way he was talking to her, she knew he wasn't alone, "I'll have to call you back," he said.

Hope was at home trying to develop ideas for his business. Rick wanted her to help him run his trucking business, and he was at home with another woman. By 10:30 pm. She still hadn't heard back from him. Hope sent him the ideas she was working on by email and texted him to check his email. Hope then texted him and said, "I see you've made your choice." Rick texted her back, saying, "with what?" Hope didn't reply; she wanted to mess with his mind. Rick called Hope and told her that he couldn't open one of the emails she sent him. She replied, "I'm doing fine, thanks for asking." Then, he asked, "what do you mean when you said I made my choice?" Hope didn't want to get into it, but Rick pushed her to tell him. Hope told Rick, "I don't want to talk about it, and I'll resend the email again." Then Rick blurted out, "bitch!" Hope couldn't believe he called her a bitch. Right there and then, Hope said to him, "no way in hell will I stay with you after you called me a bitch." He didn't care.

Hope made up her mind that she was done with him. She couldn't lay down with him anymore. Hope thought he was hurting her for months, and she looked past it but not anymore. However, she wanted him to know that he didn't break her. Instead, he just made her stronger.

So here it goes again. Hope said she wasn't going back with Rick, but she always fell back on her words. Rick didn't know how to talk to Hope. She and Rick messaged each other back and forth until her hands hurt, but every time she stopped texting, Rick got angry and told her she took too long to respond. Finally, Rick told Hope, "you're not bright when it comes to things at times." "How can that be when I'm the one running your business, doing your invoices, creating your company emails, and producing an idea for your business," she cried. She continued, "I created a website and the template for your invoices, I got your logo and your company T-shirts, and I play the role of your assistant, and I don't get paid, and that is what you will say to me!" Hope said to him, "an uneducated person couldn't do all those things."

Hope left her children at home with her sister when she should have been home taking care of them. Instead, she took care of him when he was sick and helped him run his company even when she was at home. She was angry with Rick for what he had said to her. She told Rick, "yes, I'm not bright; I should be at home with my kids." Rick was selfish. Hope knew this time when she left, and it would be for good. Hope knew that she kept saying the same thing over and over. She used to think Rick was a nice guy but hated how he talked to her at times. She had already given up a lot for him and didn't think she could give up anything more.

Rick thought Hope was looking for marriage. He said to Hope, "because of what I went through with my last marriage, I won't get married again." She didn't understand why he would say that to her. She would marry again if she couldn't get her husband back, and she would have a family again with her children, but not with Rick. She knew he wasn't for her. Hope was only with Rick because of circumstances, and she missed being a wife. She liked Rick, but she couldn't take the way he treated her anymore.

Hope made a mistake and told Rick all her problems, including what she went through as a child. She wanted to talk to a therapist, but Rick thought Hope didn't think she needed to talk to anyone but him. He gave her a shoulder to cry because of what she was going through with her daughter Renell, acting out at home and school. Now that Hope talked to Rick a little more, he sounded like she stressed him. He told her, "I'm not ready for all of this."

Hope told Rick what her father had done to her and everything that had been done to her. She told him her whole life story, and it came back to bite her in the ass. When he saw what Hope was going through with Renell, he asked her, "why don't you give the kids to their father?" Hope refused. She couldn't believe that he wanted her to give up her children. Hope told him, "You don't need to be in their lives, but I won't give my children up." Hope thought, "why would I give up my children because of a man? I didn't bring my kids into this world just to hand them over to Anthony because things aren't going well." She didn't understand what kind of a man would tell a mother to hand her children to their father.

Hope felt like Rick didn't think she was doing an excellent job with her children when he knew how their father treated them. He used to tell her to keep the kids to herself because Anthony didn't want the children. She knew he wanted her for himself and wanted her to give her children away. Rick asked Hope, "why would you want to keep the kids from their father?" He continued, "women always want to use their kids against their father." Hope replied, "my kids are my life, and I won't let anyone hurt them, not even their father." Rick said, "you only talk that way because you're not over your husband." Hope didn't respond because she knew he wasn't wrong. She wasn't over her husband, but that wasn't why Hope was doing what she was doing. She couldn't take how her husband treated their kids like he didn't love them anymore.

Rick was driving Hope up the wall. She wasn't working, and when she took the kids to school, she liked to come back home and take a nap. But Rick didn't like it. While Hope returned from taking the children to school, Rick called her twice and got her voicemail. She had left her phone home to spend quality time with her kids while walking them to school. When she returned home, she saw a text from Rick that said, "if I were in the field and needed your help, I'd be dead in the water." Hope thought, "what the hell is that? What was he doing before I came along?" Hope told Rick that she left her phone at home, and he told her, "If I wanted to depend on you, I can't because you're either sleeping during the day or forgetting your phone." Hope didn't want Rick to depend on her at this point because she was sick and tired that he didn't care about anyone but himself.

Hope was only 28 years old and had a lot going on. She couldn't be herself when she was around Rick. She had to be what he wanted her to be. At first, it was okay, but Rick changed. He kept telling her he didn't want to be in a serious relationship and didn't want to get married again, yet he wanted to treat Hope like his wife.

When she went to Rick's house, she noticed a lady's lunch bag in front of his door and two wine glasses on the counter table in the kitchen. She could see that Rick had company over the night before. Hope didn't say anything to him, but he could see that something was bothering her. Rick asked, "what happened? Do you see something in my house?" Hope didn't understand what game Rick was playing. She said, "whatever I see is none of my business," he said," good, it's my house."

Hope cooked his dinner for him but was not pleased. She told Rick, "I'll wash the dishes, but I won't wash your woman's glass." Rick got angry and said, "you always come to my house and look around like other women." Hope replied, "I saw the woman's lunch bag when I walked through the door." With anger in his voice, he said to Hope, "do you know how it got there?" Just as Rick explained the lunch bag to Hope, she knew it was a lie. Hope stopped him and said, "I don't want to hear it." She realized that if it wasn't the truth, why even hear it.

While Rick was in the bathroom, Hope went through his phone, and she saw the lady asking about her lunch bag. Hope wrote down her number, thinking it would be helpful one day. In the exact text, she saw that he said he was alone with her that same night. Hope saw that he texted the lady after Hope left and said, "you get away?" Only one thing came to Hope's mind; he was looking for sex from her.

Rick went to take a nap, and his phone rang. It was the lady calling him. He looked at the phone and put it back down. Hope knew he would produce an excuse why he couldn't answer that night, and it wouldn't be the truth. Hope wondered how someone who says they don't lie to women told the most lies. Hope knew the ones who say they don't lie are the ones who could not trust. Hope wanted to leave him, but she found it so hard. She knew she must get over the fear of being alone. "Maybe that's the reason she is still around him," she thought. Hope liked Rick but wasn't in love with him. It should have been easy, but not for Hope. She thought, "I need to find the strength to walk away with my head up high."

20.

Chapter Twenty

Hope knew all the things Rick was saying to the other women. She knew he didn't love her because he slept with many women, and she saw all the messages. They say if you look for trouble, you'll find it, so don't look for trouble." She thought about what she'd been through since she started seeing Rick, and she got angry with herself for still being with him. She thought, "I got hit in the face because of him, a woman called Children's Aid on me because of him, so why am I here?" Rick thought because of him; Hope was putting on weight. He didn't know that she was taking pills to keep her weight up. Hope was stressed out and couldn't eat anything, so she took the medication to hide that she wasn't happy.

Hope needed to find herself again and let Rick go, or she would never be herself. Hope was trying to make her music without Rick's knowledge to do it her way. She tried not to bring up music to him so she wouldn't have to lie. With everything going on with Hope and Rick, he dared to tell her she couldn't have any guy friends, or it would be over. "I don't want anyone to think my woman has a man on the side," he told her. So, Hope asked, "what if it's my brother or a family friend? What then?" He replied, "all I know is you can't have any man as a friend even if it's your brother." Hope replied, "Now you're talking crazy; not even my brother can be around me?" Rick said, "I don't want people who know me to see you in public with any guy." Hope thought he was losing his mind.

Hope was going over the conversation she had with Rick, and she thought, "It's okay for him to sleep around and have women friends, but it wasn't okay for me to do the same." Rick knew that if Hope had a chance to leave him, she would. But she knew that if a guy came around and treated her right, she would leave. Of course, Rick didn't want that to happen. He didn't know how to keep her, but he also didn't want to lose her. Hope told Rick about her best friend Neal in Barbados. He told her if she went to Barbados for a vacation, he would break up with her because he would think something had happened. She got angry and replied, "who are you to tell me who I should have as friends?" She said, "You have so many female friends, and they're not just your friends."

Rick slept with women he knew were married but thought he wasn't doing anything wrong. He got angry when Hope called them "whores," saying they weren't. Hope asked, "what do you call a woman who has a husband at home but is sleeping with another man?" "A whore," she countered. Rick wasn't happy with what she said.

A woman came to his house and spent a few hours with him. Hope found out by going through his phone. She confronted him about it, and he said she just came to talk about her man-troubles. Hope asked, "and why is that your problem? You're not a therapist." Rick replied, "we're just friends; she just wanted to talk to me about her man." She couldn't understand why it was any of his business. Hope asked, "if that's the case, why do you try to have sex with them?" "Why would a woman come to another man's home to talk about their partner? Why didn't she talk to her husband or boyfriend about how she felt." She continued, "what you're saying doesn't make any sense?"

Rick didn't want Hope to talk to anyone in her life because he knew they would tell her to leave him, and he didn't want that to happen. He didn't want Hope to talk to Michelle by saying she mistreated her brother. She regretted confiding in him about the problems Michelle and her brother Ricardo were going through. He also didn't want Hope to be friends with her friend Jen. He said she was too old to have as a friend and wasn't sexy enough. Rick never made a lot of sense to Hope. Every time Hope turned around, there was someone Rick didn't want her to have in her life.

Rick didn't even want her to co-parent with Anthony. Finally, he told Hope, "If you and your husband are friends, I'll stop talking to you because I'll think you and him are having sex." Then he said, "if you and your husband were together and we met, you'd have dated me too." "If my husband and I were together, you and I would never have gotten together," Hope responded. He looked at her with surprise on his face and said, "why would you want to be with a guy who treated you so wrong?" Hope said, "why would I want to put myself in the same mess and leave my husband to be with a man who doesn't know how to treat a woman right. Rick didn't like what she said. He said he was always straightforward with any woman he was with. Hope said, "you want me to be like your other chicks who fool around with you when they have their men at home? I've never been or will never be a whore for a man."

Hope knew she wasn't the kind of girl to be with other guys while in a relationship with someone. Rick didn't trust her or any other woman. Even though he slept with married women, he could never be involved in a relationship with a woman who would do that. Hope told Rick she never cheated on her husband even when he did her wrong. Rick told her she was foolish. "If you met me when your husband was cheating on you, you would have picked me up," he said. "That wouldn't have happened because I loved my husband, and I wouldn't have given you the time of day," said Hope. Rick got angry and said, "why would you want to be with a guy who hurt you?" Rick couldn't get past his ego, and he just wasn't a nice person.

Hope only stayed with Rick because she needed something to take her mind off her problems at home. She didn't want her children to see her cry anymore. Every time Rick hurt her, Renell would always say, "mommy, don't let him make you cry. Anytime he gets you angry, hang up the phone, and you won't have to listen to him." Hope was surprised when Renell said that. She never thought she was seeing and listening. "My baby girl, who is just eight years old, is giving me advice," she thought.

Hope looked at Renell and cried and hugged her. She knew that Renell felt her pain. Hope loved her children and knew she had to do better for them. She realized that she needed her children to see her strong woman. She didn't want Renell to grow up making the same mistakes she made. Hope knew she had to do things differently for them. She promised herself that she would be a better mother and would fix things and spend more time with them like she used to. Since Hope met Rick, she spent less time with her children. She always wanted the weekend to come to send them to their father's house when he decided to take them. Hope also had her sister, Leah, babysit for her. Hope knew that letting her sister take care of her children wasn't fair. Still, she just wanted to help Rick with his business.

Leah needed to live her life as well. Hope didn't have her sister live with her to take care of her children. But it turned out that Leah helped raise her children while she was working or helping Rick. Hope told herself long ago that she would never put any guy above her kids, but she felt like she was doing just that. She asked herself, "why did I let this get this far? Why did I let this guy make me feel this way?" Rick never asked her to take the children out because she spent most of her time with him, now that she wasn't working.

Hope learned a lot from Rick, like what you should not do when in a relationship. He thought Hope should live her life the way he wanted her to. Sometimes Hope hated being with Rick, yet she wanted to be with him. There were always mixed feelings when Rick came around. She just didn't know how to feel anymore. Her tears never stopped, being with Rick. Hope didn't know why she made him hurt her the way he did. Hope and Rick planned to see each other. She called him three times, and he didn't pick up. She texted him, but he didn't reply. She called him again for the fourth time, and he answered. He talked to her like there was someone else there with him. Hope knew that he only talked to her that way when another woman was around. Rick said to Hope, "I'll have to call you back." Then he hung up, not caring what she had to say.

She texted him back and said, "I hope those women you're putting first are worth it and have their men at home." Hope was mad at him. She didn't understand how he could plan a date with her then make plans with someone else.
Rick called Hope and wanted to come to her house. He wanted to have sex with her when he had already had sex with another woman. She didn't allow him to come to her home. He got angry and called her useless. "I hope when you reach these women's age, you can function like them. I'll be better off with an older woman instead of you. Hope was shocked, and she hung up the phone. As she replayed what Rick said to her, she thought, "why do I let him talk to me like this? I deserve better than him."

Hope wasn't happy with him. She realized that all he did was make her cry. "I do everything for him, I always have to have my phone and answer it when he calls, or he gets angry." Hope felt like she was in prison. She didn't have a life with him. She was tired of crying, and she knew Rick didn't have any love in his heart for any woman, so why was she wasting time with him? After all, Hope went through with Anthony, she should never have this happen again. Rick took Hope's kindness for weakness because she complied with his wrongdoings. Hope believed that Rick thought she couldn't get any other man, which is why he could treat her that way.

Hope prayed night and day, asking God to take her out of the situation. Finally, she said to herself, "I don't need this in my life,

I don't." She thought that she and Rick could make something out of life, but she realized they couldn't. Rick asked Hope to have his child, but she didn't want another child with another man, especially him. She thought, "what am I going to do with another child; Having another baby is wrong; It wouldn't be fair to put another child through what my kids have already gone through." Hope asked herself, "why would I bring another child into this world when it's not going to come from love. He doesn't love me, and I don't love him, and I'm sure of that." Hope knew she couldn't make someone stay with her if they didn't want to, and she surely wasn't going to give him a child just because he asked her to.

The relationship took all her energy. Rick thought he treated her like a queen and better than her ex-husband and ex-boyfriend. Rick always reminded her of her exes. Rick abused her emotionally and put everyone else above her. She couldn't have a life with him. Hope needed help to get away from Rick. She didn't know how to talk to her friends about what was going on anymore. Because of him, she couldn't talk to her sister-in-law Michelle because she didn't want to hear her say, "I told you so." She couldn't talk to her other friends, because of Rick she didn't go around them anymore. Hope couldn't get angry with her friends because they were right. Hope stopped talking to her friends because Rick told her to. He thought they didn't belong in her world. So now she had no one to call, and she felt so alone.

Rick could see that Hope was pulling away from him, so he went back to talking to Jackie. He made her believe things were over with him and Hope, even though she was still around. Rick stopped talking to Jackie because of what happened the night she and Hope got into a fight in the parking lot before Hope's show. While they weren't speaking, he told Hope everything about her because he was angry with Jackie. He let Hope know that Jackie got into an accident with a TTC bus a while back, and she sued the company, blaming them for her heart disease and why her voice box was damaged.

"Every time she goes to court, she would drink things that made her voice sound bad, and she'd win the case," said Rick.

Rick also told Hope that Jackie was a liar and a con artist. She used men and women, and Jackie enjoyed being friends with him to have her way with his women friends. He told Hope that Jackie was mad when they got into the fight because she wanted Hope for herself and couldn't have her. He also let Hope know that Jackie sent an innocent man to jail because he left her for her best friend. As well, after they'd just met, she cheated on her husband with him, and that's why he'd never be in a relationship with her. "I knew Jackie would try to keep things on him to get me in trouble as she did to the guy she was dating, who she sent to prison," he disclosed. "I remember the night you and Jackie were fighting, she told me that she was going to call the police on me," said Rick. "She was going to send the police to my home; I'll never forgive her," he said to Hope. She couldn't remember hearing Jackie say that to him, but she thought that's when they first started to argue.

Jackie tried to keep her sexuality from her daughters. That's why she and Rick were friends because her children thought that they were together, but she loved women. Hope couldn't believe everything Rick said to her.

Rick was trying to convince Hope to call Children's Aid on Jackie about her kids and call the TTC to let them know what she did to get money from them. Rick was angry with Jackie because he said he helped coach her on what to say in court, and Jackie promised that when she won the money, she would help him with his business, but it never happened. She fought with him when she won, so she didn't give him any money. Rick wanted to use Hope to hurt Jackie because he was too chicken to do it himself. Hope wasn't going to get involved even though Jackie did what she did to her. Hope wasn't going to hurt her back. She left Jackie to God. Rick didn't like it. He said to Hope, "you always let people walk all over you." "Well," she pondered, "he is right about one thing because I let him walk over me too."

Rick decided to use Jackie because of what Jackie had done to Hope. He was going to make her think they were friends again and use her. Rick wanted Hope to be on board with him on what he wanted to do. He was looking for a $5000.00 loan to take his trucking business to the next level, but he didn't have the money he wanted. Rick wanted Hope to borrow the money from the bank, but she told him her credit wasn't any good, so that wasn't going to work.

Since Jackie wanted to be his friend again, Rick asked her to help him with the $5000. But she also didn't have good credit and hadn't gotten the settlement yet from the TTC case. However, Jackie wanted him back into her life so badly that she created a charity page asking for $5000 for her medical expenses, stating that she couldn't work because of the two surgeries, and she had no money.

Hope didn't like what Rick was doing to Jackie. She didn't like Jackie, but she didn't think it was right for him to use her that way. Hope talked to Rick about it, but he told her, "I want that money, and I don't care what she has to do to get it for me." Hope was trying to get her non-profit organization started, but she didn't have the money to start it. "When Jackie gets me the $5000, I'm going to take you out for dinner and give you the money to start your foundation, and we're going to laugh at her," Rick said to Hope.

As much as Hope wanted to pay her back, it wasn't right. Hope started to think, "if he has the chance, he will do the same thing to me." Hope said to Rick, "I don't want any part of it." Hope thought Rick wanted Jackie back in his life because he wanted something more than what he said. Rick got angry, and he started to cuss at Hope, calling her foolish, saying, "you're trying to stop my business from going on." She asked in an angry voice, "what business? You can't even pay your truck to keep it running, and you have to lie and use people to get to the top, and you're still not going anywhere, so what business am I trying to stop?" "My business will go on," he stated. Rick didn't know how to stand on his own two feet and always depended on someone to improve his life. But, unfortunately, he was wasting Hope's time.

After the argument, Hope and Rick didn't talk for two weeks. She was glad that she got the break from all his drama. Now that he and Jackie were friends again, Jackie went back to her old ways, pretending to be other people and calling Hope to cuss her. Hope took time off to reconnect with her children and her sister. They went to the movies every weekend or out for a bite to eat. They were happy spending so much time together. Hope brought Jackie's calls to Rick's attention, but he got mad at her. He didn't want to believe her when it came to Jackie because he wanted to use her, so he had to keep her happy.

"You don't have anything to offer me," Rick said to Hope. Hope replied, "Now I don't have anything to offer you?" She laughed and was glad that she wasn't talking to him. She only called him to tell him to speak with Jackie, so she would stop calling her phone, but that didn't go well. Now that Rick saw that Hope wasn't calling him anymore, he called her, telling her that he missed her and didn't want Jackie, they were just friends with benefits, and the sex wasn't that good. He said, "anytime she touches me, my skin crawls." Hope laughed and said, "that's not a nice thing for you to say."

Rick wanted Hope to know Jackie was there only because she was helping him take his business to the next level, and nothing was going on with them. But Hope didn't believe him. She didn't want anything to do with him. She told him they were over, but he didn't want to hear that from her. Rick believed they had something special going on, and no woman could take that away. Rick still needed Hope to help with his business because Jackie didn't know the computer as Hope did. She felt sorry for him and promised she'd help him since she wasn't working.

Jackie tried to do everything in her power to make sure Rick and Hope didn't speak anymore. She would cuss Hope, and because Hope knew Jackie would break it off entirely with Rick soon, she wanted Jackie to feel like she was not leaving Rick.

Jackie went onto Rick's computer and found Hope's email to send a fake email to Hope to harass her. Hope had enough. Jackie took Hope to a place she didn't want to go. Hope cussed Jackie back. She wasn't going to let her get away with what she was doing any longer. Hope let Jackie know that she knew she was a con artist, what she had done to get money, and that she sent an innocent man to prison because of jealousy.

Jackie told Rick what Hope said to her. She hid the fact she was the one who started everything. Hope told Rick how it all started, but he didn't care. He was angry that Hope told Jackie things that he said to her. Rick didn't talk to Hope for three days, but she didn't care because, at that point, Hope didn't love or like him any longer.

Valentine's day was coming, and Rick called Hope. He needed her help with some pictures he wanted to put up on his Facebook business page that she created for him. He spent that whole day with Jackie taking photographs, and Jackie didn't know how to put them on his page, so Hope did it for him. Valentine's Day was Saturday, and Rick spent Friday with Jackie. She wanted Hope to know she had spent the night with him. Jackie took pictures in Rick's house with flowers he had bought for her as well. Hope went on her Facebook to see if they spent the night together as she thought. Jackie had written on her Facebook, "Thanks to my man, I enjoyed my Valentine." Hope didn't care because she was so over Rick and Jackie and their games.

Rick called Hope, wanting to go to her house to spend Valentine's Day with her after Jackie left his house. Hope was furious with Rick, so she let him come to her house. She knew he just wanted to play her as he did to Jackie, and Hope didn't have it anymore, so she came up with a plan. She let him come over. He bought her a box of chocolates and a teddy bear that said, "I love you" on the front. Hope accepted it with a fake smile on her face. Next, Rick asked Hope to cook lunch for him. After she finished cooking, he ate, and they were having a good time, or that's what Rick thought. Hope was playing Rick, so her plan would work because she knew she would break up with him for good after the night was over and not look back. She told Rick that she wanted to take some pictures with him because he was the first guy that made her Valentine's Day unique. He was happy that she wanted to take pictures with the chocolate and the teddy bear he had bought her. He didn't know what she had in store for him.

After Rick went home, Hope put the pictures on Facebook because she knew Jackie would see them. As Hope predicted, when Jackie went on her Facebook, she wasn't happy seeing the pictures. She got angry. She emailed Rick and told him, "Tell Hope she won, and she should stop now." Rick called Hope and asked her why she posted the pictures of them. He told Hope what Jackie had said in her email to him. Hope didn't understand what she had won. After all, she wasn't playing games because she didn't want Rick in her life anymore. Hope knew once she did that and Rick found out; he would get angry and get into an argument with her, which would be their end. Hope was playing them both. Jackie was 55 years old and playing childish games, calling other women, texting, and pretending to be someone else. She also called Children's Aid on Hope. She was plain evil and had no self-respect.

Rick could see that he lost Hope for good. "I have no feelings for Jackie but sympathy for her because of her condition," he said. Hope knew there was more to the story than what he said, and she wondered what kind of heart Rick had when he said the meanest things about Jackie. He thought Jackie could make him prosperous, but she had no money. All she did was fraud to get cash by using her illness to get donations for Rick while she got welfare to earn money.

Jackie walked around feeling like she was on top of the world, but Hope didn't hate her. She often picked up the phone to call the police and tell them about the innocent man she put in jail and for the fraud she was doing, but she didn't. When Hope thought about it, Jackie wasn't the one she had been angry with. It was Rick. He was the one who was hurting her. Everything Jackie had done to her, Rick made it happen. He chose not to stop it because he loved her but didn't know how to show it. Hope understood the first time Jackie hurt her, but Rick wasn't expecting it. He didn't make sure it didn't happen again. All Rick cared about was her money. Hope said to herself, "how can he get rich off of nothing? Whatever money she gave him was finished before it even started."

Hope wanted to tell Jackie what Rick had planned because she wanted to get back at him, but she didn't think Jackie would believe her. Jackie wouldn't believe the truth even if it bit her on the butt. Jackie was just being a fool for a man who had another woman. Hope should have been happy about what Jackie had done because whatever money she gave Rick, he was spending on her, but it wasn't right. Hope advised him to stop what he was doing to Jackie because it was wrong. Then Rick turned to Hope and said, "a woman like you made a man poor." Hope said to Rick, "are you for real?" "You'll always be poor because God doesn't like ugly," she cried. But, she continued, "you don't look for other people to make you rich; you look at yourself, you can make things happen for yourself and say yes, I did that." Rick was shocked that Hope said that to him. He was silent on the phone.

Hope tried not to tell him all her goals in life and what she was doing. After all, she felt he would do the same thing to her because she could help make him get rich. She wanted a guy to be with her for her, not because he saw a way out. Hope cared for him, but when she looked at Rick, she saw him as someone who wanted to live off someone else's hard work. Rick often said he didn't want any woman who didn't have good credit, a car, and money, and Hope had none of the above. Hope asked him, "why are you with me?" He said, "you're one of the lucky ones." Hope said, "no, you were the lucky one." Hope didn't give Rick the time of day, and he said, "if you get wealthy, I want my share, and I'll collect when the time is right."

Hope went a long way to give up on Rick, to focus on herself, her children, and her non-profit organization. Working with families made her realize that her problems were not that bad. She packed up her tears and stopped feeling sorry for herself. Her health was good, and her kids were happy after all they had been through. She asked herself, "what more can I ask for?" But sometimes, the little girl inside her wanted to cry out loud. But the brave woman in Hope said, "hold on a little longer; the storm will be over soon, close your eyes and let it pass." Hope told herself it was just a dream and that she should keep her eyes closed and count to ten. As she counted slowly to ten, she opened her eyes, but the storm was still there. It didn't go away, and she realized it was her reality.

Being with Rick, Hope felt used, and at times she felt he was buying sex from her with gifts. Hope didn't want to feel that way, but she did. She didn't know what kind of a relationship they had. Rick said he wanted her but wasn't doing everything to keep her. Rick told Hope that he had stopped talking to Jackie, but he lied because he never stopped speaking to Jackie. Everything Rick told Hope about her was "bullshit."

Rick wanted to get rich, so everything Jackie did was okay with him. She thought, "how could he get rich off Jackie when she didn't have a job." She had no investments, she was broke, and she had nothing going on in her life. But he was making Jackie do fraud to get money off other people and didn't care what happened to Jackie, even if she ended up in jail getting cash for him.

At first, Hope was happy knowing he had other women he was talking to because she didn't want to commit to him. She didn't want to give up her freedom, and she wasn't over her ex-husband. Then Rick made Hope believe that she could trust him and that there are still good guys out there. But it didn't take him long to show his actual "colours." Hope didn't know how to trust him or believe anything he said. Finally, Hope was happy that they were over. "No more Rick and Jackie, it's time for me to live my life for my children and me and no one else," she said.

21.

Chapter Twenty-One

Hope kept telling herself that she was going to be ok. She'd been here before, and she was going to make it through, but her heart was saying something else. It was like her life was over, and she didn't know where to go from there. She gave Rick her all, but it wasn't enough.

Hope always gave a guy everything she had, but she could never find a man to love her the way she loved them. "When am I going to find the right guy to put me first for once; Am I not pretty enough; What am I doing wrong; Why can't I find the right one for me?" she asked herself. She found comfort in talking to herself, "all this time I thought I felt something for these guys after my husband, but I didn't; Was I trying to love them and hurt myself in the process?" Hope was fighting herself to love Rick because she wanted to feel something again so all the hurt from her husband would disappear, but it didn't work.

It had been six years since Anthony walked out of her life. She still loved him and couldn't seem to get over him. She found herself dating guys just like him because she didn't want to forget him. Hope knew it wasn't healthy for her. Still, she couldn't get over him. She put up a front every day to make everyone believe that she was over her ex-husband and had moved on. But that was far from the truth, so Hope let Rick into her life for the wrong reasons. He was a waste of her time. She regretted the day she met Rick and Jackie.

Hope felt good when she talked to Rick about how he treated her and let him know that it was over between them. It was a massive weight off her shoulders. She felt stronger, and she didn't have to listen to him talking about himself anymore. She could live her life the way she wanted to live it because he didn't control her life anymore.

Hope called her sister-in-law to let her know what was going on in her life. It made her feel better because Michelle didn't judge her. She gave Hope good advice even though she was scared to advise her about her relationship with Rick. It felt good that she could still talk to Michelle. Hope wanted to tell her everything, but she was scared it would make Michelle look at her differently, but she knew her sister-in-law would find out soon. She hoped that she would understand why she didn't let her in on everything when she found out.

Now that Rick was out of her life, she could live her life the way she wanted to. She delayed her music career when she was with Rick, and now that he is gone, she doesn't have to delay it any longer. Hope wanted to be married so badly she missed her husband. Still, she didn't think he wanted her back. She wanted to go to Anthony and tell him to come home but was scared he would say no, and she would be heartbroken all over again. As a result of what was going on with Renell, Hope needed Anthony's help, but she knew she couldn't get it. Finally, Hope asked herself, "why do I miss my husband so much when he doesn't miss me?" By the way, Anthony was treating their kids, she should hate him, but she didn't; she still loved him. It had been six years since he left, but she couldn't stop loving him.

When Hope was with Rick, she gave up on finding her soulmate, or she just wanted her soulmate to be Anthony. But, unfortunately, Rick wasn't the right one for her. He didn't bring anything to her life, and all she did for a year was make him feel good about himself. She made him feel young because he was an old guy with a young girl. He wanted to make it seem like he did a lot for her, but he didn't.

Hope was there for Rick when everyone else turned away from him. She took his business to the next level when he looked for a driver for his truck. Hope spent time online looking for the right person for the business. When he wanted a business website, she created it for him and sent out the information for people to know about his business. She helped him with his invoices and business-rate sheet. She helped Rick get his business t-shirts, and while she was at work, she called the T-shirt company to make sure his orders were correct, and she got his business cards done. She also went on the road with him, helping to keep his company together. Hope helped him do some of the hands-on work. She was by his side late at night, helping him with his deliveries in bad snowy weather. But Rick still didn't respect her. Hope walked out of the relationship with her head held high. She thought, "I didn't lose anything; he's the one who lost the best thing he ever had."

One day Hope sat down and pondered on her life. Then, finally, she said to herself, "*I want those guys to know, including Anthony, that I was weak, and because of what they did to me, They made me into a strong woman. I'm not scared of being alone anymore; You took a lot from me, yet I'm still here. You made me fall on my face, but I got up because I'm strong; You left me alone in that cold bed to comfort another woman; I cried, but not for too long because I'm strong; You chose other women over me, but I got over it and you, because I'm strong.*"

Many nights Hope cried and didn't want to get out of her bed. She didn't know if she could live without the men who passed through her life. Now, she was doing fine without them. Then Hope said to herself, "Leaving was the best thing I have ever done; I'm still standing, and in the end, I was the winner, the race was hard, but I ended up on top. Thank you guys for helping me be strong."

After all, Hope had gone through and the time she had to pick up the pieces of her heart, she still had love to give. So she made a promise to herself that she would not give her love away so easily anymore. In her heart, she declared that she would not make any future men pay for the mistakes made by the men in her past.

People looked at Hope and asked, "why are you so happy? You're always smiling." Hope would smile and say, "it's God's grace and mercy." They didn't know how she just found her smile after so much disappointment, heartbreak, low self-esteem, abuse and such-like. When Hope found her smile, she looked at herself in the mirror and thought; *"I've been cold like ice since I was born but could be hot as the sun, because I don't care what other people think, at the end of the day it's only their opinion, so I'll continue to light the world with my smile."*

Everyone that wronged Hope made her cry, put her down, called her names and turned their backs on her. She wanted them to know that she had a beautiful soul, and she wasn't going to make anyone take that away from her. She refused to make anyone take away her sunshine. She had come a long way. But Hope knew she had to keep on fighting because it wasn't over yet. The more people saw her make it, the more jealous they got.

Hope had learnt that people hated her because they were mad at themself for not trying the things she was doing in life. So she practiced not getting mad with anyone. They didn't feel what she was feeling at the end of the day. She thought, "why should I make me miserable while they are happy living their lives?" "Life is too short to be jealous of someone for what they've achieved and don't know how they got it," she thought.

Grace, Hope's mother, taught her that, 'if you don't have something, do without it. It was something Hope carried with her everywhere she went. She read a passage from the Bible and the Bible:

"The reason some people have turned against you and walked away from you without reason has nothing to do with you. It's because I removed them from your life. After all, they cannot go where I am taking you next. They will only hinder you to your next level because they have already served their purpose in your life. So let them go and keep moving. Greater is coming, says the Lord."

Hope kept reading over and over and sat for a minute, thinking about her life. She realized God allowed those men to cross her path, showing her that he was real and was with her through the problems with the men in her life. Hope thought that God had given up on her. Then, she realized that he was always there and never left her side and that he took those guys out of her life. He had something better in store for her, and he showed Hope that he carried her when she was weak.

Hope wasn't angry with the men; she was angry with herself for letting them stay so long. She wanted things to be done on her timeline, but it was not God's timeline. Nevertheless, she was happier now more than ever, and she was doing what she loved to do, like singing, writing, and helping people. It was a long journey, and she knew her work wasn't over. It was just the beginning, and she knew with God's grace and mercy, he would see her through to the end.

Hope used to walk around judging women without knowing what they had been through in their lives and why they did what they did. She found out that people could make you do a lot of things. Your families can make you grow to hate them. A husband can make you fall out of love with him. Your friends can make you feel like they were better than you, and they got jealous of you because you were moving up in life and they were not. Hope learned not to judge anyone if she didn't know where they were in life. Love makes you do many things you never thought you would ever do. Friends and family pushed Hope to her limits because they thought they could.

So, Hope walked away. Sometimes she knew she had to stand up and fight, but walking away was much better than letting them think they won. Hope let them think that way because she was going on with her life while they weren't going anywhere.

Some people thought, "why did Hope stay married to a man that beat her, cheated and used her; how could she love someone like that?" But they would never understand because they've never walked in her shoes. Hope did it for her kids because she loved them. Hope knew everyone would say she was using the children to stay with Anthony, but she didn't look at it that way. When Hope thought about it, she stayed in an abusive marriage because she wanted her kids to have the family she never had. Anthony knew what to say to her to keep her down. She watched her daughter cry for her father when he wasn't around. Hope tried to let her know how much her father loved her, even if she didn't believe it was true. Hope could see her daughter's face when she saw her dad with other kids, thinking her father didn't love or care for her.

Hope could feel and understand Renell's pain. That's the same way she used to feel when she saw her father with another man's child. She knew Renell would get over not seeing her father but didn't know how long it would take. Hope's son James said to her, "Mommy, I don't miss my dad because he doesn't miss or love us." Hope wanted James to have his father in his life, to teach him the things she couldn't. She didn't understand why Anthony didn't want to be in his children's lives. All he wanted to do was come in and out of their lives and call himself a father. Hope had to be there for her kids with no help from Anthony. When they were sick, it was just her. She read bedtime stories and talked with them when they wanted someone to talk to. Hope cried because it was hard being both a father and a mother to her children, but she wouldn't change anything. "Only if their father could see what he was missing in their lives, I guess boys will always be boys," said thought.

Hope sat back and reflected on her life. She remembered all the pain she went through. She picked up a book and started to write the way she felt. She wrote, "*no one knows my pain; no one notices my heartaches; No one notices my tears, but they notice my mistakes; People only care for themselves and not others. Why can life be so unfair?*"

The more Hope smiled, the more people hated her. She asked herself, "why is it so hard to let go of my past?" She thought to herself, "*instead, I am carrying it with me into my future. Every time I try to move on with my life, people try to bring me down; I cannot help but remember my past; every night, I cry myself to sleep, hoping I will wake up to a brighter tomorrow.*" She thought, "*I care about people and care less about myself. I've learned over time; you have to love yourself first before you start loving others.*"

Hope knew that hurting herself would not do her any good. So all she could do was keep smiling and try to solve her own problems instead of letting other people's problems become hers. There were times she hated herself for being such a pushover, letting people walk all over her. She wanted to be loved for her and not for her body. No one knew how often she cried herself to sleep because of what she went through in her life. Everyone she trusted broke her heart so many times. As the tears ran down her face, she said, "they're all wolves in sheep's clothing." Finally, she made a promise to herself that she was going to pack up her tears and put herself back together. "I'm not going to put myself in a situation to be used and hurt by anyone ever again," she declared.

When it comes to bad relationships, Hope had learned her lesson, and it prepared her for the great man God has blessed her within her life, her best friend Neal, of 19 years. There were times they didn't keep in touch because of the foolish relationships. Still, Hope was glad their bond was always there and was never broken. After all, she went through in her relationships, Hope and Neal started talking more on the phone. She got herself a job in accounts receivable, and for once, she was happy living for her and her children and no one else. It felt good getting up and going to her new job, knowing that she didn't have to depend on a guy for anything, not even Anthony.

Hope thought her life was over and that no one would take her and her two children and love all three of them, but Neal proved her wrong. She was happy to move on with her life with the man she had loved since she was 12 years old. Hope said to herself, "Remember, you are in control of your destiny. Life is too short to waste it on some guy that isn't worth your time."

Hope now knew that when she prayed about things, and they didn't work out, it was because it wasn't for her. She thought, "God will never make his children suffer because he said knock, and it will open. So don't cry over a guy because it's not worth it." What should have killed Hope made her stronger, and her situation did just that. Glory be to God!

It is never a good idea to get involved with another woman's husband. They are not a boyfriend, they are a husband, and there is the meaning behind any relationship. If you put yourself in that situation where you fall in love with married women or men, it will not end well. You must take what you get because you knew it was wrong in the first place. Men will go out and play and tell you what you want to hear. They already know your self-esteem is low. They see if you are a fast girl and that's all you're going to be to them. They will never leave their wives for you. You bring excitement to them for that moment.

You are only the "side-chick" who thought you were doing a better job than the wife because he came back to you. No, that's not true because you're just a piece of meat, a booty call. You are nothing more than that to him. If a guy left his wife for you, he'd play the same game with you. How you got him is how you'll lose him. It doesn't matter if he stayed with you for six months or six years. If he never grows up, he'll keep doing that same old dance, with a different face.

Some ladies love to "harass" the wife by saying many nasty things about her, for example, "you may have the ring, but I have your man." How does that make sense when he's only seeing you in the dark and not the light because he doesn't want anyone to see him with you.

If a man leaves you night or day to be with a side chick, he doesn't love you. If a woman called you up and told you things your husband said about you, he didn't love you.

A good husband will never cheat on you or let another woman call your phone and put you down. If he cheats, you'll never know because he doesn't want to hurt you. He will try his best to keep his side chick out of your life. I'm just saying, if a man loves you and you're all he ever wanted, he'll be a one-woman man. When you marry, you become one, not you and his friends, family, and other women.

Some women stay in a relationship because they married him or have kids together. The church pastor says you must try to make it work for better or worse, till death do us part, and the church doesn't believe in divorce. So now you feel stuck like there's no way out. He beats you, and your kids see that he beats you, and they see you crying all the time, and they come and comfort you when you're crying. That is not a life you want for yourself or your kids.

In your head, you might wonder, "Is that what *'till death do us part'* meant when he kills me?" You and your children deserve better. Do not stay in a relationship if it's not working for you and your children. Even if you don't have children, there is always a way out of every situation. It's either your husband kills you, you end up in the hospital, or you choose to walk away before it's too late.

"Do you want someone else to take care of your kids if something bad happens to you in that abusive relationship?" That is a question you must ask yourself. No one can take care of your children better than you can. I get that you're thinking, "how am I going to make it if I leave him, or how is it going to affect my children if I leave?" But you're not going to know if you don't try to stand on your own two feet.

Everything that comes into your mind is just an excuse. Just because you love him doesn't mean he loves you if he's putting his hands on you. He doesn't love his children if he lets them see their mommy cry and see their father abusing their mother. That is not love. Love is when the other partner wants to share their life with you, not when they try to take it away. He'll want to build a foundation with you and your family.

Love is unconditional: When your partner loves you unconditionally, he'll accept all your faults. I know when you love someone for a long time, you'll find yourself sometimes forgetting why you love that person, but don't give up. Keep on pushing. What does not kill you will make you stronger.

Love is selfless: When you love someone, you never look at that person to see what they can do for you. Never look for anything in return. If you do something for that person, do it because you love them, not for what they can do for you. After all, if that person doesn't give you something in return, you'll lose in the end. Unfortunately, some women and men love to test their relationship. They wait and see what will happen, and they don't think about what the other person can do for them. Instead, think about what you can do to make your relationship better.

Many of us make love so tricky when it's not necessary. You love the person. You don't stay with them if you don't love them. It's crazy how you move from wanting the person to force the person to love you. Could it be we other person love for granted or person kindness for weakness? If you don't want someone let them go for their soulmate to find them

Love is kind. Love is honest. Love is faithful. Love can be a lot of things. It's up to you if you want to make it into a bad thing or a good thing. Choose what you want love to look like. Communication is the key to every relationship or friendship. You want to build that unbreakable friendship with that person in your life.

When things get hard at times, remember what brought you there in the first place and how much you mean to each other.

It says in the Bible: Corinthians 13:4-8

- *Love is patient; love is kind. It does not envy, it does not boast, it does not dishonour others, is not self-seeking, is not easily angered, keeps no record of wrongs.*
- *Love does not delight in evil but rejoices with the truth. It always protects, always trusts, always hope, and always perseveres.*
- *Love never fails, but where there are prophecies, they will cease. Where there are tongues, they will be stilled. Where there is knowledge, it will pass away.*

You don't know when you have a good relationship when you come out of a bad one. You're asking and thinking if he's doing you wrong when he goes out, and you think he's cheating. You start going through his phone, reading his text messages, looking to see who he talks to when you're not around. Now the problem comes up, and arguments happen. Yes, sometimes it's ok to go with your feelings and other times it could be wrong.

If your man doesn't give you a reason to go through his phone, don't if you think he's cheating on you. When you go through his phone and see that he's really cheating, you'll get hurt even more. They say, "what your eye doesn't see, the heart won't grieve." So don't worry about things you're not aware of. You can keep your eyes open for a sign, but if the guy does everything right to please you and is always with you, don't look. If he says he wants to go out with his friends for a night out, then let him. You can't be selfish. It's not always about you.

If your man starts to go out more often and calls you up to say he's staying the night at his friend's house, you have the right to be worried.

If your man says to you, "I don't have anything to hide," then he doesn't need to carry his phone into the bathroom or put it under his pillow while he sleeps; that's a red flag. But, on the other hand, it's ok if he puts a password on his phone. Maybe he does it if he loses his phone, *or* he could be hiding something.

If he doesn't have anything to hide, he won't mind if his phone rings and you answer it when he's not close to it. If he has nothing to hide, he'll give you the password. If he doesn't, don't get mad because you may be doing the same thing.

When your partner tells you, he loves you, judging by his actions and not words. People say a lot of things that they don't really mean. Never try to be someone else to please a man. If they can't accept you for who you are, then they're not the ones for you. Never put yourself down for a man because they come and go. You will feel the pain when they're gone, and now you're left thinking, how to get back together with him. Change for you and no one else.

If a relationship doesn't work out, don't think it's something you did. It's not worth blaming yourself and asking yourself what you could have done to save the relationship. Instead, you're looking at yourself as a loser. Look at it as they are the losers, and they didn't have what it took to be in your life.

Look at it as it was not meant to be. They weren't your soul mate. He's still out there waiting for you. Your soulmate will never come to you if you continue to cry over "spilled milk." While you're crying every day, they've moved on with their lives. It's already happened, you can't change the past, but you can change your future and learn to let things go.

I know it's hard. I feel your pain because Hope used to be you, doing everything right to make that relationship work. But it seemed like that person didn't care. Hope almost ruined a good relationship because she didn't know how to love and trust again. But Hope wasn't going to make her exes mess up a good thing for her because she had a hard time letting go of the past.

She let go of the bitterness and anger towards them. She didn't want it to take her over. Hope was angry for a long time, but she said to herself, "I don't have to live that way. You can take control of your life. It's my time to shine."

Ladies, don't lay in your bed asking yourself, "what if?" Instead, pick yourself up and put yourself back on the market. Wake up, shower, do your hair, put your makeup on, go for a walk and feel pretty about yourself inside and out. Remember, you're the only one stopping you. It's not your family, not your friends, and not your exes. Learn to love yourself before others can love you.

About the Author

Camille is the founder of the Kamille Foundation, which she started as a single mother. Camille knew that she wanted to help single mothers like herself with many barriers that faced her. So, taking all the pain that she had been through during her marriage, She started the foundation as she faced many odds, never giving up the fight to assist low-income families.

She knew what it felt like not to have enough for her and her children to eat and saw her mother's struggles as well. She knew she had to make a difference in life and break the cycle. Camille has a passion for singing, writing music, and writing. After ten years, she has finally released her first book. She believes that this book will touch the lives of the readers.